CREATI SALES TEAM EXCELLENCE

CREATING SALES TEAM EXCELLENCE

KEY STRATEGIES FOR HIRING AND DEVELOPING TOP PERFORMERS

Jeanne and Herbert Greenberg

KOGAN
PAGE

First published in 1990 as
What It Takes to Succeed in Sales
by Don Jones-Irwin

This edition published in 1991 by Kogan Page.

Kogan Page Limited
120 Pentonville Road
London N1 9JN

British Library Cataloguing in Publication Data

A CIP record for this book is available from the British Library.
ISBN 0 7494 0543 0

Typeset by J&L Composition Ltd, Filey, North Yorkshire
Printed in England by Clays Ltd., St Ives plc.

CONTENTS

ACKNOWLEDGEMENTS

It is impossible to acknowledge by name all of the individuals, companies and trade associations that have contributed so importantly to the body of knowledge which we are sharing in this book.

We do want to offer special thanks to our client companies, to the trade associations, and to the sales organisations with which we have worked for so many years. The knowledge they have provided us about their companies, their industries and the sales profession itself has contributed greatly to this book.

We also want to express our deepest gratitude to all of the members of the Caliper team who, through their specialised knowledge of various industries and day-to-day contact with Caliper's client companies, have been able to provide us with so much of the feedback and the case histories that are included in these pages.

Finally, we do want to mention two people for their unique contributions: Scott L Corwin, whose vision and strategic planning have helped bring a new direction to our company, and Patrick J Sweeney, whose counsel and overall editorial guidance have helped keep our corporate messages on course. To both of them, we are most thankful.

Jeanne Greenberg
Herbert Greenberg

PART 1

SALES AS A PROFESSION

CHAPTER 1

A PROFESSION OF OPPORTUNITIES

In striking contrast to most positions in business, sales provides an opportunity for those who want to operate with a good degree of autonomy and independence. It remains the only profession where individuals are judged according to a pounds-and-pence standard. And, for those willing to sacrifice the security of a consistent salary cheque, sales can be extremely lucrative.

For fast trackers, who are looking to make more money than their peers, seeking increased responsibility and too impatient to move slowly up the corporate ladder, there is only one option: sales.

But as inviting as all this sounds — limitless financial rewards, high visibility, the opportunity to advance at your own pace and independence — sales is not for everyone.

It takes a special kind of person to succeed in sales. First of all, salespeople have a different way of looking at the world. They sense opportunities where others fear rejection. Frowns are not signs of discouragement, they are something to be changed. Where others see obstacles, salespeople see challenges.

That is why, more than anything else, salespeople must believe in themselves. And the best salespeople we have encountered know themselves very well — they know exactly who they are believing in.

In many ways, we can compare salespeople to entrepreneurs — without the headaches, and risk, of owning their own businesses.

And, because of who they are, as salespeople grow in their positions they are constantly seeking new opportunities. According to a recent study by Heidrick and Struggles, most of today's top executives have come up through the sales and marketing ranks. This is because the best salespeople and the most effective corporate executives share many of the same qualities, including initiative, drive, imagination and a willingness to work hard.

But what attracts successful people to sales? What do they have that others do not? What, ultimately, does it take to succeed in sales?

We intend to give you a clearer picture of exactly who the best salespeople are. We will explore what makes salespeople tick, what differentiates them from people in other professions and, perhaps most importantly, what distinguishes the best salespeople from the rest of the salespeople.

The question that seems to keep sales managers constantly on edge is: why do some people excel in sales, while others who seem to work just as hard and enthusiastically fall short of meeting goals? We have advised over 15,000 firms on this question throughout the past three decades. And in this book, we will share some of our findings.

As our service economy shifts into high gear, what it takes to succeed in sales has become a little more complex. One thing that is certain is that, perhaps more than ever before, there is a growing need for the human touch. As technology opens new doors, overwhelmed customers find themselves looking for someone to guide them through the labyrinth of possibilities they face. Many products and services are difficult to distinguish from the competition. So, above all, this process depends upon trust. This trend underscores the growing importance of truly professional salespeople.

That is because the things being sold in today's economy are not really products or even services. What the best salespeople truly sell are solutions — solutions which meet exactly the particular needs of each client.

Throughout this book, we will be taking out our psychological pens and sketching a portrait for you of the kinds of individuals who have what it takes to make it in this game where there are few clear-cut rules, and where the odds are inextricably stacked against success — but where the opportunities and challenges are virtually limitless.

First, though, allow us to draw back the curtains of time to see what it has taken historically to make it in sales.

In the US, when Eli Whitney was developing his 'mass production' technology, a fellow named Eli Terry tried the same techniques on his own product line — clocks. Soon, he had a method for assembly-line clock making. But money was scarce. Clocks, even assembly-line clocks, were expensive, and, more frequently than not, Terry returned home after a hard day on the road with a tired horse and a wagon still weighed down with timepieces.

Finally, the enterprising Terry figured out an unorthodox merchandising technique: a free trial with no money down. This offer astounded potential customers. And before they could fully recover from the first surprise, Terry would spring the second one: if they kept the clock, he would accept partial payments spread over a period of time. Within three years, Eli Terry, the father of the instalment-buying concept, had become the largest clock manufacturer in the world.

What distinguished Terry from most of his contempories was the imagination and energy he brought to selling his merchandise. Undoubtedly, there were others with similarly fine clocks, maybe even superior ones. But then, as now, product quality alone was not enough. The extra spark that was, and still is, needed is superior, inventive salesmanship. The same kind of creative selling abilities Terry demonstrated are still what makes the difference between success and failure.

Today, executives have at their disposal a dazzling array of techniques and technologies for selling. But sales remains an extremely personal business.

After a product or service has been conceived, the feasibility studies completed, the production technology developed, the marketing plan completed, the market testing concluded, the advertising and public relations plans conceived and implemented, the merchandising and promotion materials produced and distributed, there still comes a point where one person must persuade another to buy the product or service.

In a world characterised by the most precise calculations of variables in the overall marketing milieu, the salesperson remains almost entirely a mystery.

We hope to help solve this mystery. The people we are about to describe for you are rare individuals, but they are not impossible to find. In our work, we have found that approximately one out of every four individuals today has what it takes to succeed in some form of sales, either consultative, or relationship-building, or display sales, or the hard and fast-driving closers. However, only a few of those one-out-of-every-four individuals with sales ability end up using their innate talent. And, as we are all well aware, far too many people who are completely lacking in sales ability wind up selling. The result is that sales has often received a professional black eye. But, more about that later.

For now, we would like to concentrate on those who do best in sales. For starters, they do very well . . . in fact, exceedingly well financially. The median compensation in the industrial and service sectors is £20,000. And that figure is dragged down considerably by a large number of people in sales who should be doing something else. The truth of the matter is that it is not uncommon for top salespeople to make (or, more precisely *earn*) more money than their sales managers. Sales superstars sometimes even earn more than the owners of their companies. Some companies have salespeople earning hundreds of thousands of pounds annually. All of these head-spinning figures prompt the question: what special skills or motivations explain why many salespeople earn more than we pay the prime minister of the country . . . or, for that matter, even as much as a star footballer.

Sales, perhaps more than any other profession, is a psychological testing ground. Ten years ago, a survey rated product knowledge as a salesperson's most important attribute. But just recently, a similar survey has found that product knowledge has been surpassed by honesty, integrity and professionalism. The best salespeople say unanimously that they would leave their jobs if they did not wholeheartedly believe in their product or service.

Prospects, meanwhile, go through a precise psychological order when making a buying decision. First, they judge the salesperson's integrity. People today simply will not do business with someone unless they are sure they can depend upon them. Then, a prospect will determine whether the salesperson's company can back up its product or claims. Next, they determine whether what is being offered, regardless of price, will take care of their needs. Price becomes the final determinant of whether they will place an order.

The salesperson who succeeds is the one who works as an assistant to customers, helping them do their jobs better. To accomplish this, salespeople bring several qualities to the table, including empathy, persuasiveness, persistence, patience and resilience.

And the very best salespeople make it look so easy and natural. While understanding thoroughly the advantages of the products or services they represent, they are well-versed on the weaknesses of their competitors . . . and they seem to anticipate their customers' evolving needs. To cap it all, they make it look as though they could do it all while walking in their sleep.

Super salespeople are extremely attentive to each client's needs, and totally intent upon seeking an ideal solution to each client's unique problems. In the end, such individuals are problem solvers. They are the ones who solve problems better and quicker than their competitors.

For such work, salespeople enjoy an unusual degree of independence, a chance to make money commensurate with their abilities and limitless opportunities. They are, in many ways, their own bosses. When it comes down to it, few individuals in other professions can say the same.

A glance through the recruitment advertisements in the back of almost any newspaper demonstrates that the appeal to salespeople starts with money. One headline reads: 'If money talks, you could be screaming.' Another starts out: 'Money. You're in sales because you want it.' Still another: 'Unlimited earning potential.' Does all that sound a bit over the top? It is little wonder that the overwhelming majority of those individuals who are attracted to such advertisements are dreamers with little chance of succeeding.

While money may be an initial motivator, we have found that the top salespeople earn so much that, as one of our clients put it, 'After a while, money loses its ability to inspire you.' The superstars are constantly striving to improve themselves. They have a need for accomplishment. So they make a game out of creating new challenges and going after the 'impossible sale' to maintain their enthusiasm. These needs, as we will discuss in more depth later in this book, are far more basic than money to the true salesperson.

These same recruitment advertisements try to attract people who are seeking 'independence'. One job advertisement highlights that you can 'make your own hours', another says you can 'run your own show', another will allow you to 'sell your own way'.

The picture that develops is of a highly paid independent professional who is often the sole representative of a company and is a trusted confidant to his or her clients. Such an individual (and that is a word that has lost much of its meaning in today's job market) is out there proving him or herself every day. They are on the cutting edge, in a black and white world, where they either make it or they do not. There are really few jobs holding that level of continual suspense. But that is what the best salespeople thrive on.

So, for all its advantages, why has sales, historically, received such bad publicity? Why are there so many jokes about the travelling salesman? Why are there so many negative phrases about the profession, such as 'selling you down the river' and 'selling out'?

Our studies show that the real reason the sales profession has suffered in terms of prestige is because four out of every five people now selling should be doing something else — for themselves, for their company, for the profession and certainly for the sake of the prospects they encounter. But because these salespeople do not have a natural talent, they try to fake it and, in the fast-talking process, sell themselves, and all the rest of us, short.

Unfortunately, these are the kind of salespeople whom we all seem to come across more frequently than we encounter the true professionals. They are the types that make you want to ask them, 'Why don't you do all of us a favour ... and get another job?'

We hope this book will help eliminate the hackers and pave the way for true sales professionals. We hope to provide insights which will enable managers to uncover people with natural sales ability and which will help individuals to determine whether they have what it takes. If we can contribute in the slightest way towards this goal, we feel we will be providing an enormous service to the business world, and to the unfortunate customers who unwittingly come across the lion's share of misfitted, mismatched and ill-equipped salespeople.

Why, you might ask, is it so difficult for executives to find talented salespeople? We believe it is because most recruiting practices start out by looking in the wrong places for the wrong things. This is curious to us since the cost of recruiting and training a salesperson is extremely high for a company. A recent survey relates that the total annual cost of supporting a salesperson is approximately £50,000 for the industrial sector and £47,500 for the service sector. Considering that the cost of closing a sale in many industries has jumped from £342 to over £2,800 in the past 15 years, it is not surprising that marketing operations are under increasing pressure to perform more effectively. Business executives today understand that marketing productivity represents a critical advantage — one that dramatically impacts the company's bottom line.

Still, in the hiring process, we have found there is, almost universally, entirely too much concern with external superficialities (what salespeople are supposed to *look* like), and not enough concern with what is inside (whether they are *motivated* to succeed in sales). This seems to have been the case throughout time. For instance, an article in the premiere issue of *Sales and Marketing Management* 70 years ago noted, 'Large men command attention, providing that they are physically well-organised and their muscle tone and health is all that it should be. Large salesmen are more likely to depend upon their size and bluff to succeed than they are to make use of every ounce of their grey matter. Smaller salesmen must make up for this deficiency in height and brawn by using their minds more effectively. They must either have more courage and elf-reliance, more tactfulness and friendliness, or more intellectual resourcefulness.'

Sometimes, the more things change, the more they seem to remain the same. We can only assume that the continued emphasis on external factors, such as size and appearance, is due to a lack of understanding that sales is fundamentally a game of motivation.

If we can convey one thing in this book, it is that succeeding in sales has to do with what is inside of you. And, when push comes to shove, no one can give a salesperson the desire to succeed, the need to persuade, the ability to bounce back from rejection, the ability to understand the needs of others or any of the other qualities that are needed to succeed in sales. These are all inherent gifts which some of us have in larger quantities than others. But they are not gifts that we can package neatly and give to someone else.

In addition, we have found that the best salespeople, regardless of their field, share one other characteristic. Ben Feldman, the most successful life insurance salesman in the world, summed it up best when he was asked, 'What is the best shortcut you've discovered for getting to the top?' 'Shortcut?', Feldman repeated. 'I've never been able to discover any shortcut around hard work.'

It is important to keep in mind that a piece of coal and a diamond both consist mostly of carbon. But it would be fruitless to give a jeweller a piece of coal and ask him to polish it until it becomes a precious gem. Yet, that is what many sales executives are asked to do every day — to create salespeople out of individuals who are not fundamentally suited to the task.

Having assessed over three-quarters of a million individuals in our work, we are convinced that the majority of people have the potential to be winners in this world. What it takes is an understanding of our inherent strengths, and then getting ourselves into positions where our limitations are not of consequence, and our strengths are allowed to shine.

With this in mind, we will examine why, with all its advantages, the sales profession continues to suffer from high turnover and poor productivity. Then we will look at the key motivations and personality dynamics critical to sales success. After that, we will try to provide you with a clear understanding of the specific internal motivations that distinguish the best salespeople.

Next, we will show you how to develop a thorough understanding of the specific requirements of a sales job and how to determine whether an individual possesses the necessary qualities to succeed.

We will then deal with the 'how to'. We will discuss how to maximise the productivity of a company's existing sales team, approaches to recruiting sufficient numbers of applicants, and special techniques for identifying individuals who have what it takes to make it in sales.

With this backdrop, we will examine, in depth, the qualities needed to be a successful salesperson in six industries: life insurance, property and health insurance, cars, property, banking and high technology. We are using these industries — a representative cross-section — as a way of explaining the differences to be found among successful salespeople in varying sales situations.

We will conclude by examining how sales has changed and how the profession may be projected through the coming decade.

It is our hope that this book will help executives improve their ability to upgrade the productivity of their sales team and help them to bring into sales the kind of high quality individuals that the profession deserves. We also hope that the information contained in this book will help individuals to determine objectively whether sales is for them and, if so, in what area.

Ultimately, for people who have what it takes, sales can be a very lucrative profession, offering many opportunities.

CHAPTER 2

THE SALES PROBLEM

If the sales profession is indeed so attractive, offering the high income, personal freedom and limitless opportunities discussed in the previous chapter, why is there any problem in recruiting and retaining highly productive, professional-level salespeople?

Whenever sales and marketing executives get together, poor productivity and high turnover are invariably key topics for discussion. These executives are constantly seeking ways to reduce the incredibly high cost, in both time and money, of recruiting, selecting and training salespeople, only to have the majority leave, be dismissed or, at best, turn out to be mediocre producers. While striving to solve these problems, they nevertheless seem to accept, as a fact of business life, that 80 per cent of all sales are made by only 20 per cent of the sales force. The staggering, wasteful costs stemming from this situation are endured because they are thought to be inevitable. The resulting high turnover among those 80 per cent who are fumbling along is, in turn, accepted as a necessary cost of managing a sales force. The fact is that neither the universally accepted poor productivity among sales forces nor the high turnover need be inevitable.

Our studies show that 55 per cent of the people earning their living in sales should be doing something else. Quite simply, they do not have the personality attributes that are needed to succeed in sales. Another 20 to 25 per cent have what it takes to sell, but they should be selling something else. These individuals could be successful in some selling situations, but they are only marginal in their current sales position. This leaves approximately 20 per cent of salespeople who genuinely possess the personality attributes needed to succeed in selling, and who are selling the products or services best suited to their personality. The same studies indicate that this 20 per cent of properly placed people are precisely the same individuals responsible for selling 80 per cent of what is sold.

Unfortunately, we have found, with some consistency, that a small percentage of each sales force is overwhelmingly successful, while the vast majority barely hang on, leave or are dismissed. But it need not be this way. A realistic goal can be that a majority of a company's sales force can consist of people as effective as the highly productive 20 per cent. The results of having such a sales force are exciting to think about. Just imagine two-thirds, three-quarters or four-fifths of a company's sales force selling at the level of the current top 20 per cent. We leave it to you to do the maths. That final figure would not even include the reduced costs that would result from less turnover, recruiting, training and managing of novices.

A more objective approach to recruiting and selecting sales personnel can result in a significant increase in the percentage of productive people. It is a matter of looking at the sales profession in a new way.

But before looking at the way to dig out of this hole in which the sales profession finds itself, let us try to understand how we got here. Why is it so difficult to identify people who have what it takes to succeed in sales?

Our studies show that most salespeople are hired for the wrong reasons. Most hiring approaches do not predict whether someone has what it takes to succeed in sales.

Depending upon the industry, there are two prevalent hiring approaches, both completely different, both predominantly doomed to failure. First there are the traditional, but invalid, hiring criteria. There are companies and industries in which the hiring process is selective, but their hiring criteria have absolutely nothing to do with predicting whether someone has what it takes to succeed in sales. And second, there is what we term the 'warm body approach'. Those companies and industries just need someone to fill a pair of empty shoes, so they take their chances with anyone who walks through the door.

INVALID CRITERIA

Regardless of how selective a company might be, they cannot hope to make correct hiring decisions if their selective criteria are incorrect to begin with. These companies often use extensive application forms, have multiple interviews, check references carefully, and, in short, take many of the steps that are required in making a logical, thoughtful hiring decision. This process is often costly, but is thought to be worth it, again because of the importance of that decision. But, as most human resource executives and sales managers will confess, despite all of this time, money and effort, wrong decisions are the norm, and so the poor productivity and turnover continues.

When we speak to groups, we jokingly describe the candidate typically sought, legalities aside, as the young, white male, 25 to 35 years of age, with 20 years of experience, with multiple, advanced degrees, who is earning £36,000 a year, but will go to work for you for £12,000. We go on to say that even if you could find this paragon, who commenced his working career at the age of four, the likelihood is that you would be hiring another inappropriate person. In fact, our studies have revealed that the odds are about four-to-one that you would be hiring the wrong person. The reason is that these same studies, which will be described later, have proved that age, sex, race, formal education and even experience are invalid predictors of sales success. Most people today will at least pay lip-service to the notion that sex and race are inappropriate criteria. Besides, the law is very clear that these criteria cannot be used. But, we have found that in presenting our findings to managers, there is much argument about the other three criteria. Let's look at the arguments and see where they go.

Age

There are two specific views relating to the question of age. The predominate one is that management wants young people who will make a career with their company. Somehow, in their minds, youth becomes equated with longevity, energy, openness — and a willingness to learn. Of course, the arbitrary age cut off varies, but the desire for youth predominates. Yet, haven't we all interviewed recent graduates who, among their first questions, ask, 'What is your pension plan?' Do you really want 40 years' longevity with a young person who is worried about his or her pension plan?

Our studies show that young people are no more or no less willing to learn than their older colleagues, and the likelihood of longevity with your company may be even less because they have not thought through their career choices. Your job may be part of their experimentation and, of most importance, they may simply not be appropriate for the job.

On the other side, there are those companies who seek 'older, more stable people'. Part of that thinking relates to the image thought to be conveyed by an older, 'more mature person' and, of course, age is also connected with experience, which we will talk about next. Again, the situation comes down to the individual. There are some 50-year-olds who are less mature than many teenagers, and do indeed, over the long run, manage to convey that lack of maturity. On the other hand, we have all met 22 and 23-year-olds who in bearing, demeanour, and knowledge convey a far older and very definite professional image. The issue, as in so much that will be discussed in this book, comes down to the qualities possessed by each individual regardless of age. In the long run, there really is no magic formula.

Would it not be better to hire a 50-year-old who is appropriate for a job and who will give 10, 15, or perhaps 20 years of high productivity, rather than that 22-year-old waiting for his or her pension, who will provide 40 years of mediocrity? Similarly, would that same firm not prefer to hire a young person who is mature, open and anxious to learn rather than an older, so-called mature person who has floundered around through life and now comes to that company on the road to mediocre retirement? Simply put, it is not how old a person is, but who that person is.

Experience

Of all the invalid hiring criteria that managers use or misuse, experience has been the most difficult for us to debunk. It is simply much easier to hire someone with knowledge of your product or service, or a person with a 'long-term track record'. Someone with this kind of experience can be up and running quickly, and does not require the kind of basic training that is required by someone without experience. Yet the price is high for taking this easy road.

First, we should look at who this 'experienced person' is who is being pirated from a competitor. Why is this individual willing to give up all the benefits of seniority and customer relations in order to start all over again with you? The reality is that this is probably an individual who has performed just well enough not to get fired—classic mediocrity—and who is looking to find an elusive pot of gold at the end of a non-existent rainbow with another firm. The widespread practice of pirating from one's competitors has always resulted in nothing but the recirculation of mediocrity.

Perhaps an unrelated and yet appropriate example might help to make this point. Let us pretend that you are a coach of a professional rugby team, and it is not really important in this fantasy whether you actually know or care anything about rugby. You are looking to recruit players. You now have two candidates to consider. The first is 5ft 7in tall, weighs 9 stone and had excellent credentials in playing school rugby. He also has an encyclopedic knowledge of the game. He can quote statistics, discuss strategies of every past game and so brings to his candidacy every value of the experienced person. The other candidate is 6ft 4in tall, weighs 16 stone and can run 100m dash in 11.5 seconds. However, he has hardly ever seen a rugby game. He knows nothing about strategy and would not know the difference between a pass and a tackle. If you are that coach, would you hire the experienced young man, or would you be willing to put the time and effort necessary into teaching the exceptional physical specimen? In other words, wouldn't you rather teach the second man rugby than have the little expert attempt to put his expertise into practice on the field?

Our problem in conveying this point to managers is that, although we know that this comparison is apt, it is not nearly as visible in the job situation. The difference is as pronounced, but exists within the individual's psyche, rather than being manifested externally. The ability to sell is not demonstrated visibly as is the 6ft 4in, 16-stone frame, nor is the obvious lack of such ability clearly visible. Yet, hiring the so-called experienced person who does not have the fundamental sales dynamics permitting him or her to succeed in sales is just as inappropriate as trying to make a professional rugby player out of the 5ft 7in young man.

It is important to add that there are, obviously, some situations in which a firm will find individuals possessing the necessary sales dynamics qualifying them to sell its products or services who have experience to boot. That obviously presents a 'best of all worlds' situation. Perhaps someone may have done a brilliant sales job in Glasgow and be moving to London. So, the company has someone with the talent, who can be up and running immediately with little effort. But the real world does not normally present those wonderful situations.

Most things are trade-offs and what we are suggesting, in the strongest possible terms, is that a manager should be willing to trade lack of experience and lack of product knowledge for real dynamic ability to sell. The lack of knowledge can be overcome by training, but the lack of fundamental ability to do the job cannot. Just as we discussed with regard to age, it is still the individual's inherent abilities that must be the focus.

Education

It is amazing how many managers indicate a college degree as an essential requirement for their sales positions. In many instances, when this requirement is probed it becomes obvious that there is actually no connection between having a college degree and selling their specific product or service. Of course there are many technical sales situations that require a college degree, as well as extensive knowledge in a particular field (computers, electronics, etc). For the most part, however, we have found little relationship between a diploma and an individual's ability to learn. The ability to obtain product knowledge quickly and to learn effective sales techniques is fundamental to selling effectively. But that ability is not necessarily proved by the fact that an individual possesses a college degree. By equating a college degree with intelligence, and more importantly growth potential, managers are effectively eliminating many excellent candidates who are more than sufficiently intelligent, but who do not happen to have the degree.

Again, what is critical here is that the individual must be the primary focus.

The manager should ask, 'Is the content involved in obtaining a degree really important to this sales situation?' If the answer is 'yes', then, of course, a specific degree should be required. On the other hand, if the answer is 'no' then the manager should seek other means of determining whether an individual possesses the ability to acquire the product knowledge and sales technique needed to succeed in that specific job. While it might be convenient to use the lack of a college degree as a simplistic screener in the selection process, all of our studies reveal that a college education has little to do with sales success in many industries. Of most importance, the possession of a college degree, in and of itself, clearly cannot in any way assist in predicting sales success.

THE WARM BODY APPROACH

At the opposite end of the spectrum are those thousands of companies and many industries which, though they certainly do not call it that, rely on what we term the 'warm body approach' in their hiring of salespeople. The way it works is that little or no salary is paid in lieu of sky-high commission rates for people who 'are willing to meet the challenge', 'will work hard', 'are career-minded', 'have real ambition' and 'want to get ahead'. Since no salary is paid, the theory is that anyone who wants the job should be brought aboard. People who hire on this basis say, 'What do I have to lose? If the individual sells one property or one life insurance policy, I'm ahead of the game.' The result is that a continual mass of recruitment advertisements are run in the newspapers, and a revolving door is set up for masses of people who decide to take a shot at these 'great opportunities'. But, since four out of five of them have no sales ability, most of them only last long enough to bother their relatives, friends and a few unsuspecting prospects. And so the turnover carousel continues. This warm body approach has, in fact, damaged the image of many industries, while creating huge, though often hidden, costs for the companies employing it.

When we focus later on the property and life insurance industries, we will deal with the real costs of this warm body approach in these specific industries. For now, suffice it to say that the costs of conducting an ongoing recruitment and selection process, continuing to train incapable individuals and then supervising them until they realise that they are in the wrong place at the wrong time are virtually incalculable. On top of this, these inappropriate people will inadvertently burn a company's precious prospects. Once these figures are added up, it becomes clear that the mere fact that salaries are not paid does not offset the true cost of hiring inept salespeople.

Another unfortunate result of this approach is the direct, negative impact on sales as a profession. If it is so easy to obtain one of these sales jobs in a warm body-oriented industry, what kind of status can be accorded someone who holds such a job? Job status is derived from the fact that it takes a particular expertise to be a member of the profession. Engineers, physicians, lawyers and accountants all hold their jobs because of recognised professional skills, knowledge and training. But salespeople in one of the warm body industries know that almost anyone walking the street could be filling their shoes.

An even more serious result of the warm body approach is the fact that four out of five salespeople with whom the public comes in contact are essentially incompetent. Thus, most people grow up with an exceedingly negative view of salespeople. Many of us remember that very pushy life insurance salesman who knocked at the door or that brush salesman or encyclopedia salesman who invariably came at inappropriate times and would not take no for an answer. We all, of course, look askance at the tyre-kicking used car salesman, and we have all heard stories of swindles conducted by fast talkers. So why would anyone want to join a profession with such a negative image?

Of course, not all companies or industries use this warm body approach. There are many cases where the selection of salespeople is more judicious. Many sales positions pay substantial base salaries, plus incentives; and many companies, due to the nature of the specific sales situation, are keenly aware of the enormous cost involved in the training required even to begin to sell the particular product or service. And, of course, in this high-tech era, there are increasing numbers of companies and industries in which specific technical know-how is a prerequisite to selling. The problem is that, even in situations where there is emphasis on carefully selecting the right person for the right job, in most cases the wrong criteria are employed for making that final hiring decision.

In this chapter, we have attempted to answer the fundamental question, 'Why, given all the opportunities in the sales profession, is there difficulty in finding and retaining highly productive people?' The high turnover rate and the lack of status caused by the numbers of inappropriate salespeople currently selling, using the warm body approach and hiring for the wrong reasons go a long way, we feel, towards explaining why professional sales is not one of the most important and one of the most sought-after positions in the business hierarchy.

The real sales professionals, on the other hand, are an exciting, dynamic group of people. After getting to know them, as we have, you quickly realise why they are the leading life insurance people, why they win national awards for computer sales and the like. It is these professionals that should be representative of the sales profession, but unfortunately they only represent approximately 20 per cent of that profession.

We will next delve into the personality attributes that are shared by the top 20 per cent of salespeople — those who sell 80 per cent of what is sold. Then we will look at ways to replace the old, outmoded, invalid hiring criteria, and, of course, the warm body approach, with recruiting and hiring methods that can attract productive people. We will explore how to select, develop and manage those individuals who are best suited to a company, selling a particular product or service. Ultimately, we will describe an approach that will help you reach, or at least approach, the situation where 50 per cent of what is sold is sold by 50 per cent of your salespeople, and your sales force more closely approaches, in its totality, the level of productivity currently represented by that magical 20 per cent.

PART 2

WHAT IT TAKES

Successful salespeople possess special personality attributes enabling them to succeed. Unlike many jobs where mediocre performance can be disguised and an individual is able to at least get by despite intensely disliking the job, the salesperson's success or failure is revealed immediately by bottom-line numbers. The very nature of the sales job precludes success for those who do not possess the fundamental motivation to sell.

In this part, we will first talk about motivation in general and then discuss the four central qualities, including the specific motivations, that are key to success in sales.

As we discuss these central qualities — these key motivational forces — it should be kept in mind that though possession of these central motivational qualities is essential to sales success, simply possessing them by no means ensures success in a specific sales job. Thus, this part will be devoted to examining the basic foundations upon which the question of what it takes to succeed in sales must be built. The next part will deal with the additional qualities that are needed to succeed in specific sales situations.

CHAPTER 3

THE MOTIVATIONAL KEY

The key element that separates the 20 per cent of all salespeople — the 20 per cent who sell 80 per cent of what is sold — from the rest is their motivation to excel in a very special way. Only by understanding what motivates an individual from within can we know what it really takes to succeed in sales or any other occupation.

Companies are continually looking for ways to motivate their people. Motivational speakers are featured at company meetings and industry conventions. Incentive plans are developed and contests are held. In most companies there is an endless sequence of carrot and/or stick programmes designed to motivate. Unfortunately, virtually all of this attention to motivation deals with external rather than internal motivation. Our work over the past 30 years has proven to us beyond question that the real key to productivity is not external motivation but, rather, that which is generated from within the individual — what we term 'internal motivation'.

Motivation is commonly defined as an incentive that persuades someone to do something. We pay salespeople commissions to motivate them to sell — a positive motivation. On the other hand, there is the threat of firing if people do not come to work on time or if they fail to work diligently. The annual review serves as another motivator, theoretically driving people to do their best for the purpose of earning salary increases or promotions. These are the classic carrots and sticks.

But it is our view that entirely too much emphasis is placed on these externals, and not nearly enough on what is the critical key to effective job performance — internal motivation. In the long run, the external motivations have little bearing on how well, or how poorly, an individual will perform. Of course people want promotions. Of course they want the highest commissions they can receive. And, of course, they do not want to be fired. However, these carrots and sticks do not create effective, productive work.

The true motivation that causes individuals to excel comes from within. It is this inner motivation which distinguishes the 20 per cent of those who succeed in the sales profession.

Internal motivation relates to what impels us from within to act. We need no one to tell us to eat when we are hungry. Similarly, when we are tired, we sleep because of our internal feeling of fatigue. When we are thirsty, we drink. We need no one to motivate us to enjoy the sunshine or to listen to a symphony (if we love music). Whether inner motivation is physiologically based (hunger, thirst, fatigue) or based on learned motivations (music, golf, fishing, sports etc) we are impelled to satisfy those motivations from within, and often we will even fight external resistance to satisfy these motivations.

When we look at internal motivations impelling us toward specific job functions, we are, of course, dealing with far more complexity than the easily described motivations of hunger and thirst. It is a simple matter for people to recognise that they are hungry, as it is simple for someone else to understand when an individual says, 'I want to eat because I am hungry'. When, on the other hand, one is dealing with job-related motivations, there is neither the individual's own clear-cut recognition of these motivations, nor is there the simple possibility of revealing these to another. When we talk about ego-drive in Chapter 5, we will be looking at one specific example of an internal motivation — the need to persuade. Yet, can you imagine an individual saying to someone else, 'I want to sell because I get specific ego gratification from having someone else say "yes" to me'? Yet, as we will see, that is precisely what is occurring. It should be added that here the matter becomes even more complicated, because some people are much more in touch with their inner motivations than others.

Without labouring the point, it is important to understand that, while all inner motivations impel us to action as clearly as hunger and thirst, we are not always aware of these motivations. Still, there is nothing more important in determining the effectiveness of an individual in a job than to understand his or her basic inner motivations, and to gear the job placement, training, compensation and supervision to those motivations. There is nothing more basic to the individual than those inner forces — those inner needs — driving that individual.

But because inner motivation seems so difficult to understand, many managers focus on the more obvious, but less effective, external motivations. For instance, many sales organisations set aside a particular month as 'Super Sales Month'. All of the salespeople are listed on a board, and each individual's sales are noted on a daily basis. This public display is, of course, designed to motivate everyone to compete. At the end of the month, the top producer (see page 173) will receive an all-expenses-paid trip for two to Hawaii with all the frills.

As expected, everyone works hard during that month, sales increase and someone wins the glamorous trip. Aside from the wonderful time the top producer has in Hawaii, however, the story does not have such a happy ending. Two results somehow tarnish the lustre of the exercise in external motivation. First, to no one's surprise, the winner of the contest has been the top producer consistently for two years. Second, and much more important to the success of the company, although sales increased during the contest month, they dropped substantially over the next couple of months, and the year's results consequently were the same as they would have been without the contest. What the external incentive did was generate some additional activity for a short period of time and cause people either to delay sales in order to close them in that month or hurry to push them into that month. But the overall totals were not affected. Simply put, sales, and individuals, found their level.

It is, of course, much easier to hire 'motivational speakers', or to set up contests of this kind, in the hope that such external processes will increase productivity. Externals, whether incentives or threats, are tangible, and so we reach towards them as solutions. Everyone walks out of a room feeling wonderful after being exposed to a dramatic, motivational speaker. Still, we cannot help but wonder whether the productivity increase is any better than it would be if the participants had gone to a good play or a good concert, after which there is also a wonderful feeling.

The truth is, although it is much more difficult to uncover, it is the inner motivation that determines how well an individual will do in a specific job. These inner motivations are much harder to deal with because you have to delve below the surface to uncover and understand them. Interviewing, conducting psychological testing, and checking resumes and references are all focused on uncovering some of these motivations. How effective we are in this quest determines how successful we will be in our hiring. The plain truth is, if we hire people whose motivation and abilities suit them to the position, then and only then can some of these external motivational approaches have a positive effect on productivity. Without the proper internal motivation, the externals can create motion but not consistent achievement.

We should add here that, as strongly as we deny the power of externals to create productivity, we certainly have seen situations where externals can place important limits on that productivity. It is certainly possible, for example, to set up a compensation system that runs counter to the motivation of the people receiving that compensation. If highly driven salespeople, with tremendous persuasive motivation and entrepreneurial orientation, are placed on a salary, even a high salary, with little upward mobility, this will de-motivate them. The incentives — the commissions — will not in and of themselves act as a motivation, but their absence, for certain individuals who need enormous up-end potential, can act as a disincentive.

A number of years ago, we ran into a classic case of this disincentive with one of our clients. We were asked to do a study on their sales operation to attempt to solve a problem that had plagued the company for more than a decade. They felt they were hiring effective salespeople. Most of their new hires started quickly and over the first couple of years were highly productive. However, counter to the experience of most companies who lose salespeople early in their careers, this company found that there was a high turnover between the third to fifth years of their salespeople's careers, and a parallel flattening out of sales productivity.

When we tested the sales force, we found that the company did have an unusually high number of strongly driven, highly motivated people. Instead of the usual 20 per cent of effective salespeople, their staff consisted of more than 50 per cent who we would have recommended for hire on the basis of their sales dynamics. When we investigated further, we found another unusual fact. The high turnover rate in the third to fifth year was largely among the salespeople with strong dynamics. The marginal people, those who were just getting by, were hanging on and were making a career of their mediocrity. This was puzzling. Normally, people leave because they are not being productive and so are not making a living. Here it was the productive people who were leaving.

As we studied the situation further, the reasons became clear. All signs pointed to the company's sales compensation plan. What occurred simply was that when a salesperson's level of sales became 'too high', their sales territory would be split. The reasoning, as we found out from interviewing management, was that a salesperson could not possibly handle too large a territory since there was continuous follow-up involved in most sales. Thus, once a salesperson had too many clients, the reasoning went, they could not possibly service those clients.

As rational as this sounds, the net result of this splitting of territories was that it removed the most productive salespeople's incentive to do well. People with drive are normally willing to risk earning little or no money at the beginning, but they cannot tolerate a limit on their top potential. This splitting of territories created an absolute upward limit and therefore destroyed the motivation of the few people the company counted on to be productive. On the other hand, the mediocre salespeople probably never reached a high enough production level to demand a split of their territory and so they hung on with their mediocrity.

We suggested that rather than split the territory of the highly productive people, the company provide these top producers — these inner-motivated people — with a service assistant whose job it would be to help in the ongoing servicing and follow-up as the salesperson's number of accounts increased. Rather than destroying up-end incentives, we felt it was important to give the top salespeople the ability to deal competently with their ever-expanding book of business. The result was that, within a year, the turnover among the productive salespeople was reduced by two-thirds. As might be expected, higher productivity substantially increased in proportion to the increased tenure of the effective salespeople. Within one more year, the company was able to effect important savings through reducing the number of 'senior account representatives' and supporting most of these people with lower-paid service assistants.

This is not to suggest that one compensation plan can fit all situations. Far from it. There are other cases where an individual's major motivational pull is towards security, consistency and stability. In these instances, an up-end incentive system, regardless of its potential, could be viewed as too risky and therefore clearly de-motivating.

We will discuss compensation in more detail later. But suffice it to say here that we should look towards externals to make certain that they do not demotivate, but we should rarely look towards them as a key factor in increasing individual or overall productivity.

We should underscore the point that money motivates virtually everyone to some degree, but truly effective individuals in any field of endeavour are motivated by more than money. For them, money is a symbol of achievement, not a motivational factor in and of itself.

The case of George provides a classic example of how internal motivation really is the dominant factor, regardless of how positive the external motivation is thought to be. George was an operations manager for one of our corporate clients, who was well on his way towards becoming vice president of operations. He had been on the job for ten years, received substantial salary increases each year, and enjoyed all of the requisite perks that go along with the rising star.

We were contacted by the current vice president of operations, who George was destined to replace due to that vice president's imminent retirement. He was concerned because, during the last six months, George's work had fallen off and he had confided to friends that he was thinking of leaving the company. The vice president asked us to test and interview George to determine what the problem might be, as the thing they wanted least was to lose this exceptional employee.

After evaluating George's test, the problem became apparent to us, though it took several in-depth interviews to convince George that the problem was, in reality, what we thought it to be. As an operations manager, George's work obviously involved a great deal of detail, much co-ordinative work and substantial overall administrative skills. Within this operational function, there was little or no opportunity to persuade. What the test showed, however, was that George possessed enormous persuasive motivation. He needed to convince people as a key means of gaining personal gratification. Lacking this opportunity on the job, he exercised his desire to persuade through a substantial degree of political involvement and some fund-raising activity for the former student's association of the university from which he had graduated. What was clear, however, was that as the job made increasing demands on him, both in terms of responsibility and time, the opportunity for these external persuasive outlets diminished and, with the vice presidency and the demands that it would impose, might disappear entirely. Added to this was the fact that, although George was able to cope with the detail required in the operations job, his inner motivation was not that of a real detail-oriented individual. He could tolerate detail but did not really enjoy it. Thus, despite the fact that George was successful in his job, the job demanded that he do things that he was not motivated to do and was blocking him more and more from doing things that he was motivated to do. Thus, success and the intended externals that go with it were not enough to provide George with satisfaction. Rather, the deprivation of his inner motivations was causing him to want to leave his job despite all of the external trappings.

When we shared this with George, he was totally astounded. To paraphrase, 'I really believed in your test until now, but when you say to me that I have sales ability, you lose your credibility.' He continued by telling us that he had never sold anything in his life and that the last thing in the world he would want to do would be to sell. He backed that up by pointing to his degree in finance and to his ten years of exceptional success in operations.

After a while, however, George began to see how his politics and fund raising activities really provided him with more personal gratification than his day-in and day-out work. He also began to connect both intellectually and emotionally the fact that these activities were in effect sales, and that it was the sales process that he enjoyed so much. It then became clear to him how the lack of this sales process created his primary frustration with his operations job.

The result of this was our startling suggestion to corporate management that a mid-career change be made for George right within the company. To cut a long and happy story short, this change was made after much protestation, and within two years, George was one of their top sales producers, again heading toward a vice presidency; this time vice-president of sales — a position directly attuned to his internal motivation.

Despite all of the external motivations that could have been provided, George would have left his job and sacrificed his fast career track just because his much more basic internal motivations were not being fulfilled. This is true even though George was not consciously aware that it was sales which really excited him. He was just vaguely dissatisfied with what he was doing. Despite this lack of conscious awareness, he would have given up the externals because of the internals. And this is the key to everything we are saying. If the internal motivation is there, and externals do nothing to inhibit it, but, rather, act to enhance it, people will succeed on the job. External motivation can never get the job done if the internal motivation is absent.

To help better understand internal motivation, think for a moment of the laziest person you know. Most likely, that individual is working for your company. When you look at this 'lazy person,' ask yourself if he or she is too lazy to get up at four o'clock in the morning to go fishing, or to stand in the hot sun swinging a golf club, or to work in the garden, or to play bridge or to do one of a hundred other enjoyable things. The answer is 'of course not'. What you are really saying when you think about that 'lazy person' is that the person is too lazy to do what *you* want done. The reality is that this so-called laziness, with few exceptions, is really a lack of inner motivation to do 'what they're supposed to do'. Provide them with an activity that coincides with their inner motivation, and they will work as hard as anyone.

This is our basic thesis. If an individual possesses the inner motivation to do a job and is given the proper training and supervision, he or she will succeed. On the other hand, if an individual does not possess the proper motivation required to perform successfully in a specific job, all of the training and incentives in the world will not make that individual highly productive. That 'lazy person's' willingness to work hard at fishing, golf or bridge is really typical of all human beings. We will work at what is fun for us — at what we enjoy. If we enjoy our work because that work satisfies our inner motivations, we need no one to tell us to work harder — we will do it because we want to, because it is rewarding. If, on the other hand, we hate what we are doing because it runs counter to our basic motivational forces, we might make motions, we might do our best because it is our responsibility, but we will never really be happy and will never really achieve at a top level, regardless of external motivations.

Before discussing the key motivational factors essential to sales success, it is important to emphasise that, while we have found that it is virtually impossible for an individual who does not possess these dynamics to be successful in sales, the mere possession of them by no means ensures success in a specific sales job. It is essential to begin by possessing these dynamics — empathy, ego-drive, ego-strength and service motivation. The possession of many other attributes, however (which we will discuss later), determines whether an individual will succeed in a specific sales job. With this in mind, we can turn to a discussion of these central characteristics. Before doing so, however, it might be interesting to review the events leading to our discovery of these characteristics.

In the late 1950s, we were asked by an insurance company to determine what they could do to reduce the enormous turnover among their agents. That company, like so many in the life insurance industry, was experiencing 60 per cent annual turnover of new agents, and nearly 90 per cent turnover in three years. If they could discover a test, a structured interview, or any other method of reducing their turnover, even by 5 per cent, the economic impact would be enormous.

We spent three months exploring hundreds of tests, interview guides, biographical and demographic appraisals, and even handwriting analysis to uncover a way to identify people with the potential to succeed in sales. The result of our three-month effort was a very short memo, which essentially read: 'There is nothing we can find worth the paper it is written on.'

We found it amazing that at a time when the boundaries of outer space were being explored, there was still very little understanding of what goes on inside people. Why was it conceivable to plot a lunar landing, but so difficult to predict whether someone had the qualities needed to succeed in sales? So we spent the next four years exploring what kind of people are motivated to put themselves on the line, day-in and day-out. What kind of people feel a need to persuade others? What does it take to endure the enormous amount of rejection which characterises the sales profession? From this research we discovered the central characteristics needed to succeed in sales.

CHAPTER 4

THE IMPORTANCE OF EMPATHY

The first key quality we found to be of critical importance to sales success is empathy. We define empathy as the ability to sense the reactions of another person. It is the ability to pick up the subtle clues and cues provided by another in order to assess accurately what they are thinking and feeling. Empathy does not necessarily involve agreeing with the other person's feelings, but it does involve knowing what their feelings or ideas are.

Empathy is not sympathy. Objectivity is lost in sympathy. Someone once said that 'empathy is placing oneself in the other person's shoes, but sympathy is putting them on and feeling the pinch'. Sympathy involves a feeling of loyalty to another person and, thus, the loss of objectivity. If you identify with and feel the emotions of another, you cannot view them in a dispassionate, objective and helpful manner. Thus, in order to sell effectively, an individual must understand how a prospect or client is feeling, while still maintaining one's own sense of identification, one's own purpose and one's own objectives. A salesperson simply cannot sell without this invaluable and irreplaceable ability.

Because sales involves evasions, objections and changing of course by the prospect, salespeople need to be empathetic enough to adjust their presentation and approach. Understanding the need of each customer and selling them an appropriate solution is part of a building-block process that starts with someone who is empathetic enough *really* to hear what is being said and *really* to feel the needs of the prospect, including clear recognition of hidden agendas and hidden objections. It is more often these hidden agendas and objections which defeat a sale than the clearly stated ones which can be dealt with more easily. Only with sufficient empathy to recognise the real needs of a prospect can those needs be met through the product or services being sold.

During the course of our early research, we identified empathy as the single basic ingredient common to all good salespeople.

The successful salesperson, while he or she may genuinely like the prospect and, hopefully, sincerely wants to serve the prospect well through the product or service, nevertheless sees that prospect as a means of achieving the end of making the sale and, therefore, as a means of gratifying that salesperson's ego needs. Where sight of this goal is lost, the salesperson, though he or she may be well liked, will be less effective in terms of the ability to overcome objections and close sales.

We overheard a conversation in the office of one of our client companies that illustrates this point well. The sales manager was berating one of her salespeople for failing to close an important prospect. The sales process had evidently been going on for more than three months, and both the salesperson and his manager felt that the prospect had a real need for their service.

In response to the manager's criticism, the salesman explained that the president of the prospect firm was extremely busy. He went on to describe the absolutely staggering schedule followed by the president, and how difficult he found it to add to his pressure. He went on to say, 'When I did get to see him, I felt I only had part of his attention, and that he always had one foot out of the door.'

What was happening here was that the salesman so identified with the customer's pressures that he failed to keep his objective in mind, which included providing a service that would in the long run actually help alleviate some of those very pressures.

The over-identification with one element of the customer's problem — the president's busy schedule — prevented the salesman from meeting his own objectives — making the sale — and simultaneously prevented him from really providing an important service to the customer.

In order to understand how empathy functions, or, in fact, whether it functions to a sufficient degree, it is important to realise that *functional* empathy relates entirely to motivation. No one really knows whether an individual is born with differential empathetic capacity. In fact, we do not really know with any degree of certainty whether people really lack the capacity for empathy or absolutely possess that capacity. What we do know, and what is critical to all of our discussions about what it takes to succeed in sales, is that in a behavioural sense, people vary widely in their ability to make *functional* use of their empathy. The point we are making here is that, whether or not there is some sort of built-in empathetic capacity within an individual, the key factor relates to each individual's motivation to use their empathy.

There are many people who choose to perform on the surface of life. They deal with what is tangibly in front of them and tend to accept what is said and what is done on its face. They are not interested in exploring what might lie behind the statement or action and really spend little of their energy thinking about the motivations or needs of others. These may be perfectly nice, friendly, outgoing individuals. In fact, they may, if given other personality attributes, literally be the life of the party. They may even be right there when someone needs help, especially physical help. The key, however, is that they do not probe beneath the readily recognisable. If someone falls and is injured, they will respond to this, but they are not likely to recognise the psychic pain that another might be experiencing. Simply put, these people do not think about reading other people, and so are not motivated to do so.

There is another kind of what we might term 'blockage' to empathy. That is, there are those individuals who might be extraordinarily intelligent, and who may even possess some motivation to understand others. They may, however, be so rigid that they use their intelligence to defend their preconceptions and screen out empathetic feedback that might be contrary to their own ideas or attitudes. They may simply screen feedback so that it conforms to what they want it to be, rather than to what it actually is.

There are, on the other side of the coin, those individuals who are motivated to read and understand others. They probe beneath the surface and are constantly examining situations and individuals in terms of underlying, rather than surface, factors. It is these people who are motivated to use empathy — to open up their receivers — and to take in the feedback from others. You can almost relate these three groups to owning a hi-fi receiver. The first does not bother to buy one. The second may own a fine receiver, but either does not turn it on or, at best, permits it to function defectively through a great deal of static. The third turns it on and makes sure it functions at its fullest capacity.

This brings us to another significant point. That is, there are no moral values attached to empathy. Salespeople who are providing a product or service that is genuinely needed by a prospect use their empathy as a key tool in persuading the prospect to make the right decision. On the other hand, the con man will use empathy to find the weaknesses in victims that will cause them to act in a way that will injure them, but help the con man.

Empathy reminds us in this context of the split atom, which may be used ultimately to destroy mankind or to save us, to level cities or to cure cancer. By itself, the atom will do neither. What counts is how it is used. As with the atom, empathy itself does not determine the ways in which it will be used. Other factors influence this determination.

When we first started to explore the qualities needed to succeed in sales, we felt that empathy was the sole key to predicting sales success, and indeed there proved to be a high correlation. However, as we ran studies in company after company, a pattern emerged indicating that, although empathy was clearly essential, it was not enough. Invariably situations would arise where top management agreed that certain individuals possessed empathy, but nevertheless were producing poor sales results. A case from our files illustrates the problem in these situations.

Frank, a property salesman who we tested at his manager's request, appeared to perform his sales role perfectly, but, mysteriously, he rarely closed a sale. He educated buyers about local property values, worked with great energy to find available properties at the right price and style, and expertly guided potential buyers toward the best financing arrangements and mortgage institutions. Throughout the process, he cultivated his customers to the point where he was deluged with golf and bridge invitations. But when the customers signed on the proverbial dotted line, it was usually with another salesperson, frequently from another estate agency.

Frank, like so many people following this pattern, was empathetic enough to develop excellent relationships with customers and associates, and to maintain existing accounts. But he rarely brought in new business. The simple fact was that he could not 'close' the sale.

So often, as in Frank's case, we were told that these individuals presented a product or service well, developed excellent relationships with customers and associates, and maintained existing accounts, but rarely brought in new business.

It became clear from studying hundreds of cases such as Frank's, that, while the irreplaceable feedback provided by empathy is absolutely essential to sales success, empathy alone is not enough. What is needed is the motivation to use the empathetic feedback as a tool for persuasion. We call this motivation ego- (or personal) drive.

CHAPTER 5

PERSONAL DRIVE AS A MOTIVATIONAL FORCE

What is there about salespeople that sets them apart from their colleagues in other professions? Why don't they look for jobs in which they can drop an anchor in calmer waters and face a judgement of their abilities only when it is time for their annual salary review? Why do they endure rejections even though they could be avoided? Actually, the answers to these questions are one and the same.

Ego-drive is a special basic personality quality that makes the salesperson want and need to make a sale in a personal, or ego, way. Individuals with ego-drive feel that the sale has to be made. So, the prospect is there to help fulfil a personal need. To the top salesperson, getting a prospect to say yes provides a powerful means for ego enhancement. His or her self-image improves dramatically by virtue of achieving that yes and diminishes with each sales failure. Whether the yes involves commission is far less relevant than the yes itself. To the ego-driven individual, 'Yes, I will go out with you', or 'Yes, I will join your club', or 'Yes, I will vote for your candidate', or 'Yes, I agree with you' are just as satisfying as 'Yes I will buy your product or service'. If an individual really has ego-drive, he or she needs that yes — regardless of what the yes is — as a key means of satisfying the ego-drive.

How people view themselves underlies most of their ambition and motivation. We seek approval, we want acceptance, we enjoy our associates' acclamation for a job well done. For the fortunate among us, the path we choose in search of self-enhancement becomes our career.

Engineers are gratified by designing complex equipment, building bridges or planning a dam. Artists achieve gratification by expressing themselves creatively. Teachers achieve through the accomplishments of their students. Carpenters, tailors and repairmen achieve gratification by exercising their craftsmanship. In the same way, top salespeople enhance their egos through persuading others, frequently in a face-to-face, one-to-one situation.

What salespeople seek is an opportunity to turn others around to their point of view. That is why top salespeople never really retire. Characteristically, after reaching the mandatory retirement age, they head a local fund drive or put their energy to work fighting for one civic cause or another, perhaps even entering into politics for the first time. Even when they no longer need the money earned in a lifelong process of persuasion, they are still strongly driven to persuade. Persuading is like breathing for the ego-driven individual.

The strongly motivated career salesperson or sales manager who retires at the company's compulsory retirement age seems young, fresh and vigorous, virtually until the last day on the job. If they find other ways to channel their energy, they appear to maintain youth and vigour for years. However, if they spend their post-retirement months and years pottering around the house or relaxing in the classic retirement community style, their former associates are frequently shocked to note how much they seem to age in only a year or two.

Ego-drive should not be confused with the usual perceptions of drive, willingness to work or aggressiveness. For example, a bank president may be extremely ambitious, driven, hardworking and aggressive, but still not have an inner need to persuade. Ego-drive is a particular means of gaining self-enhancement by persuasion of another person; it is not to be confused with a general desire to get ahead or to achieve.

Strong ego-drive alone does not assure success in selling. Ironically, unless properly balanced with empathy and other key personality characteristics, it can spell disaster in selling.

The reason is simple: salespeople whose ego-drive is in overdrive are 'too hungry' for the close. They are so driven to conquer in a one-to-one situation that they tend to bowl customers over, rushing towards a close without listening to possible objections, or even relating the product or service to the prospect's needs. Such a salesperson, by the sheer force of his or her personality, may produce some sales. But he or she will miss many sales which a more sensitive, more balanced salesperson would have achieved in similar circumstances. And such salespeople often offend or alienate potential customers and, in the process, burn territory for their company.

Clearly, then, a balance must exist between ego-drive and other basic personality characteristics if a salesperson is to be genuinely successful. We can illustrate our point here by considering the case of Jack, a salesman for a major computer firm. On first appearance, Jack would impress any potential employer with his prototypical sales abilities. Yet, he was among the least productive members of the sales force. When we examined his personality dynamics in detail and then checked his profile against his job, the reason was clear: Jack's job was to sell large computer installations to the government.

Success was defined as selling two major installations per year. The financial rewards for these two sales were enormous, but Jack's ego-drive was so intense that he simply could not tolerate the infrequency of closings. His need for the close impelled him to push too hard in his desperation to achieve a quick sale, and so he met with failure.

This does not mean that Jack had no value as a salesman. It simply means that his personality dynamics were wrong for the particular job in which he was slotted. He was transferred to another division of the company which provided time-shared computer services — payroll, accounting and the like — primarily to small and medium-sized businesses. His success was almost immediate. The reason was that he had several closing opportunities per day and, given his level of ego-drive, was able to convert more than his share. The reality for Jack was that his up-end financial opportunity was somewhat less in the new situation, but the opportunity for satisfying his ego-drive was greater.

We have learned from dealing with thousands of Jacks and their employers that the salesperson with an over-abundance of ego-drive can, if his or her drive is tempered by other qualities, be exceptionally successful with essentially hard-sell and small-ticket products.

The evidence is clear that no single salesperson would be equally effective in all sales jobs. (This is one of the most critical, and often overlooked, factors in attempting to build a sales force.) Some people's personality dynamics suit them to a particular kind of selling, but no person is ideally suited to all kinds of selling.

With that fact in mind, we will in later chapters discuss the various personality characteristics which are needed to succeed in different types of selling. But empathy and ego-drive are the two characteristics most important in identifying the basic sales personality.

The question that invariably arises in discussions about the dynamics of a successful salesperson is: are these abilities inborn or are they developed? Is ego-drive something — a genetic quality, perhaps — that exists in the individual from birth, or is it something that can be developed in anyone through training and motivation?

There is no way to know the exact role genetics or socialisation plays in any behavioural trait. As in most human functions, the answer probably lies somewhere between nature and nurture. Undoubtedly, there are some inherited qualities that provide the kind of climate in which ego-drive is more likely to develop. Yet, there is no provable evidence to indicate that genetics alone is responsible for ego-drive. What appears to be the predominant factor in the existence of ego-drive — as in the development of other personality characteristics — is childhood and early adolescent experience.

For example, a young boy may be well endowed with physical strength as a result of inheritance, good food and other environmental factors. As he develops, he finds through athletic accomplishment and feats of strength that he receives a great deal of approval. He is able to throw and catch a ball better than his five-year-old peers. At the age of six he may be praised for defeating an eight-year-old bully in a fight. At the age of nine he becomes the leading bowler for his school cricket team and helps win a championship. All these things have brought him ego gratification, the self-enhancement we all seek. Is it surprising, then, that as a teenager he goes out for his secondary school cricket and football teams and yearns for a first-class cricket career or a starting slot with Liverpool or Spurs? Since he has achieved his gratification primarily through athletic prowess, he would hardly be likely to anticipate adult gratification in a sales career. Not persuasion, but physical accomplishment, would be his likely means of achievement.

In this example, as in most, it is almost impossible to separate the role of nature and nurture. Certainly the boy could not have achieved his primary ego gratification through physical accomplishment were it not for the potential with which he was born; but neither could he have achieved this satisfaction if he did not have appropriate nutrition, motivation, care and a conditioning environment. But it is clear that by the time this young man is 20 or 21 years old, his motivational pattern will be set. He is what he is, and his means of receiving gratification are what they are, regardless of the nature/nurture balance.

Ego-drive develops in the same way. For example, another youngster's early gratification is gained through talking and interacting with people. Either because of inheritance or the stimulation of his environment, or perhaps a combination of both, he is an early talker, and at 18 months he has a surprisingly broad vocabulary, for which he is praised and commended by parents and other adults. Early in his childhood, he learns that he can accomplish more by persuasion than by temper tantrums, and gradually he comes to enjoy the process of persuasion as much as he does the ultimate goal of persuading someone else. This learned response strengthens as he matures, converting a simple childhood lesson into a direction and a career — sales — that allows him to profit from a gratifying pursuit.

The development of the ego-driven personality does not appear to follow a classic pattern. People develop the desire to persuade for many reasons. But it is quite certain that these reasons are rooted in childhood experience. Putting aside 'born' or 'made' theories, we know that ego-drive exists in young adults to the precise degree that it will continue to exist for the rest of their lives. A person who is not basically motivated to persuade others cannot be trained to derive primary satisfaction from selling. You cannot train him or her to use what they do not have. Only a person with ego-drive can be trained to use what he or she has in a maximally effective way.

Ego-drive is to the salesperson what fuel is to a car engine. Without fuel, the car engine cannot move forward. With fuel, but without steering, the car constitutes a hazard and is valueless. Ego-drive is that fuel, while empathy provides the steering.

CHAPTER 6

THE EMERGING FACTOR OF SERVICE MOTIVATION

For many sales positions, there is a motivational force parallel to ego-drive that can be as important to success as ego-drive itself. While the ego-driven individual derives personal gratification from getting the yes, the service-motivated individual derives the same gratification from receiving the 'thank you', 'you did a good job', 'I appreciate that', etc. The feeling of approval provides the same gratification to the service-motivated person as the closed sale does to the individual with ego-drive.

More often than not these two motivational forces do not exist in the same individual, and yet on first impression, for example in a job interview, the two may easily be confused with one another. We will discuss the reasons for this confusion later, but suffice it to say here that that confusion leads to many hiring mistakes and many wrong decisions relating to training and developmental approaches to improve individual productivity.

What is becoming more and more true in the 1990s is the fact that success in increasing numbers of sales positions really demands that an individual should possess at least some degree of both of these motivations. Where both are demanded, and only one exists, failure is likely to be the result.

This situation is illustrated by one of our multinational client companies, which acquired a medium-sized US company whose products fit extremely well into our client company's product mix. The smaller company was acquired at an extremely advantageous price because, for several years, it had lost market share and in the last couple of years had lost substantial sums of money. This was in spite of the fact that the company's product was at least as good, and perhaps better, than that of most of its competitors. We were asked to conduct an audit of their sales and management team to see how much of the problem rested with the quality of that team.

After assessing nearly 500 salespeople and their managers, the problem was easily diagnosed. Simply put, some 90 per cent of their 'sales' people did not possess sufficient ego-drive to allow them to sell successfully. Many had empathy, and a good many more possessed qualities that permitted them to do an exceptionally good service job. Thus, what the company was calling 'salespeople' were in reality very good servicers.

Early in its history when the company held a prominent position in the market, and the product was novel, in great demand and virtually sold itself, these service 'sales' people were able to 'get away with it'. They literally took orders for the product, and the most they had to sell involved getting retailers to push the product just a bit more. As the situation changed, however, and competition, with aggressive salespeople, entered the market in increasing numbers, these so-called salespeople were swept away by their more effective competitors. It was clear that nothing changed in terms of the nature of the people, but with competition the nature of the job changed radically. Most of the company's existing people did not possess the personality attributes that would allow them to change with the situation, and the result was accelerating failure.

When we presented these findings to management, they expressed no surprise. They, too, felt that many of their people, especially the long-tenured ones, were more order takers than real salespeople. Yet, they correctly said that the nature of their product absolutely required service as well as sales. We agreed that the job could not simply involve closing sales, but had to require effective, outstanding ongoing service as a follow-up to that closed sale. What was clear, then, was that this company indeed needed salespeople with empathy and sufficiently strong ego-drive to close more effectively if they were to be able to compete. Their salespeople had to be motivated to persuade — to get the yes — as a means of gaining personal satisfaction, but while also being motivated to come through and enjoy being told, 'Thank you', 'You did a good job', and 'I appreciate that', as a parallel key means of deriving ego-gratification. This need we term 'service motivation'.

Service-motivated people have strong inner motivation to come through and a strong need for approval and appreciation. As we mentioned earlier, all people find means of making themselves feel good. For the ego-driven person, getting someone to say yes provides enormous personal gratification. For the service-motivated person, 'Thank you, you did a good job' provides the same kind of gratification. It is critical to service-motivated people that they be liked, and they work as hard to accomplish that as the ego-driven person does to achieve the yes.

In order to gratify an individual's service motivation, he or she has to have the ability to get things done in a timely manner. He or she must have the attitude and conviction that if they have committed themselves to do something, they will get it done, and it will be done right. Their word is their bond.

Certain qualities are critical if an individual is to fulfil his or her service motivation — to do a good service job. Obviously, people skills are essential together with a strong sense of responsibility. Yet, it is not good enough to 'yes' someone to death or smile in the most ingratiating way. Strong personal organisation and the ability to handle detail well, without being absorbed in it or using detail as an excuse for delay, are key tools for service effectiveness. Service people have to judge the legitimacy of a customer complaint and be willing to take the responsibility for making a decision about the best way to resolve the situation. But here lies a common problem: if you are motivated to look good, to receive approval, you do not want to make a mistake and risk looking bad. Thus, indecisiveness and inaction are endemic among too many people in service roles. What they tend to do is take what they consider the safe way and do nothing, rather than take the chance of being wrong. Also, in an effort to be liked, the service person may tend to promise anything, but unless he or she possesses the wherewithal, both practically and in terms of personality, to fulfil the promise, bad service is obviously the result.

As we indicated earlier, many people who possess strong service motivation lack strong ego-drive. Thus, finding people who possess both is not an easy task, given the inherent contradiction between the two motivational forces. More often than not, companies find they have one or the other, but not the combination. Ego-driven people typically tend to be impulsive and individualistic; they have less of a need to please or seek approval, and they dislike detail and follow-up. Service-motivated people, on the other hand, tend to be cautious team players who are oriented towards detail work and are good at follow-up; they have a strong need to be liked and approved of. These service-motivated individuals are absolutely essential to the good functioning of most companies. Selling without quality service will guarantee eventual failure as certainly as failure to sell the product in the first place. Most successful salespeople will be the first ones to state how critical the sales support provided by service people is to their own success. In fact, service as a profession is becoming an increasingly important and respected role in our changing society.

The problem only occurs where service motivation is confused with, and so substituted for, persuasive motivation or ego-drive. It is when the service-motivated person with little ego-drive attempts to sell, or the ego-driven person with little service motivation attempts to provide service, that problems arise.

What increasing numbers of sales roles require are people who possess both of these motivations to a rather strong degree.

Still, when making a hiring decision there is potential confusion between ego-drive and service motivation. We can recall a situation that illustrates this point. A couple of years ago one of our senior account executives recommended that a client should not hire a particular applicant for a sales position. There was a heavy moment of silence followed by, 'But she came across so well in the interview. What is wrong?' Our account executive replied, 'From our analysis, I can see that this individual is very intelligent, and probably made a pleasant impression. The right questions were asked, and a warm, friendly, and genuinely likeable demeanour was conveyed. In fact, the applicant probably came right out and said that the interview was enjoyable and your firm was impressive. She may have even written you a thank-you note or called to express her continuing interest.' The client thought a moment, and then said, 'That is exactly right. That is exactly what happened. Even the thank-you-letter. So, what is wrong?'

What was wrong, and what our account executive tried to explain to our client, was that the applicant's motivations were not those needed by that client for that specific sales role. The applicant made the good impression because she was strongly motivated to do so. She possessed service motivation. Thus, during and after the interview, she worked very hard to be liked, to come across as nice, and to do everything in her power to create a positive impression on the part of the interviewer. Making that impression might have got her the job, because the impression was condensed into a one-hour interview. That impression, however, is seldom sufficient to allow an individual to succeed in sales, in an ongoing way, without the motivation to sell (ego-drive). Simply put, selling is far more difficult than simply making a good first impression. Yet, how many people have been wrongly hired because of that first impression with the invariable moan six months or a year later as the individual is dismissed. 'But he or she looked so good in the interview'? In the hiring process, it is necessary to distinguish first impressions from inherent personality qualities.

It is particularly important for managers to separate ego-drive and service motivation, which may on the surface, over a short time-span, look similar, but which are in reality very different dynamics. In most instances, despite the good impression that the strongly service-motivated person conveys, such people simply are not sufficiently motivated to sell nor, again typically, can they or do they want to take the rejection involved in sales. So, most purely service-motivated people will be sales failures.

Yet, despite this admonition, it is important to re-emphasise that there are those individuals (though they are difficult to find because of some of these inherent contradictions) who do possess both motivational forces in sufficient degree to succeed in sales roles requiring good service follow-up. We were in fact able to assess a number of these individuals for our client who is slowly replacing the pure servicers as they either change jobs or retire. Our client will, in fact, end up with a smaller sales force, but with people who can both close sales and do the servicing that continues to be a vital aspect of the job.

CHAPTER 7

RESILIENCE

When all is said and done, selling is a game of trying to beat the odds of rejection. Rare indeed is the salesperson who can close a sale in two contacts. Regardless of the industry involved, the person who is attempting to persuade another individual is more likely to be rejected than to be accepted. What happens then to the persuader (the individual who likes himself or herself better as a result of getting someone else to say yes) when the inevitable rejection occurs? The individual feels diminished. But the key here is that the salesperson nust never feel totally diminished. When one fails, he or she obviously does not feel too good, but the essential question is: does that person have the resiliency — or what we call ego-strength — to bounce back from that rejection?

Ego strength is really the degree to which an individual basically likes him or herself. If an individual possesses great ego-strength, then the failure can motivate them towards the next try.

Persons with ego-strength feel as badly as anyone would when they encounter failure, but they react to that failure much as the hungry person does to missing a meal: they are all that much hungrier for the next opportunity.

The failure, though disappointing, does not destroy the individual's view of him or herself. It is not personalised but, rather, creates a disappointment — a lack of fulfilment — that the next opportunity will correct. On the other hand, when people do not have sufficient ego-strength to react with resiliency, if there are not enough good feelings about themselves, they take the rejection personally. They feel that the no is a no to them and is further proof that they are indeed not very good, not really worth while. They are, therefore, very hesitant to seek another situation that could incur yet another rejection because, even if they have the desire to persuade (the ego-drive) the pain of the potential rejection is simply too great to run the risk.

Another serious problem where there is a lack of ego-strength results from the sheer intensity of the conflict within the individual. As we said, people work very hard to like themselves, and so the individual who inherently lacks a good sense of self (ego-strength) is putting forth enormous effort inwardly to find ways to like him- or herself better. This inner conflict takes up so much of the individual's energy that there is literally no time and certainly no energy to invest fully in a job. The preoccupation is with self and anything external must of necessity take a back seat. Their occupation with their conflict thus makes it difficult to work in a consistent way, particularly where there is a good deal of pressure or confrontation involved.

Many years ago, when we were only vaguely aware of the importance of ego-strength, we ran into a situation that taught us, in a most dramatic fashion, its importance.

We evaluated a sales applicant for a client and strongly recommended that the client hire the individual. He had outstanding empathy and possessed more than enough ego-drive to close sales effectively in that company's situation. He also had a strong sense of responsibility and clearly possessed the desire to succeed.

Sure enough, the young man started out like a house on fire. Within a month after the training period, he was in the top 10 per cent of the sales force and, to say the least, we had a very happy client.

Three months later, we received a panic call from the sales manager. To paraphrase, the manager told us, 'Jim simply stopped producing (ie selling) about a month ago. As you know, we thought he would be the best person we ever hired, but all of a sudden it all seemed to come apart. He has not made a sale in the month and what is making it worse is he is beginning to come in late, take long lunches and some days does not even show up at all. He has obviously got the ability, but what do you think could have happened?'

We re-evaluated the test and determined, again, that Jim had all the ego-drive and empathy that we had originally thought he did. But what we began to see as we examined the results of his behavioural test is that he really did not have good feelings about himself. His ego-strength was clearly lacking. As we discussed the situation in more detail with the manager and interviewed Jim several times, the picture became clear. Given his ability, Jim successfully closed a number of sales in succession. Someone with less ability would never have made those sales, but anyone, regardless of ability, could not continue at that sales pace. Inevitably, rejection pushed Jim out of the super sales level. Statistics being what they are, those rejections came in three out of every four sales attempts, and simply put, Jim's lack of ego-strength made it impossible for him to deal with them. He was not able to look at the rejections as statistics inevitably catching up with him, but rather saw them as the truth finally being told. The early successes he viewed as simply a fluke, and the real Jim was represented by the failures.

As a means of desperately trying to turn the situation around, Jim pressed hard, acted inappropriately and literally drove away prospects to whom he would have sold earlier. The more he pressed, the more he failed, and the more he failed, the more he came down on himself. Finally, despite his obvious sales talent, Jim was dismissed.

Jim and thousands like him remind us strikingly of a cricketer who is the spring batting phenomenon. He tears the cover off the ball during spring training and continues at this almost impossible pace into the first week or two of the season. Within a couple of months, he is back down the batting order and soon after has faded out of memory. Why? Obviously, he had batting talent. However, nobody hits sixes steadily, so, like Jim, the phenomenon hits the inevitable slump that is going to bring him *down* to a still lofty batting average. If he had the ego-strength, he might maintain his averages through a hall-of-fame career. However, again like Jim, lacking ego-strength, the phenomenon comes quickly down on himself. He changes his swing and, in his desperation not to fail, guarantees failure by doing things differently — by getting away from the natural talent that brought him his success.

The case of Cathy illustrates the role of ego-strength in quite a different way. When we evaluated her test, we saw an individual who had excellent empathy, was highly intelligent, and possessed both a strong sense of responsibility and fine personal organisational skills. Our only doubt related to her ego-drive. She definitely had some persuasive motivation, but she lacked the intense need to persuade that characterises most highly productive salespeople. She got pleasure from the close — from getting the yes — but not the typical kind of intense satisfaction that strongly ego-driven people receive. Thus, we felt that she might miss some closes because of this lack of intense drive.

Given her other strong qualities, especially her good sense of self (her good ego-strength), we suggested to our client that Cathy be hired. We also suggested that, if at all possible, she be provided with training in the area of closing skills to try to bolster her only moderate ego-drive.

Cathy was hired, and for the first month or two we and our client were concerned because she started extremely slowly. In the first two months she only made one sale, although as our client described it she did have a number of prospects on the line.

Slowly, however, the situation began changing. A few of the prospects became customers and the number of prospects steadily increased. Within six months, Cathy was functioning in the middle of the sales force, and by the end of the first year, was high in the second rank of salespeople. Now, four years later, Cathy is still functioning well up in the second rank of the sales force, and though not a top producer, she is well above average and an important, strong contributor to the company's bottom line.

Unlike Jim, Cathy's rejections came early. Because of her lack of intense ego-drive, she did not close sales early and often. Rather, she experienced the rejections and failures that are so typical of novices. But, again unlike Jim, because of her good sense of self (her good ego-strength) she did not view the rejections in a personal way. She saw her failures as the inevitable result of inexperience and of the price she had to pay to gain that experience. Because of many other strong personality attributes, she would not accept no as final, but continued to consider them as prospects in need of folow-up and, of equal importance, she was able to continue looking for more prospects without fearing their rejection. In the long run, she had enough ego-drive to convert some of those initial rejections to closings and, with increasing know-how, slowly but steadily to improve her initial conversion ratio.

The difference between Jim and Cathy can be summed up this way: Jim obviously had more drive and possessed the potential to function near the very top of the sales force. His lack of ego-strength, however, made it impossible for him to actualise that talent because he could not deal with the inevitable rejection that even a superstar must experience. On the other hand, Cathy, with less inherent talent, could function to the top of her potential because she felt good enough about herself, and strong enough within herself, to do so.

Ego-strength, then, is quite simply an individual's feeling good enough about him- or herself to accept rejection, not as a personal affront, but as part of life. The individual with ego-strength has the ability to leave the rejection behind and go on from there. Those who accept themselves, who possess ego-strength, operate freely and fully, and allow themselves to function at or near the top of their capacity.

CHAPTER 8

THE CENTRAL CHARACTERISTICS FOR SUCCESS

There is an enduring stereotype of the successful salesman. He stands 6 ft tall with a halfback's physique and a bone-crushing handshake. He is an incurable extrovert with an unending supply of hilarious jokes. He likes people in groups and is dependably the life of any party. He is great on the golf course and is ready to converse, at least superficially, on almost any subject.

Recognise him? Of course. The legend has survived for generations, and today is so thoroughly ingrained in our culture that it appears not to be subject to change. In fact, it is so much a part of our heritage that an entire branch of folk humour — the travelling salesman joke — is rooted in it.

In truth, the typical top salesperson is often strikingly dissimilar to this idealised portrait, a fact that can be verified at any number of annual sales meetings, where the 'Salesperson of the Year' award often goes to a middle-aged, somewhat balding fellow who is 5 ft 6 in, has a slight paunch, and wears rimless glasses, or to an ordinary-looking woman who no one could mistake for a halfback.

In our work we have found that relying upon this sales stereotype is as expensive as it is fanciful. Salesperson after salesperson is hired because he or she conforms to the stereotype, only to fail in the field. (We have seen more sales vice presidents surrounded by gregarious, athletic-looking failures than we care to remember.)

The fact is, sales success is only remotely related to external characteristics. The stereotypical attributes of the successful salesperson are demonstrable nonsense.

Two primary observations should be made on the subject of what makes a good salesperson:

1. As we have emphasised in earlier chapters, determining factors are internal, related almost entirely to the individual's personality; and

2. There is no one person, regardless of his or her personality dynamics, who can be equally successful in all types of sales situations.

Let us look at why this is so. The four major personality characteristics that we have been discussing — empathy, ego-drive, service motivation and ego-strength — do not exist independently. They affect one another — sometimes positively, sometimes negatively.

In the inherently successful salesperson, empathy and ego-drive exist in a dynamic relationship, where both combine to reinforce and fulfil the potential of each characteristic.

People with strong ego-drive have maximum motivation to use whatever empathy they possess. People with fine empathy are equipped to direct and temper their ego-drive.

Naturally, there are a number of possible permutations of empathy and ego-drive. A person may have a high degree of both empathy and ego-drive (ED), little of either (ed), or a mixed combination (either Ed or eD). For example:

ED Salespeople who have a great deal of both empathy and ego-drive will almost invariably be at or near the top of the sales force as long as they have sufficient ego-strength and other qualities needed for the specific position.

Ed Salespeople with fine empathy but too little drive may be splendid human beings, but in many cases will be unable to close effectively. They are usually well liked and, from all appearances, should be among the best salespeople on the staff. But they never quite make it. While they develop very good relationships with prospects, they never convert them to clients. Salespeople with fine empathy but very little drive get along with and understand their prospects, but they lack enough inner hunger to move those final few inches to a completed sale. This is not to say that such individuals will never sell anything. In fact, there are somes sales situations in which these individuals may perform reasonably well. They may succeed in selling to doctors for a pharmaceutical house, for example, or in selling the government a large-scale installation. These are instances where service and relationship-building are more vital than the close. But where fast and frequent closes are the requirement, such individuals will not succeed, despite their congeniality, personableness and sensitivity.

eD A salesperson with much drive but too little empathy will, by sheer force of personality, bulldoze his or her way through to some sales, but also will miss a great many. In the process of making an occasional sale, such salespeople may cause enormous damage to their employers' professional reputation. Again, there are some specific sales situations in which these bulldozers can be reasonably effective. For instance, they may do well selling used cars in a city car dealership. Or they may be effective selling life insurance. In other words, he or she may succeed in situations where the immediate close is the name of the game, the potential market is unlimited, and the likelihood of repeat business is minute. But this particular bulldozer's strength begins to wane as soon as the sales situation requires follow-up, service and relationship-building—in short, where repeat business and the development of a stable market are important. Then, even if their number of sales seems acceptable, they can be like termites, causing unseen harm to the firm's professional reputation.

ed   Someone without much empathy or ego-drive simply should not be in sales. A potential employer would save much time and money by determining this in advance, before hiring, training and then losing him or her. This does not mean that such individuals are failures as human beings. Non-salespeople might be excellent at hundreds of other pursuits: engineers, accountants, computer programmers, technicians, operations personnel or any number of non-selling activities. Where they are destined to fail, both themselves and their companies, is as salespeople. It is tragic that many such individuals, with little or no chance to succeed in selling, none the less carry on a perennial and futile quest for success. This makes for a double waste. First, they fail their employers at the job they have chosen and, secondly, they fail themselves by not choosing a profession at which they could succeed. These individuals without sufficient empathy and ego-drive account for 55 per cent of the individuals now attempting to earn a living in sales. Ironically, within the same companies in which they work, there might be any number of openings for jobs which they might fill with distinction and profit.

As we said at the outset of this section, an individual cannot sell successfully without possessing, to a reasonable degree, empathy, ego-drive, and ego-strength. In ever-increasing numbers of sales situations, service motivation must be added to the mix. People, however, are not neatly slotted into distinct categories. Most people do not either have empathy or totally lack empathy. People are not distinctly separated by having ego-drive or totally lacking persuasive motivation. And most of all, people do not either have ego-strength or lack it. Rather, people function on a continuum, and so, as we look at their ability to sell, we have to look at how much or how little of each quality they have and how these qualities integrate with the strength of the other qualities. For certain sales jobs there can be too much ego-drive, while others need as much as possible. Certain jobs require only moderately strong persuasive motivation, but a high degree of service must go along with it. Many sales jobs can tolerate somewhat reduced levels of ego-strength, but others demand high degrees of that quality.

In short, few people possess optimum amounts of all these central qualities. The human condition involves trade-offs. As we look at an individual and determine whether that person is suited to a particular sales job, we need to look at how much of each of these central qualities he or she possesses and how these attributes may interact with one another to produce a motivational pattern within that individual. Next, we need to look at the real requirements of the sales job to see how that pattern fits those requirements. Then, we must still go to the next step and look at additional qualities beyond these central dynamics that might be required for success in the specific sales role. Then and only then can we predict with some confidence that an individual is indeed suited to the specific sales job and would be likely to succeed.

In Part 3, we will turn to the process by which the individual's unique personality attributes are matched to the job as a key means of predicting success on that job.

PART 3

JOB MATCHING

As we discussed in Chapter 2, one of the key reasons for high turnover, poor productivity and the fact that 20 per cent of salespeople sell 80 per cent of what is sold is the inappropriate approach management takes to the hiring of salespeople. Both the warm body approach and the use of inappropriate hiring criteria lead directly to hiring inappropriate people who are virtually guaranteed to be unproductive, and who will turn over quickly at great cost to themselves and to their employers.

In this part we present job matching as an alternative to these two invalid approaches to hiring. In Chapter 9 we will talk about step one in the job matching process — understanding the job. Chapter 10 will deal with step two — understanding the personality attributes required for the job. Here we will deal with qualities beyond the central dynamics that really determine, given an individual's possession of ego-drive, empathy, ego-strength and service motivation, whether or not an individual can succeed in a specific sales job. Then we will be talking about matching the strengths of an individual to the functional requirements of the job and examining the role that a fatal flaw might play in preventing effective job performance, even if there is a match of personality strengths to the job requirements. Finally, in Chapter 11, we will discuss the bottom-line results of substituting job matching for the old approaches to hiring.

CHAPTER 9

UNDERSTANDING THE SALES JOB

As we indicated in the last chapter, the fact that an individual possesses all of the key sales dynamics central to success—empathy, ego-drive, service motivation and ego-strength—does not mean that that individual will be effective in your specific sales job. If we look at that individual from the perspective of vocational guidance, we would certainly suggest that the driven, empathic individual possessing ego-strength should be in a career in which successful persuasion is central to success. That does not mean, however, that a person's persuasive ability will ensure that he or she has the many other key attributes necessary to succeed at a highly productive level in a particular sales position. It is for this reason that we have never simply looked at the central sales dynamics in order to help our corporate clients determine whether or not an individual is suited to a particular sales job. Rather, we look at what we term the job match to make that decision.

This section will be devoted to this 'job matching' process, which begins with an understanding of the job for which an individual is being considered.

Though it is obvious that all sales jobs involve, at their core, the ability to persuade, the range of these jobs is virtually limitless. Sales jobs range from quick-closing, hard-selling, short-term, commission-only positions to an opposite extreme where the persuasive element is camouflaged and only takes place once or twice a year at the end of a long process. This same range can include positions requiring numerous closes per day to positions in which one or two closes in a year could produce as much, or more, income.

Similarly, many sales positions require little or no technical background or skill, while others require the salesperson to be a technical expert in a particular product or service.

Some sales jobs presume that the individual customer will buy once and likely never again, while in most other sales situations, a one-time only buyer would be disastrous.

Numerous additional examples of these extremes could be cited, but we hope these are sufficient to make the point that saying a position involves sales is far from sufficient to provide an understanding of the nature of that position. As we begin to look at the job matching process, let's review some of the key elements that are necessary and some of the key questions that must be asked to develop an understanding of the specific sales role sufficient to know what personality attributes might really be required for an individual to fill that role successfully.

PRODUCT OR SERVICE

The first question to be asked is, 'What is the nature of the product or service to be sold?' Even here it is not sufficient to say, for example, computers, cars, property or pharmaceuticals. Within these broader categories of products and services are numerous subdivisions, each of which requires many differing individual qualities and work processes to sell them successfully. For example, it is a very different job to sell personal computers over the counter in a retail store than it is to sell large mainframes directly to business, government etc. Both can be technically categorised as computer sales, but there the similarity ends. Thus, as simplistic as it may sound on the surface, it is important to understand, and to convey to potential jobholders, the full nature of the product or service being sold. Along the same line, and as part of the understanding of this product or service, the potential customer base must also be understood. PCs may be sold to businesses, incidentally, but they are sold over the counter to many personal users as well. We know of few mainframes that are sold directly to individuals. Residential property is obviously sold to individual home buyers, while commercial property is sold for business purposes. The purchaser of a Mercedes, Porsche, BMW or Rolls-Royce is likely to be a totally different customer to the buyer of a Honda, Vauxhall or Ford. Selling proprietary drugs to pharmacies is very different to selling pharmaceutical products to doctors or dentists, and yet both might be termed pharmaceutical sales.

This critical difference was brought home to us a few years ago. A pharmceutical firm expressed interest in working with us and began by having us evaluate a substantial cross-section of their 'pharmaceutical' sales force. Since this was in part a test of our accuracy, they did not provide us with production/sales data or explicit job descriptions until we had already made judgements as to the productivity of their salespeople.

Given this lack of information — the impossibility of making a real job match as part of our analysis — all we could do was evaluate people on the basis of their empathy, ego-drive and ego-strength, and assume that people who were strong in these dynamics would in fact be the best salespeople. When the production/sales data was presented after we had completed our evaluations, it was found that our predictions landed far from the mark, and in fact, in many instances, people with strong ego-drive were at the bottom, while people with moderate to extremely mild ego-drive were performing exceptionally well. Empathy seemed to hold up as a predictor, but ego-drive and ego-strength failed, and so our overall judgements did not prove out.

After we were provided with job descriptions, we were able to explore the reasons for our lack of predictive accuracy. The reason that we discovered exemplified the critical importance of defining the job before making the decision as to whether or not an individual is really suited to that job.

What we found was that the sales force we evaluated should in reality have been broken down into two sales forces: proprietary and medical sales. The proprietary salespeople's job was to visit pharmacies, present their proprietary products, and get the pharmacy to purchase more of those products. The salesperson was literally charged with walking out with an order from each visit. The sale was tangible, and success or failure was determined by the value of the contract in pounds with which that salesperson walked out of each pharmacy. Several closes a day was the name of the game.

On the other hand, the medical salespeople literally never closed a sale. They would visit doctors, leave samples of various prescription drugs and talk with the doctors about the value of the drugs. They would leave the doctor's office hoping that they made a sufficiently good impression so that the doctor would think of their particular antibiotic or blood pressure pill when they prescribed to patients. They literally never closed and only got feedback as to whether or not they had succeeded in general by quarterly, half-yearly or annual reviews of how their area was doing. Thus, when we fully understood the nature of these two radically different jobs, both called 'pharmaceutical sales', we were able to determine why our earlier analyses, without this information, had to be incorrect. If an individual had too much ego-drive, he or she simply could not tolerate the lack of closing involved in the medical sales position. They literally would have no opportunity to gain the satisfaction that an ego-driven person needs from hearing a yes. Thus, it was not at all accidental that the very people we would have predicted, on the basis of ego-drive, as being successful in this medical sales position did in fact fail.

On the other side of the coin, we would have predicted failure on the basis of moderately low ego-strength, which is correct in most sales situations. However, in the medical sales position, the potential for rejection is relatively low. The medical salesperson with empathy is providing the doctors with samples, information and hopefully with a pleasant break from a highly stressful day. The lack of ego-strength, therefore, might not, unless it is too serious, reduce the ability of a medical salesperson to do a good job. On the other hand, both the lack of ego-drive and ego-strength would be totally destructive in proprietary sales.

The list of similar titles with drastically different job functions goes on, and some of these differences will be studied in detail in future chapters. Suffice it to say here that in order to make a rational judgement on who can fill a particular sales job, we need to understand the product being sold, the resultant nature of the prospects being solicited, and the very process through which success can be attained.

FREQUENCY OF CLOSE

Related closely to the above is the issue of how many opportunities for closing the sales job presents. As we said earlier, many sales jobs require multiple closings per day, or at least per week, in order to be successful, while many others offer relatively few, but extremely important, closing opportunities. If, for example, an individual has extraordinarily intense ego-drive, and perhaps possesses the impatience that frequently goes along with that kind of drive, that individual hungers for closes as a key means of satisfying that drive. Thus, regardless of the compensation, a sales situation that provides two or three closing opportunities per year would simply not satisfy that individual's ego-drive. He or she would not have sufficient fun; there would just not be enough closing to keep that person happy. On the other hand, for the individual who has moderate drive but possesses great consultative skills, service motivation, persistence etc, the job requiring frequent closes might prove too taxing, while the ability slowly to develop an account for those two or three closes over the year would be ideal. Thus, it is really critical, even before understanding the person, to determine the frequency of closing opportunities available so that an individual geared to that level of close could be properly matched to the specific job.

LEAD PRODUCTION

It is a far more difficult sale when cold calling is demanded. The cold caller must, out of necessity, experience far more frequent rejection, often of a far more abrupt, even nasty, kind than the individual who follows up leads that have been furnished. The warmth of these leads also determines, in large measure, who can or cannot be successful in their conversions of prospects to customers. Thus, a very clear definition of the job must be made internally and presented honestly to the candidate as to the nature of customer conversion, cold leads, cool leads, well-screened leads etc. Very different people will be successful depending on an accurate definition of this aspect of the sales role.

NATURE OF CUSTOMER

We touched on this subject when we talked about differences between the Rolls-Royce and the Ford, and differences between the residential and the commercial property customer. The topic is important enough, however, to explore in somewhat more depth who the customer is. Many individuals would be highly successful at selling individual consumers a tangible product, but would fail totally if faced with the necessity of making a full-scale, well-developed presentation to a committee or a board of directors. Others could deal extraordinarily well at a lower- to middle-echelon level (eg with a purchasing agent, branch manager, office manager etc), but would find it extremely difficult to deal on the boardroom or managing director level. Still others would be effective in selling to one person but would lose effectiveness if that individual has to work his or her way up the chain of command in order to get the final sign-off. Thus, it is critical not only to know to whom we are selling (companies, individuals etc), but on what level the sale is initially made, and on what level the final purchase can be approved.

TECHNICAL BACKGROUND

The technical background required for a specific sales job relates closely to the question of 'Who is the final purchaser?' If microcomputers are being sold to office managers who for the most part know little about the technical aspects of the machine, somewhat less technical proficiency will probably be sufficient on the part of the salesperson, so long as that salesperson can speak accurately about the machine's capabilities and its potential benefits to the customer. On the other hand, if the buyers are engineers, heads of data processing divisions, etc, that salesperson had better be exceptionally proficient in the technology, or his or her credibility, and so the credibility of the product, will quickly be lost.

Thus, as we look at the specific customer, we must at the same time make a determination, given the nature of that customer, as to how much technical know-how the salesperson must have, or at least how much technical ability that salesperson fundamentally possesses so that he or she can quickly and expertly acquire sufficient knowledge.

SUPPORT

Large numbers of salespeople relish their positions because they are able to function in a totally independent manner. This is one of the great attractions of the sales profession to many people. Being a salesperson is to some the closest possible approach to being an entrepreneur, without the risks inherent in investing in your own business. These are people who want, and need, little support, and who function best in situations where they are left on their own. On the other hand, there are equally successful salespeople who need support and, perhaps, the structure and the security that go along with such support. They want to know that, if they lack information, there is a technical apparatus ready to come into the situation and help them. They want to have a sales manager who will help them close that critical deal, or writers and research people who will help them develop that all-important presentation. These are the team players — the people who work effectively in an integrated team approach, each member doing his or her part.

This support requirement relates closely (although it is not identical) to another key part of a valid job description: 'How much travel is there? Does the job require working in the home or a branch office, or is there a great deal of individual field work?' The more an individual is in the field (the more a job takes the salesperson away from the home office), the less secure they are, and the further away their support system is. Also, since they are far away, there is no sales manager to say, 'Here is what to do today, and here are your plans for tomorrow.' Such a salesperson must do it all.

Perhaps a case from our files might serve to illustrate these two, as well as some earlier, aspects of the critical job description.

Several years ago, we helped place an individual in a large city car dealership. He had the empathy, ego-drive and ego-strength necessary to sell, plus some other important qualities that allowed him to sell for that dealership in the context of the highly competitive city area. Indeed, the individual turned out to be as successful as we had hoped, becoming their leading salesperson in less than two years. A sales recruiter, knowing of that individual's success, recruited that young man for another dealership selling the same make of car. When we received permission from the first client to discuss this individual, we suggested to our other client, in the strongest possible terms, that they should not hire this highly successful salesman. The second client was in the Midlands and was located off a motorway junction, not near any large city area. They were surprised at our non-recommendation and, given the fact of his success, plus the obvious sales dynamics he had, they made him the offer. To put it simply, they made him an offer he couldn't refuse. Within six months, our second client contacted us and asked if there was anything we could suggest that could be done before they had to face the unpleasant, but necessary, task of firing the young man.

Why did we urge that client not to hire the individual, and why did this highly successful salesman fail miserably in the new situation? The reason certainly cannot be found in understanding the product, since the product being sold was identical. Nor can the answer be found in the nature of the customer, because the customers were virtually identical. Rather, the answer must be sought through understanding how the leads were produced and, perhaps more importantly, the nature of the structure and support system provided.

In the first case, our strongly driven salesman got his leads in one very simple way — people walked through the door. Being located in the centre of a large city, the dealership had no lack of walk-in traffic. True, many of these were simply browsers, but some were potentially serious buyers, and others, once they were in the showroom, could be converted into customers if the salesperson was effective enough. The leads were there; they would buy now or probably not at all, and so it remained only for the salesperson with strong sales dynamics to close those prospects on the spot. Further, the city area dealership had a strong sales management team to approve deals, finance and insurance people to deal with those aspects of the sale, and, in general, a strong support system to help the salesman close the deal, both in terms of closing technique and, more importantly, in terms of the myriad details necessary to maximise the deal, both for the dealership and for the customer.

In the Midlands situation, on the other hand, the job called for the salesman/assistant sales manager to leave the dealership to produce prospects. Relatively few individuals casually entered the showroom, and so prospects had to be created through country club memberships, solicitation of businesses, referral programmes etc. Not only did a structured outside system have to be developed to create prospects, but that system had to be fully implemented by the salesperson in a structured way, and the total deal had to be carried through from beginning to final contract by that salesperson. Thus, the support system so badly needed by that individual was absent, and though the prospects (the potential customers) were essentially the same, the process of securing these customers was radically different.

Our story did have a moderately happy ending, though by no means in the grand old Hollywood tradition. We were able to save this man's job by suggesting that he be brought back into the dealership and begin functioning as a real assistant sales manager. What we suggested was that other salespeople go out to generate the leads, to do the country club work, to solicit the business etc, and bring the prospects they generated in to our hero. Then, he could use his enormous closing ability and other sales talents to help close the deal. That provided him with some of the team play he needed, and at the same time eliminated, or at least substantially reduced, those aspects of the job for which he was totally unsuited. And, after a couple of years of this, he returned to work for another city area dealership, at which he is currently their leading salesman.

This case really provides an excellent example of several areas of job description. How prospects are provided, the support system, the need to travel and the nature of the sale itself all played a role in defining an individual's success in one situation and abject failure in another. Even an element as simple as the fact that the city dealership could do very well with its thousands of potential one-time buyers, while the Midlands situation demanded repetitive buys, could have, by itself, explained the entire process; but when you add the multiplicity of factors we discussed, it was no great feat on our part to have predicted failure in the Midlands situation. Our Midlands client made the mistake of thinking selling is selling, and that selling their particular product equalled selling the same particular product in a city area. The client was not willing to examine in detail the different natures of the two positions. Had they done so, they could have avoided a great deal of pain, time, money and effort on their part, and on the part of the individual involved.

To conclude, there are a number of other questions that should be dealt with in defining a specific sales job.

- To whom does the salesperson report?
- Does the salesperson have any secretarial or administrative help?
- What is the compensation plan — salary, salary plus bonus, commission only etc? (We touched on the implications of this question earlier.)
- What is the career path of the position? (Does it lead to bigger and better sales, or is the next step management? If so, management potential should be part of the consideration.)
- Are we dealing with tangible or intangible sales?
- Are we dealing with small-ticket or big-ticket items?
- Are sales cyclical or consistent through the year?
- On average, how many contacts does it take to close a sale?
- Is the job in a big city, suburb, town or rural area?
- How large is the sales force?

- Is the company known in the market, or is part of the sale selling the company name?

There are more questions to consider, but if companies and sales managers do no more than develop their job descriptions using the questions outlined here, they will have taken a major step towards achieving the job match that is the key to sales success. The exercise of putting together such a job description for their own edification will substantially improve their ability to make judgements concerning who can fill the job. In addition, presenting a job description of this kind to individuals in line for promotion, or to applicants, will help these individuals immeasurably to determine whether they really want the particular sales position, given a clear description of *all* its aspects.

So now, hopefully, we have a better understanding of the job—of our sales job. Now, for the second part of the job matching process, let's turn to a discussion of those many other personality qualities, beyond empathy, ego-drive, service motivation and ego-strength, that an individual requires to fill the wide range of positions called sales.

CHAPTER 10

PERSONALITY AND THE JOB MATCH

As we indicated when discussing the central qualities required for sales success, the possession of empathy, ego-drive, ego-strength and even service motivation does not ensure success in a particular sales position. When people possess these qualities, they should certainly be in a position in which persuasion is central to success. What that specific position is, however, depends upon the possession of a number of other attributes. Once the nature of the specific sales job is understood, as we discussed in the previous chapter, the personality attributes needed to succeed in that job can be determined.

Let us look at some of these qualities that can be as crucial to success in specific sales jobs as the central dynamics themselves.

These attributes include the ability to grow on the job; to be an effective decision maker; to be good at, or at least tolerate, some degree of detail; to organise work and time; to communicate effectively; and to work, where required, as a team member.

GROWTH

Whether an individual has the ability to grow in a job should be a major concern. The ability to grow, which is closely related to the ability to learn, is a necessity in most sales jobs and in virtually all management jobs. But while growth is related to one's ability to acquire new information and view situations from a fresh perspective, it is not merely a reflection of IQ. Some individuals, while possessing an outstanding IQ, are so opinionated, rigid and dogmatic that they use their intelligence to reinforce and defend preconceptions. In other words, they use their intelligence to build a wall around themselves, selecting evidence supportive of what they already believe to be correct and ignoring all conflicting ideas and facts. Such individuals use their intelligence to keep themselves from growing. More than once, we have discovered an individual with an IQ of 165 who was incapable of growth in even simple job situations.

Growth involves intellectual capacity, of course, but it truly manifests itself in empathy, sensitivity and the flexibility of mind that receives and ponders — and sometimes accepts — new ideas and methods.

DECISION MAKING

In many situations, the ability to make quick, correct decisions can save a sale from being lost. In some ways, this ability surpasses in importance the salesperson's need for intelligence. Should the price be cut? Should a special guarantee be offered? Should the close be pushed for? Should another meeting be scheduled at which technical assistance can be brought in? Is this customer a genuine prospect that should be pursued, or one that is just looking for diversion, enjoying the attention that hopeful salespeople lavish? Is the customer picking the salesperson's brains for technical information without any real interest in buying? What should the salesperson do when the purchasing agent wants to refer him or her to the vice president? How does the salesperson react when a customer accuses his or her company of giving poor service?

Even with generous shares of empathy and ego-drive, a poor decision maker can fail as a salesperson by acting too impulsively and be even more destructive by not acting at all, out of fear of making a mistake.

An overly impulsive salesperson may immediately cut prices, wildly promise extravagant benefits, accuse competitors of outlandish practices and behave in a way that is irredeemably embarrassing. This hasty, impulsive, impatient decision maker tends to be poor on follow-up. Yet, given empathy and the ability to grow, such individuals may learn from their mistakes. With experience and a course in time planning, such impulsive salespeople may partially or even fully overcome this tendency.

But the non-decision maker has less opportunity to learn from mistakes, because those mistakes are due to inaction, rather than judgemental error. Consequently, the results are difficult either to trace or to measure. Because such overly cautious individuals cannot decide to make a fractional price cut, they may fail to secure a million-pound order, but no one can accuse them of having made a 'mistake'.

It is hard for anyone to learn from mistakes that are camouflaged or rationalised out of existence. It is this failure to learn that poses the largest problem for the overly cautious decision maker. Overly cautious people fear the possible results of their actions and, therefore, never act decisively. So they lose critical opportunities, and rarely sell effectively.

Shrewdness and judgement are also critical attributes which play a part in the decision-making process. As we want to balance willingness to act with a strong sense of responsibility in order to temper hastiness, we also want to include the shrewdness, insight and good judgement component of good decision making. We look for an individual who will take a risk, learn from whatever mistakes are made and, by and large, make astute decisions.

DETAIL

The ability to handle some degree of detail work is also important in many sales jobs in spite of the stereotypical salesperson who despises and, indeed, cannot cope with even the smallest amount of detail.

Many salespeople do, indeed, exemplify this stereotype. To the hard-driving, impulsive salesperson, detail is an abomination; it is a form of torture to write a sales report. Yet, there are thousands of good salespeople who are capable of coping with detail adequately and some of them are even good at it. In thousands of sales jobs, detail is an inescapable part of the operation. for example, how could a property salesperson sell a house or a commercial property without involving him- or herself in detail? How could a person begin to sell complex equipment and machinery and stay clear of detail? Without the ability to handle details, is there any way, even with an abundance of drive and empathy, that an insurance salesperson could sell securities or an agent sell estate planning programmes?

There are, of course, some sales jobs that require less ability to handle detail than others. Car salespeople, if they have a sales manager to back them up, need only moderate detail ability. The encyclopedia salesperson, the door-to-door cosmetics salesperson, the vaccuum cleaner salesperson and the person on the soft drink route all have the required details built directly into their canned presentations and they need relatively little inherent detail ability. All this clearly indicates why knowledge of an individual's ability to handle detail is critical in assessing potential in any given sales job.

ORGANISE WORK AND TIME

The ability to organise one's own work, in combination with initiative, also needs to be considered in determining a person's sales potential. Many sales jobs, by their very nature, bring customer and salesperson together and so permit the salesperson with significant ego-drive a reasonable number of customers, regardless of whether he or she has done preparatory work. But in many other sales jobs, even outstanding salespeople could starve while they waited for the customer to come to them.

The nature of those sales jobs requires that salespeople find customers, then use their ego-drive to close sales. In these sales situations, individuals without the ability to organise their work are likely to sit all day waiting in vain for a prospect to persuade. They are like the lonely person on a Saturday night who wishes for a date but cannot quite manage to dial the number to get one.

The case of Sandra exemplifies this point. An insurance agency asked us to test their entire sales and management staff. Sandra, we found, possessed outstanding empathy and ego-drive, exceptional intelligence and all the prerequisites of an outstanding salesperson. Yet, she was not succeeding.

Why, in view of Sandra's strong central dynamics, was she failing? She was an impulsive, driven salesperson who intensely disliked detail, had little or no capacity for self-starting and who had a low level of organising talent. She was simply incapable of going through customer cards or prospect lists with painstaking care or engaging in routine follow-up activities.

Though the job was called 'sales', the primary means of retaining and expanding business was through what is known in the industry as 'x-dating'. What this means is that the salespeople had to keep close tabs on their account files so as to be aware of when their policies were coming up for renewal (the 'x-date'). It was at that point that the salespeople were supposed to contact the customers, discuss their current insurance and look to opportunities for increasing amounts or broadening coverage. Sandra's lack of detail ability and personal organisation made such careful record-keeping and folow-up virtually impossible. She much preferred the rejections involved in looking for new customers to the paintaking detail work involved in working through customer record cards.

We advised the managing director that Sandra would never be appropriate if her job continued to involve detail follow-up. Yet, we did not want our client to lose an individual possessing Sandra's high degree of sales dynamics. Sandra was installed in a purely outside sales role and she was replaced by one of the agency's customer service representatives who had too much ego-drive for a purely service role. The customer service representative possessed the detail ability and personal organisation skills needed to follow up on x-dates, but still had sufficient ego-drive to take advantage of the sales opportunities presented during these follow-ups.

Without these job shifts, the agency would have lost a valuable salesperson in Sandra because she was attempting to fill a sales role with a job description not suited to her personality. They would also have lost a customer service representative who had too much drive to function in a purely service capacity. With these shifts, both people were retained, and both were made more productive. Sandra filled a role not requiring so much detail ability, while the customer service representative was placed in a role using her detail ability and personal organisation skills, but also allowing her to satisfy her persuasive motivation.

COMMUNICATION

The ability to communicate is also critical. Empathy, a vital component of communicative power, makes it possible to receive a message from the customer and understand it correctly. However, having empathy is no guarantee of being able to communicate ideas effectively and clearly to the customer. Some sales situations require no more than standard forms of communication, but other situations require as high a degree of communicative ability as that needed by a top sales trainer or a first-rate teacher.

Clearly, selling is communicating in one form or another. In virtually all one-to-one sales situations, the effectiveness with which the desirability of the product or service is communicated determines whether or not the sale will be made. The ability to receive accurate feedback from a customer, coupled with effective presentation skills, which address the customer's reaction, is, at least in selling, two-way communication at its best. Where the salesperson lacks empathy, the conversation that is thought to be a meaningful sales dialogue is in reality several alternating monologues. The salesperson is talking at the customer, the customer talking at the salesperson and no real communication is taking place. On the other hand, if the salesperson has empathy, and so genuinely understands what the customer is thinking and feeling, but is unable to translate that understanding into good presentation skills, the empathy could be wasted and the sales failure would be just as complete as if the empathy did not exist in the first place. Thus, real communication involves both the ability to gather vital feedback from the customer and the ability to use that feedback in order to effectively communicate the product or service in terms of how it will meet that customer's needs.

THE TEAM PLAYER: THE ABILITY TO DELEGATE

One of the most overlooked attributes of the successful salesperson is the ability to function as a member of a team. Usually this attribute is related to his or her ability to delegate. In any discussion of management talents, delegation of responsibility is always stressed; but strangely, in discussions of a salesperson's talents, it rarely is. Yet, at times, the ability to turn a job over to another or bring in required help can make the difference between success and failure. The ego-driven salesperson, by definition, wants the thrill of conquest and is more often than not the ultimate individualist. Yet questions often arise to which the salesperson does not know the answer. Perhaps the most intelligent, most credible (and most honest) answer that any stumped salesperson can give is, 'I don't know, but I will find out'. Unfortunately, some salespeople appear to be constitutionally incapable of that kind of reply. Instead, they are more inclined to blunder along, faking answers they don't have, frequently misleading the customer and, quite likely, losing him or her forever. It follows that one of the key requisites of a successful salesperson is the ability to bring in technical help when necessary, and to make use of the manager's skill and experience. In short, the salesperson must often be able to play as part of a team, not just as a wheeling-and-dealing individualist.

The sports world offers a close analogy. Many a team laden with superstars has stumbled and failed because each individual star played for himself, instead of submerging his strength into the body of the team. So it is with a salesperson.

ASSERTIVENESS

Many people may possess ego-drive (the motivation to persuade) and yet are not assertive enough to ask for an order, in spite of their intense desire to get that order. A time comes in every sales situation when, after the presentation, the gathering of customer information and all of the other elements that go into a sale, the prospect has to be told, 'please sign here'. It is at that moment of truth when the customer gives the final yes-or-no answer, when the salesperson's assertiveness or lack of it can mean the difference between success and failure.

The term *assertiveness* is frequently confused with aggressiveness. Assertiveness is not pushiness and, in fact, should never really be perceived as pushiness, aggression, attempted dominance etc. Rather, assertiveness is the ability which enables an individual to get other people to do willingly what they might not spontaneously do on their own. Assertiveness allows an individual to have a special effect on others which commands their respect and admiration, and causes them to respond in a positive way to what that individual is asking or suggesting. Assertiveness involves the ability to get a positive response from others and use that response to bring about a desired attitude or course of action. Putting it in simplest terms, the assertive salesperson is willing to ask for the order and is capable of asking for it in a sufficiently effective way to ensure that the prospect will willingly give that order.

AGGRESSIVENESS

Aggressiveness is often confused with assertiveness. The two, however, are distinctly different and, in some instances, even opposite qualities. Where assertiveness, as we just discussed, involves getting people to do what you want them to do without pushing, aggressiveness is precisely that pushing. *Agressiveness* is defined as the willingness to actively oppose someone else's position, interests or point of view, even if it could adversely affect that other person. Unfortunately, too many salespeople, particularly those with some-what deficient empathy, are purely aggressive, as opposed to genuinely assertive. People do not want to be pushed into making a decision, and so the psychological difference between real assertiveness and aggression is far more than an academic distinction. Yet, there are sales situations in which aggression of a certain kind is essential. For example, there are many telephone sales situations in which the salesperson is simply blocked from talking to the potential prospect. Pounding away at the locked gates often requires simple, though hopefully polite, aggressiveness. After all, you cannot use empathy, ego-drive and assertiveness on a prospect with whom you have no contact. This can mean multiple conversations with a secretary before finally wearing her down and getting through to her boss, the prospect. Interestingly, once the door is opened, the prospect often will say, 'How could I say no after such aggression and persistence?' and 'You really must believe in what you're doing if you were willing to work that hard to arrange a meeting'. Once can look at these multiple calls as simple persistence, but the reality is that while persistence was certainly involved, each conversation had to include a pushing, polite but still a pushing, towards the goal of eventually talking to that secretary's boss. Simple persistence (the willingness to make 18 phone calls without the aggressive push) would probably not have changed the goal.

Here again is a perfect example of why, though we talk about individual qualities, they cannot really be viewed separately. The aggressiveness we have just described would have done no good without persistence and without empathy. There had to be ego-drive to persuade the secretary to let the call through, empathy so that the secretary did not become angry and persistence to keep trying. All of these qualities, not one, had to come into play to achieve the goal. In fact, we should really mention another quality — ego-strength — because there was a great deal of rejection on the road to achieving the goal.

SHREWDNESS

Shrewdness is the ability to read between the lines and to further process information, rather than accept it all at face value. There is certainly a relationship between this attribute and empathy, yet they are very different in the sense that empathy deals with the understanding of the person, while shrewdness deals more with insights into a situation. Here again, the combination of empathy and shrewdness really makes for the ideal salesperson, particularly where you are dealing with more complex conceptual sales, as opposed to the sale of a simple, tangible product. Often, a prospect will tell the salesperson what is needed on one level, but shrewdness will allow the salesperson to read between the lines, and to get to the next level of real need. In fact, many salespeople will relate instances in which their insight — their shrewdness — allowed them to ascertain needs of which the customer was not even aware. Shrewdness and empathy allow the salesperson to act as a consultant, helping customers ascertain their real needs and, hopefully, meeting those needs through the product or service being sold.

Again, there are many sales situations in which shrewdness is less important because the situation is simple, and what is on the surface is all that is really there. In other situations, however, shrewdness can prove to be as important as some of the central dynamics themselves.

SENSE OF INNER URGENCY

The individual with a great deal of inner urgency needs to get something, or everything, done 'right now'. There is a need to move quickly. The individual with inner urgency needs to make things happen immediately and finds delay extremely frustrating. Typically, he or she cannot stand long deliberation over a subject, but rather is motivated to act, and keep on acting, until a successful outcome is achieved. To individuals with inner urgency, there is no waiting for a call, but it is much more satisfying to pick up the phone and make the call themselves.

Individuals with little inner urgency will be much too laid back, complacent and even passive. Even if they possess ego-drive, they are likely to feel that closing opportunities will present themselves and they feel little need actively to seek those opportunities. When such individuals are presented with a prospect, their ego-drive will allow them to close effectively. But if they seriously lack inner urgency they will not be proactive but, rather, will only be reactive. On the other hand, individuals with too much inner urgency could be so bent on immediate response that they could make bad judgements. In trying to get an immediate decision, they could end up with a negative one.

In understanding inner urgency we should look at this quality in relationship to ego-drive and to impatience, with which qualities it can easily be confused. Ego-drive is the need for victory, but that does not necessarily imply that that victory has to be immediate. Ego-driven individuals with the *right* amount of inner urgency will not let grass grow under their feet — they will move with all deliberate speed. On the other hand, they will not act recklessly and perhaps wrongly just for the satisfaction of this need for immediacy. However, we have seen many potentially successful salespeople, even with a great deal of ego-drive, who simply do not possess enough inner urgency to impel them to look for ways of satisfying that drive. For example, we can recall one young man who we tested and found to have ample amounts of empathy, ego-drive and ego-strength. He turned out to be, in fact, a reasonably successful salesperson, though, as our client told us about a year later, he never achieved the top performance level that would have been indicated by his level of ego-drive. After some investigation, we found that his conversion ratio (number of closes to number of contacts) was quite high. What we found, however, was that his number of contacts was among the lowest on the sales force. After several interviews, it became apparent that he made no effort to maximise the number of calls he would make in a given day. If one call was completed at 11:30am, rather than try to make an additional call before lunch, he would use that time to take a somewhat longer lunch. If a call was completed at 4:30pm, he would not rush to get to someone's office by 4:55pm, but instead would take the opportunity to beat the traffic and go home. Individuals with inner urgency would probably have made those additional two calls because they would have the need for immediacy that would drive them to use the time to get the work done. The result, given this young man's conversion ratio, would likely have been at least one additional sale per day.

What we see here is an individual who is making full use of his ego-drive; once he was in front of a customer, he closed that customer effectively. His lack of inner urgency, however, substantially reduced the number of these closing opportunities. The result was adequate, though not outstanding, sales performance.

As we said earlier, inner urgency is also confused with impatience. The difference is that, while someone can be terribly impatient, the individual with inner urgency will act to obtain immediacy, while the individual who is simply impatient may be bothered by delay, but not necessarily do anything about it. An individual, for example, may be terribly impatient while experiencing the inordinate waits typical in doctors' surgeries, but the individual with inner urgency is likely to walk over to the nurse, tell her it's impossible to continue waiting and either get seen earlier or reschedule the appointment. Mere impatience does not denote action. Inner urgency, for good or ill, most often leads to action.

SELF-DISCIPLINE

Self-discipline involves the inner motivation to do what is needed to be done, whether or not the task involves something that the individual really wants to do. In other words, self-discipline is the inner motivation to do what one should do rather than what one may want to do. There is again an obvious connection between this attribute and inner urgency. If a salesperson has enough self-discipline, he or she might try to make that final 5:00pm meeting, even though the inner urgency to do so is absent. They would do so because they should, not because there is the inner desire to do it. On the other hand, the individual with inner urgency will make that meeting because he or she wants to—because such a person has the need to get that little extra done during that day. As you read this you might ask, what is the difference? If the salesperson in fact makes that meeting, aside from academic interest, why do we care if it is because of inner urgency or self-discipline? We do, in fact, care because, as is the case with so many things we are discussing in this book, we do those things we like to do and want to do much more effectively than those things we have to do or are forced to do by external pressure. Thus, if the individual makes that meeting at 4:55pm, because he or she is compelled to by their inner sense of urgency, they are likely to pursue that meeting full tilt, making every effort to make that meeting effective and successful so as to satisfy their need for immediate results. On the other hand, if the meeting is carried through because it should be done, but the individual is basically yearning to be home or to be playing golf, the process may be carried out in a *pro forma* way to satisfy their self-discipline, yet not be done with the intense enthusiasm that might result in the closed sale. Obivously, if someone possesses both the right level of inner urgency and the self-discipline to plan and organise work and time efficiently, you have the best of all worlds.

Many other qualities could be touched upon, but we hope that the above discussion has essentially made the point that, as important as empathy, ego-drive and ego-strength are to sales success, one must not stop there in determining whether an individual will be successful in a specific sales job. The job match — making certain that the individual's central qualities match the functional requirements of the particular sales job— is the critical factor in that determination, and many attributes beyond the three or even four central qualities play a key role in making for that job match.

CHAPTER 11

THE JOB MATCHING PROCESS — SELECTING SALES WINNERS

With the information about the job in hand and the individual being considered for that job, the actual job matching process can now take place. As we discussed in Chapter 9, the first step of this process is to define the job. What is needed here is an understanding of the hour-by-hour, day-by-day functional requirements of the job, which will enable the holder of that job to attain the goals and objectives set by management. In other words, what is needed here is not simply a job description, but a thorough understanding of what the jobholder needs to do to achieve success in the job.

The next step is to determine what qualities are needed by an individual to perform effectively in that job. For example, if the Midlands car dealer that we discussed in Chapter 9 had evaluated his job, he would have determined that individual initiative, persistence and patience were three critical attributes required to do *his* job. Completing the kind of job analysis we discussed should permit management to determine the qualities an individual must have to excel in a particular position.

The third part of the job matching process is to look at the individual being considered and determine whether he or she has the qualities needed for the job.

Only if there is such a match need the fourth step be taken. If the strengths of the individual match the strengths required by the job, the fourth step involves determining whether there is a fatal flaw.

THE FATAL FLAW

All human beings are made up of an enormous package of motivations, abilities and attributes. All of us are in the top 2 or 3 per cent of persons possessing some particular qualities or abilities. But then, we are also in the bottom 5 or 10 per cent for some other qualities, and, more than likely, somewhere in the middle for other qualities. No human being is, or can be, everything.

There is a great myth that is represented by the following statements: 'You can be anything you want to be', 'All you have to do is work hard enough and you can do it', and 'There is nothing you cannot achieve'. All of these add up to the idea that because winners work so hard anything they touch turns to gold. On the other hand, the losers fail at anything they attempt. However, we must say that expressions such as these, and the entire concept of the winner/loser, is nothing but rank, destructive nonsense. We have found that the winners in this world all share one thing in common. They are lucky enough or skilful enough to be doing a job for which they are ideally suited. Winners play to their strengths. They do not attempt jobs for which they are unsuited.

On the other hand, losers are trying desperately to do something totally alien to their basic personality. In sales, losers account for 80 per cent of the people scratching, clawing and fighting over 20 per cent of what is not sold by the professionals. Losers are in effect trying to be what they are not; that is why they lose. However, if those losers in sales were to become administrators, teachers, lawyers, engineers, accountants or whatever they were ideally suited to, they might quickly be converted to 'winners'.

The key is for individuals to play to their strengths, do the best they can to improve their trainable weak areas and not be particularly concerned with the fact that they possess, as do all human beings, a number of weaknesses. The key to success in selling, as in all other professions, is playing to your strengths, being the best at what you are and playing away from your weaker areas.

We think that this is a terribly important point to understand as we look at ourselves, at people we are currently supervising and those who we are considering hiring. No one can be everything and so the key word, as you are dealing with people, invariably is 'trade-off'.

So we go back to the central job match and to the fatal flaw. One trade-off that cannot be made is the match between the functional job requirements and the key strengths possessed by the person who must fill that job. The fatal flaw comes in when we look at the weaknesses of an individual and determine whether those weaknesses would make it difficult for the person to do the job in spite of their positive attributes.

The word 'non-trainable' is extremely important to understand as we look at this fatal flaw. There are those weaknesses, as we said, that are simply a basic part of the individual and, regardless of training or motivation, really cannot be expected to be substantially altered. If, for example, people simply do not enjoy the persuasive process — if they seriously lack ego-drive — you might, through training, prop them up to some degree in terms of tools or techniques, but you will never really make them enjoy selling and, as a result, you will never really make them an effective salesperson; nor should you. That lack of ego-drive is simply too basic to the personality, and the reality is that such an individual simply should not be selling. On the other hand, if someone has some weakness in time planning, that person might be helped with a good time planning programme. A bit more difficult, but still possible, is a situation where an individual is inconsistently assertive. Again, depending on degree, a good assertiveness programme *might*, under certain circumstances, help the individual assert him- or herself with more consistency. Certainly, where the weaknesses involve lack of knowledge or lack of a particular skill, and the individual has enough intelligence, openness and willingness to learn, such weaknesses will not constitute a fatal flaw. On the other hand, if that knowledge requires a four-year degree, then it indeed might fall under the fatal flaw category.

Thus, if we focus on the fact that all people have strengths and weaknesses — that nobody can do everything — and we look to match appropriate strengths to the real requirements of a job and make certain that there is no nontrainable fatal flaw among the individual's myriad weaknesses, then we have a job match, with the resultant likelihood that, given training and proper supervision, the individual will perform at a high level of productivity in the position.

RESULTS OF JOB MATCHING

Earlier we said that the existence of so many inappropriate people in sales jobs is traceable, in part, to the fact that people are hired for the wrong reasons. We mentioned that, letalities aside, age, sex, race, experience and formal education are frequently used as hiring criteria, and that our studies have found that these criteria are invalid. It is appropriate here to describe the most comprehensive of these studies, not only to debunk these invalid criteria, but to show how the job matching process, if substituted for these invalid criteria, could indeed go a long way towards solving the high turnover, overall poor productivity and the 20/80 pattern that characterises sales across industries.

JOB MATCHING FOR BETTER SALES PERFORMANCE

The results of our comprehensive 14-industry study were published in the September/October 1980 issue of the *Harvard Business Review*. With their permission we present excerpts from that article.[1]

The findings we report are based on our study of more than 360,000 individuals in the United States, Canada, and Western Europe since 1961. (Author's note: Our consulting firm, Caliper Corporation, has currently evaluated more than 750,000 individuals.) The study covers 14 industries:

Automobiles	Banking and Finance
Chemical Manufacture	Business Forms Manufacture
Life Insurance	Data Processing
Media and Publishing	Farm Equipment
Pharmaceutical Manufacture	Heavy Manufacturing
Real Estate	Printing
Stock Brokerage and Mutual Funds	Property and Casualty Insurance

The seven industries in the first column characteristically have a high turnover of salespeople, while those in the second column have a lower turnover.

A random sample of individuals who were hired after testing were selected from each of these industries, and performance data gathered. They were then compared by industry, and on the basis of age, sex, race, experience, and education. Finally, they were compared as to whether or not they had been recommended for hire on the basis of their possession of appropriate dynamics for their specific sales job. In other words, they were compared as to whether or not they were appropriately job matched.

Under 40s versus Over 40s

The worship of youth has long been recognized as a feature of the American culture. The myths relating to the value and attributes of youth have done wonders for clothing designers and cosmeticians. Few others, however, have benefited from our neurotic obsession with youth. It is not our purpose, however,

---

[1] Reprinted by permission of *Harvard Business Review*, 'Job Matching for Better Sales Performance' by Jeanne Greenberg and Herbert Greenberg, September/October 1980. Copyright © 1980 by the president and fellows of Harvard College; all rights reserved.

to deal with the tragedy of setting aside people at the very time that they can contribute most to society. Rather, let us focus on the sales talent that industry loses in the over 40 age group.

When comparing the on-the-job performance of people over 40 with that of their under 40 counterparts, we found no statistically significant difference. Nearly the same percentage of individuals in the older and the younger groups performed in the top quartile of their sales force in 6-month and 14-month periods. The same similarity between the groups held for second, third, and fourth quartile performance.

Even in turnover rate, the two groups remained extremely close, although the older group did turn over at a slightly lower rate.

Men versus Women

For a number of years, of course, it has been illegal to discriminate in employment according to sex (as well as race, age, national origin and so on). But women continue to be substantially barred from many occupations in which they could succeed perfectly well. Real estate is one of the few industries that over the years has offered women excellent opportunities to actualize their potential in sales and management.

Can women be the same rich source of talent in other fields? How well do they perform in sales in comparison with their male counterparts? The results show, beyond statistical question, no performance difference between men and women, even in industries such as stock brokerage and auto sales, which until recently were considered exclusively male bastions. Virtually the same percentage of women and men performed in the top quartile of their sales forces after 6 months and 14 months.

Moreover, the two groups had virtually the same failure rates, whether failure is described as fourth quartile performance after 14 months or as termination because of poor performance.

Blacks versus Whites

The law and a sense of justice tell us we cannot discriminate against individuals because of race. The data indicates clearly that it is not good business to do so, if for no reason other than self-interest. Blacks perform on the job as well as their white associates.

We should point out that the blacks in these sales forces are essentially middle class, so this group is not representative of all American blacks. But the group is representative of black individuals applying for or holding jobs in the cross-section of industries presented in this study. What would be the results of a study of a less advantaged group of blacks, for example, participants in an antipoverty program who have little work history, little schooling, and little exposure to the middle class world?

The answer, based on our experience with more than 7,000 individuals in federally sponsored programs in the 1960s, is that, when placed in positions suited to their real abilities, less-advantaged blacks perform at high levels. Of the more than 3,000 persons placed in jobs under an antipoverty program, less than 3 per cent were fired because of inability to perform. True, others left for a multiplicity of reasons; but the fact emerged clearly that, when they were placed appropriately in jobs suited to their abilities and were given proper training, counseling and supervision, people from disadvantaged groups did well on the job.

Experienced versus Inexperienced

Experience is usually a principal criterion for making hiring decisions. Someone with experience in a particular industry, in selling any product or service, or even in doing unrelated work in the same industry, enjoys a great advantage in applying for a sales or a management position in that industry. Yet we found little difference in performance between these experienced individuals and those with no experience. The person with no experience, given training and supervision, is as likely to succeed as the person with two or more years of experience.

As in the results previously discussed, in the high-turnover areas there were no discernible differences.

There is an old saw that 20 years' experience can reflect one year's bad experience repeated 20 times. Our findings confirm that this is often the case. Too many people cling tenaciously to their unsuitable jobs and do just well enough not to be fired. Thus they accumulate years of experience. It is these individuals — the 80 per cent in the wrong jobs referred to earlier — who make the value of experience nil as a prime criterion for the selection of successful salespeople.

College versus High School Educated

Though the following is a direct quote from our *Harvard Business Review* article, we should add an updated note here. During the nine years between the publication of that article and the writing of this book, much has occurred leading towards additional emphasis on education. The emphasis on more and more high-technology products and the increasing emphasis on the consultative rather than the hard sell has geared the sales profession more towards the better educated individual, especially on the highest levels. With this said, however, our more recent studies continue to show that degrees *per se*, or number of years of education *per se*, is not a good predictor of sales success. Where education really is essential, the necessary level must obviously be a requirement, but using education itself as an absolute criterion continues to be a fallacy.

As a value to be cherished and encouraged in our society, education cannot be challenged. The use of formal degrees as an absolute criterion for judging someone's potential effectiveness in a sales or a sales management job, however, must be challenged.

Obviously, in certain specialized fields, complex technological knowledge is required to sell the product. The computer salesperson must know the technology necessary to deal with the specialist in the company that may purchase a new system. Of course, intimate knowledge of the product or service is necessary in all sales situations. But normally such knowledge is obtained through the company's training programs, not through a college degree. Our probing research shows that people with little education, given the basic intelligence, can be as successful in many sales jobs as those with college degrees.

Unlike the four other criteria discussed earlier, we found some industry-to-industry variations according to levels of education. The college graduate and the multi-degree recipient slightly out-performed the less educated competitor in industries characterized by big-ticket, highly technical sales and by sales requiring lengthy follow-up. These differences however, seldom reached 5 per cent.

As in the examination of the other hiring criteria, virtually no differences surfaced in the proportions of salespeople who were fired or who quit during the two periods.

Job Matching Approach

In view of these findings, an obvious question arises: If these long-used criteria are invalid, what criteria can industry use that would better predict job performance? The answer is, "Criteria that make a better match between the person and the job."

The experience of companies that have tried to match applicants with their sales openings shows distinct differences in performance. A final aspect of the survey was a comparison of new hires in terms of whether they were job-matched.

Persons who had been matched in the first six months with appropriate sales positions out-performed, to a statistically significant degree, those who had not been matched. Moreover, the differences widened after 14 months. Finally, the turnover rates of job-matched individuals were much lower in all cases.

For the purposes of clarity, we reformulated the data from the study so that performance could be compared among individuals still on the job after 14 months. We compared the performance of those individuals whose personality dynamics matched the job for which they were being considered against those who Caliper did not recommend but who were hired because they met the old criteria or because 'they looked so good in the interview'.

Tables 1 and 2 present this comparison for both high turnover and low turnover industries.

Table 1 *Performance of those in high turnover industries who were job matched compared to those who were not recommended*

Measurement period after hiring: 14 months	Top half
Job matched	85%
Not job matched	17%

Note: Sample sizes – 4,362 people who were job matched and 8,740 who were not job matched

It can be seen from these figures that 85 per cent of the individuals recommended for hire on the basis of their appropriate personality dynamics (still on the job) were performing in the top half of their sales force after 14 months, while only 17 per cent of the individuals hired who were not job matched were performing at that satisfactory level. In the low turnover industries, 76 per cent of those recommended were performing at that high level, while only 21 per cent of those not job matched were doing as well.

There is another important difference revealed by the study. In the high turnover industries, 57 per cent of those individuals hired by the old criteria were no longer on the job after 14 months, while only 28 per cent of those who were hired on the basis of job matching resigned or were fired. The turnover difference was even more dramatic in the low turnover industries, where only 8 per cent of the recommended individuals resigned or were fired, while 34 per cent of the not recommended group were no longer with their companies after 14 months.

As we wrote in the *Harvard Business Review*, 'While error free personnel selection will remain an impossible dream, this study points out a direction business can take to reduce such errors.' We are convinced from this study and many other smaller studies that we have conducted within individual industries and across the industry as a whole, that if job matching replaced the old invalid hiring criteria, the sales profession, because of the quality of its people, will

Table 2 *Performance of those in low turnover industries who were job matched compared to those who were not recommended*

Measurement period after hiring: 14 months	Top half
Job matched	76%
Not job matched	21%

Note: Sample sizes — 1,800 people who were job matched and 3,961 who were not job matched indeed achieve the level of productivity and professionalism to which its importance entitles it. There is no doubt in our minds that if management moves towards job matching in its hiring of salespeople, and if many existing salespeople who have sales talent but who may be selling the wrong product or service are allowed to shift positions, the sales profession will be characterised by the quality of what is now only the top 20 per cent.

PART 4

BUILDING A WINNING SALES TEAM

Until this point, we have spent a good deal of time dealing with the psychology involved in what it takes to succeed in sales. We have talked about sales as a profession, dealt, at least to some degree, with the problems holding the sales profession and salespeople back from achieving their full potential, and talked about the central dynamics needed by an individual if he or she is to succeed in any kind of sales. We then talked about the job matching process, which included a review of many other qualities beyond the central dynamics needed to succeed in specific sales situations. Finally, we looked at the job matching process and compared its results to the use of old, traditional hiring criteria; we found that by using job matching a far higher level of sales productivity could be achieved.

It is now time to begin dealing with the 'how to'. We will begin this part with a bit more discussion of our theory of the salesperson as a manager. Then, before talking about recruiting and selecting new people, we will discuss how to examine an organisation's existing sales team as the first step in upgrading the productivity of that team. Following this, we will explore, in detail, sources of potential sales talent, recruiting that talent and all of the steps involved in effective selection of productive salespeople.

We hope that by the end of this part the reader will be able to begin integrating the theory of what it takes to succeed in sales with some ideas about how to use that theory to build an effective sales team.

CHAPTER 12

THE SALESPERSON AS A MANAGER

To promote the star salesperson to a managerial position often induces a classic application of the 'Peter principle' (the proposition that each member of an organisation tends to be promoted until he or she reaches a position beyond his or her capabilities). This practice seems, on reflection, to be almost purposefully self-defeating, since it removes that rare breed, the top sales producer, from the opportunity to produce sales and places him or her in a job for which their competence may be, at best, questionable. Yet, this practice would appear to be the rule rather than the exception. In fact, it is almost institutionalised by some company recruiters who promise young people that a beginning in sales is the sure, and usually the straightest, road to a managerial career.

The philosophy underlying this strange practice is that 'if a person can sell successfully, they can manage with equal success'. This is like saying that since cabbages and strawberries both grow close to the ground, they taste equally good boiled and served with corned beef.

On its face, the assumption can be recognised as fallacious. Certainly, some salespeople can manage, and some managers can sell. But the physchological realities strongly favour less than desirable results when the roles are indiscriminately interchanged.

Most frequently, managers live to regret promotion of their strong sales personnel into management jobs. The first and most obvious result is the loss of an outstanding salesperson and the gain of a mediocre, or worse, manager. The misfortune is compounded by a secondary consequence: the former sales-person who fails as a manager often will not, indeed cannot, go back to the sales force of the same company, since this is a tacit admission to his or her associates of failure. They will be more inclined to leave the company, sometimes to take a sales job with a competitor, on whose behalf he or she begins to exercise the sales abilities that then take business from the former employer.

This problem will come as no surprise to many experienced managers. In fact, when discussing it, they almost invariably tell us that they know the automatic promotion of top salespeople to managerial responsibilities is an unwise policy. But more often than not, they follow this acknowledgement with a shrug and an admission of bafflement: 'Where else can we find sales managers?' or 'Our people want to be promoted or rewarded, in some way, for good and faithful performance. What else can we give them?'

No matter how genuine their frustrations, their solutions are short-lived. But there is a rational approach that can lead to a permanent solution: reward your good salespeople in the most imaginative and suitable ways, but promote to management only those individuals who have the ability to manage.

There is solid scientific evidence that argues for the concept that sales and managerial abilities are not necessarily correlated. In fact, the personality dynamics that make a top salesperson and those that make an excellent manager are frequently, if not mutually, exclusive, or at least in unremitting conflict.

The movement of salespeople up and out of selling into inappropriate management jobs is such a persistent business weakness that the point is worth exploring further. The clearest and most acute point of conflict between the two sets of inherent personality characteristics is the way in which the individual's ego is gratified. By definition, top salespeople experience enormous gratification when someone says yes to them. But how does this desire for personal conquest fit in with a manager's absolute need to delegate, specifically, the sale and the close? How does he or she sublimate this insatiable need for personal victory? How do they start, like a footballer past his prime, to teach the newcomers the tricks of the trade — or, as here, the techniques of the close?

This is only one facet of a complex problem, but it serves to illustrate the point. The highly driven salesperson who, because of great ego-drive, leads the company's sales charts may be totally incapable, because of that same quality, to lead its other salespeople.

On many occasions, exasperated managers have told us that a sales management spot has just come up in the company, and that several top salespeople are lusting after it. Our advice is unvarying: give your best salesperson anything that is feasible — a big private office with a thick rug and a huge desk, increased commissions, dinners in their honour — anything to show the degree to which their performance is valued and appreciated. But under no circumstances make them managers without being certain they have the proper dynamics to manage.

It may be difficult to make them understand that, in the long run, neither they nor you will benefit by the wrong promotional move. Though difficult, the attempt must be made.

The underlying problems seem to be rooted in the salespeople's perception of the managerial role. First, they frequently feel that greater status is attached to managing than to selling. The salesperson in the field often perceives the manager to be the person who 'has made it'; they have their name and title on the door to the big office, are under less pressure to produce and are judged only occasionally, and then only on the basis of others' performance.

It is in response to just such perceptions that many efforts have been made over the past four decades to professionalise sales. What is generally meant by this is the upgrading of the image of selling, not only in terms of the public's view of the salesperson, but also in terms of the salesperson's view of him- or herself.

However well intentioned, many of these efforts have been simplistic and shallow, suggesting, for example, that associations of salespeople or substitute terms to describe the job of selling might make the salesperson happier. What has not been done adequately to reach the professionalisers' goals is to convey certain facts to the public and to the trade about the salesperson, including facts about the special abilities salespeople need, industry's dependence upon salespeople, their rarity and the prodigious amounts of energy and money spent to train them. Further, it is necessary to communicate the fact that compensation for the successful salesperson is high — so high that of all people in business earning over £12,000, 80 per cent are salespeople. Finally, there is a need to communicate the most important fact of all: that sales offers rich opportunity for fulfilment and non-material personal gain, including maximum opportunity for freedom to do a job in one's own way.

Therefore, salespeople should be careful to avoid managerial jobs unless they are convinced that their best talents and greatest opportunities for gratification lie in managing.

Admittedly, these are not easy points to sell a particular salesperson who hungers after the prestige and ease that he or she thinks are concomitant with a managerial position. We were recently asked by a client to speak with his top salesperson, who he feared would resign if not moved into management. The manager, a friend of long standing, foresaw the consequences of that step, and he valued the man too much to lose him, either before or after a promotion. So, he gave the man and his wife an all-expenses-paid holiday with a room at the best hotel in town, theatre tickets, a driver and a car, and luxury restaurant reservations. His only official business was to come to our offices for a chat.

The dialogue was remarkable. Frank told us that his boss might just as well have saved his money because, although he appreciated the gesture, he was leaving the company. Why? He had been refused a sales management spot which, by seniority and performance, he should have been offered.

Frank said of his boss, 'He promoted a guy—put him over me—who could not sell his way out of a wet paper bag; now he can go to hell!'

We sympathised, then got on to other subjects, primarily selling. Since we had tested him previously, we knew more about him than he could ever have suspected. We knew he loved to sell, that he was tremendously driven, that he had absolutely no tolerance for detail, that activities such as planning territories and sitting in marketing meetings would bore him intolerably.

'I love selling. It's my whole life' he told us, and then launched into story after story of his sales triumphs, which still brought him a noticeable glow of pleasure.

The situation was clear. His feelings were hurt. He felt that he was not appreciated and that his honour had been impugned when a promotion went to someone less deserving. He rejected the unconscious suspicion that he would dislike the management job and kept insisting that he should have it.

Our job was cut out for us. Our first strategic move was to point out many of the things he already knew about the management spot, with emphasis on those of its features likely to be least attractive to him. Secondly, we reassured him that his boss 'loved' him, and valued his services and their relationship so highly he would not abet any plan, no matter how innocent, that would make him unhappy, even at the risk of losing a top salesman and a friend. Finally, we stressed a fact he may not have known: ultimately, he probably would earn between £6,000 and £9,000 less in the managerial spot. There was a ceiling on the earnings of managers, but none on those of salespeople, many of whom build up excellent incomes on the basis of accumulated sales.

The talk about money and unpleasant managerial responsibilities no doubt had its effect, but what turned the trick was the assurance that his boss valued him so highly.

Frank went back home the next weekend, and a call the following Monday morning from his boss verified our private prophesies. Frank was back on the job and raring to go.

Here are some of the things we told Frank that might be repeated almost verbatim to the salesperson determined to inherit the title, if not the responsibilities, of a manager.

Tell him or her to be prepared to do the following.

- Sublimate your own ego; let the people under you get the glory.
- Learn how to handle detail, for there will be lots of it, including, in addition to your own reports and administrative record-keeping, all of the sales reports and expense vouchers of every salesperson in your territory.
- Organise your own activities and those of your sales staff.

- Induce your staff to act without forcing compliance, an exercise which requires infinite quantities of patience (a characteristic not notably abundant in top salespeople).
- Make decisions of a more far-reaching nature than those that affect a single sale; this requires that you gather and evaluate all pertinent information and consider the consequences of your decisions.
- Plan and analyse — for countless hours — prospect lists, advertising programmes, and marketing plans, instead of dealing with people.
- Expect to attend frequent meetings, listening to the problems and complaints of your salespeople and justifying their performance — and your own — to your supervisors.
- Handle such personnel chores as firing people you like or recommending that they be fired.

These are only a few in a long catalogue of sales manager responsibilities — tasks which can be anathema to the good salesperson.

There is, of course, another dimension to the matter of the salesperson turning manager. There are thousands of potentially excellent managers who are now engaged in selling. So, executives looking for a sales manager would be foolish to overlook the possibility that the right person for the job is already on the sales force.

If all salespeople were perfectly qualified for selling, we would postulate that the odds were strongly against finding good managers among them. But many do not belong in selling. Large numbers of this group may perform reasonably well or even excellently, not because they are best suited for selling, but because their personality dynamics suit them for a broad range of activities, not the least of which may be managing.

Every salesperson should be studied as a potential manager, virtually from the day they are hired. The reasons are obvious: if the manager is promoted from the sales ranks, he or she will begin their first managerial day with an intimate knowledge of the company's products, clientele, sales force, sales problems and policies.

The benefits of the qualified person being promoted to managerial responsibilities are so clear, in fact, that we have for many years evaluated and reported the managerial potential of all salespeople we have assessed.

The fact that there are so many salespeople who cannot manage does not invalidate the fact that there are many who can. Danger lies only in the belief that competence displayed in one area can be assumed to indicate competence in all other areas; or, for that matter, that demonstrated incompetence in a single activity is a guarantee of general incompetence.

The fact is that we have found far more people in the middle of a sales force who have turned out to be well-qualified managers than we have found at the very top. Again, they have tended to have somewhat less ego-drive and so are able to tolerate delegation better than their more strongly driven, perhaps more productive, sales colleagues. Also, a person with less ego-drive (though, again, this is not an absolute) tends to have better tolerance of detail and a more balanced ability to make decisions and to handle work in a more organised way. Again, this should not be thought of as an absolute, since certainly there are those few top people in sales forces who have become outstanding managers. The point again, is that when you are looking for a salesperson, you are looking for sales dynamics (empathy, ego-drive, ego-strength, service motivation etc.), while when you are looking for a manager you are trying to determine whether they have leadership ability, the ability to delegate, the ability to make good management decisions, the ability to handle detail, the ability to co-ordinate and follow up on the work of others etc. If all of these qualities happen to be combined in the same individual, that makes for the best of all worlds due to the values inherent in promoting one of your own salespeople to manager. If such a combination does not exist, then, whether on board or not, if you are looking for a sales manager, be certain that the management dynamics may exist regardless of outstanding sales performance.

As in so much that we have written in this book, the critical element here is matching the dynamics of the individual to the dynamics required by the sales management job. It is only through matching relevant dynamics that you are likely to fill the job successfully.

So, before concluding this chapter, let's explore in more depth the qualities an individual needs to succeed in the sales management role. A number of these qualities overlap attributes that are required to succeed in certain sales situations. To succeed as a sales manager, the possession of most of these qualities, again regardless of sales ability *per se*, is essential.

Among extremely effective executives we have worked with there are flamboyant extroverts as well as those who are painfully shy. While some stick to the straight and narrow, others give eccentricity a new meaning. Some are self-centred, while others are generous to a fault. For every manager who suffers over decisions, there is one who seems to make decisions with great ease and aplomb. Some have broad interests, while others know nothing except their own area of expertise.

Leadership, as James MacGregor Burns points out, is one of the most observed and least understood phenomena on earth. Still, when we delve below the surface, we believe there are certain consistencies to be found among successful managers. To be effective, managers have to sense opportunities, formulate new possibilities, build coalitions with peers and convince those in positions of higher authority that their proposed innovations will help achieve corporate goals.

We can thus define the work of a manager as planning, organising, integrating and measuring.

PLANNING

To set objectives, a manager must have access to appropriate information about the company's standing, competitive ideas and trends in the market-place. An effective manager must be able to synthesise and analyse this information in a manner that balances the business's immediate needs with those of the future.

Of course, such an individual must be a competent decision maker, possessing a strong sense of personal responsibility and the willingness to make quick, appropriate decisions. Such decisions must be thoughtful and based on knowledge of all available data and possible consequences. On the other hand, an effective manager must be willing to take the risk of occasionally being wrong in order to act with the speed and decisiveness which many situations require.

The overly cautious individual is likely to be so fearful of being wrong that he or she would prefer not to act at all rather than take a risk. The ideal decision maker, on the other hand, combines thoughtfulness and responsibility with the courage to act, and the intelligence and flexibility to make generally sound judgements and learn from mistakes.

ORGANISING

After objectives are set, a manager has to be able to organise the resources within his or her purview. This, again, takes analytical skills in order to effectively classify the work, divide it into manageable activities and select employees most suited to completing the task at hand. This requires the ability not only to plan and organise the manager's own work and time, but also to plan, organise, co-ordinate, and follow up on the work of others.

Once objectives are set and resources organised, a manager must motivate and communicate. This is where leadership comes into play. More than 40 years ago, Bertrand Russell called power the fundamental concept in social science 'in the same sense in which energy is a fundamental concept in physics'. Leadership is the ability that enables an individual to get other people to do willingly what they have the ability to do, but might not spontaneously do on their own. Leadership implies that an individual has a special effect on others that commands their respect or admiration and causes them to follow that individual. This implies a certain amount of assertiveness in the sense that the leader projects some part of his or her personality on others. Some leaders influence by personal example, others by persuasion, and yet others through understanding the motivations of others. But, most importantly, a leader wins others over by influencing their willingness to act, rather than by forcing their compliance. Effective leaders strive to become aware of the abilities of others, in order to guide them towards goals they can realistically attain.

Delegation skills are often what separate good managers from better ones. The capable delegator is an individual who, while he or she may personally be able to do a certain job just as well, if not better, realises that keeping the work would be an inefficient use of time and possibly would interfere with the development and best utilisation of others.

There are two types of individuals who strongly resist delegating: (1) the highly impulsive, driven individual who personally wants the gratification of completing a job and so is unwilling to provide that opportunity for gratification to others; and (2) the overly cautious perfectionist who fears that no one will do the job with the same amount of care and responsibility.

The ability to delegate combines the willingness to allow others to do a job with the capacity to accurately assess their ability to do so.

INTEGRATING

In order to make a team out of the people who are responsible for various jobs, a manager must be able to communicate clearly, concisely and convincingly. A manager must have the ability and desire to convey ideas, knowledge and skills to others. He or she must be able to listen as well as talk, and have enough empathy to sense whether messages are being understood.

Still, even though communication is a two-way process, it must be under the leader's guidance and direction. To communicate effectively, a leader must be able to combine assertiveness and empathy, and display personal behaviour that encourages a positive response from colleagues and subordinates.

One management quality which, as often as any, differentiates the effective salesperson from the productive sales manager is detail ability. There are, of course, many sales jobs requiring detail ability or at least a tolerance of detail, and there are few management jobs, definitely including sales management, that do not require at least a reasonably good ability to handle detail.

The ability to handle detail requires a combination of personality dynamics which enables an individual to organise work in a systematic way. It also enables him or her to deal effectively with activities which are repetitive and structured. At one extreme, a person with too great a need for personal organisation and structure may tend to become so overly involved in day-to-day detail that they may lose sight of the real meaning of the activity. At the other extreme, a person may be so impatient and intolerant of order that he or she will be undisciplined in the planning and execution of his or her work. This lack of self-management could hamper the individual even in functions not normally requiring a great deal of detail involvement. The individual with good ability to handle detail enjoys, or at least is comfortable with, order or structure, and yet is not so enmeshed in detail that he or she loses sight of the broader picture.

MEASURING

Once objectives are set, work organised, and goals communicated, an effective manager must establish yardsticks against which performance can be analysed and appraised. Such measurements must be approached with consistency in order to be fair. Those individuals one is managing will find their responsibilities acceptable if they have the security of a clear authoritative structure. It is management's task to set clearly understood objectives and establish standards by which to meet those goals.

On this light, a manager must be able to develop people, including him- or herself. The ability to learn and grow requires considerably more than the possession of intelligence. Natural intelligence must be combined with sufficient empathy and flexibility to permit an individual to acquire new ideas and formulate new methods. In many cases, even people with well-above-average intelligence lack the capacity to grow because they use their intelligence rigidly, to defend and justify their preconceptions, rather than genuinely to seek or accept new approaches. On the other hand, many individuals with only average intelligence have the potential for growth because their openness, flexibility and empathy permit them to make full use of their abilities. Thus, for an individual to have good growth potential, he or she should combine natural intelligence with the openness and flexibility to seek, acquire and try new approaches.

UNIQUE COMBINATION

In essence, while managers approach their work with varying styles and approaches, we have found that there are basic characteristics needed to manage effectively, regardless of the situation.

To be effective, a manager must be able to analyse situations, willing to make decisions and take risks, able to communicate effectively, capable of commanding respect from others, able to delegate and motivate, consistent and fair and willing to encourage growth in others as well as oneself.

Rather than trying to fit into a prescribed mould, the best managers we have worked with are those who understand thoroughly their inherent strengths and limitations. Then they build a team by doing what they do best and hiring others whose strengths complement their limitations.

In the final analysis, there is no single profile that is ideal. But, in our assessment of over 750,000 individuals, we have not come across a single effective manager who did not possess all of the above qualities.

Allow us to close with an analogy. In sports, we have known that the moment a new record is set every athlete throughout the world acquires a new dimension of accomplishment. For years no one could run the mile in less than four minutes. Then Roger Bannister broke through the old record, and soon runners from every neighbourhood athletics club were approaching the mark, while another generation of leaders began to break new barriers.

In human affairs, the distance between the leaders and the average remains constant. If leadership performance is high, the average will increase. With this in mind, the easiest way to raise the performance of an entire company is to raise the effectiveness of its management.

CHAPTER 13

THE SALES TEAM

How many coaches, managers or chairmen of professional sports teams spend time fantasising how wonderful it would be if they could replace their entire team with one of the great teams in the league? What a wonderful fantasy suddenly to have your football team, which has not made any cup finals in years, replaced person for person by the members of the team of the League Champions. A wonderful fantasy though this may be, such dreams really do not come true. What is true is that the only way the cellar dweller, a team perpetually at the bottom of the league, can be turned into champions is through painstakingly building that team into a winner. Coaches do this through maximising use of a team's existing talent to make the very best out of what currently exists. Since you cannot suddenly replace 11 football players with an equal number of better players, the key thing that must be done is to make the best use of the talent you have on hand. There are, in fact, as all sports fans well know, many teams that perform far beyond what their talent level would indicate because they are able to maximise the talent that does exist. On the other side, many talented teams fall short throughout the years because they are not able to do just that.

The first step in building a winning team, whether in sports or in business, is to get the most out of what you have, then add to the team. In football this is done by trading and buying players; in business it is done through recruiting and selecting productive people.

START WITH THE MANAGER

For the purpose of this discussion, let us look at the sales team as one unit led by a sales manager. In a large organisation, there may be many of these teams divided into districts and regions, but each of these teams really must be viewed separately, and worked with separately, if real progress is to be made.

A team must be viewed as a totality, and not simply as individual elements. Every team has particular strengths and weaknesses. We should start, however, with the leader — the sales manager.

The first thing to do is gain a thorough understanding of the strengths and weaknesses of the individual leading the sales team. Most managers fall into one of two broad categories. In the first group is an outstanding salesperson replete with empathy, ego-drive, ego-strength and service motivation, but seriously lacking some key management attributes. That individual needs a group of self-reliant, well-disciplined, self-starting salespeople reporting to him or her. In all likelihood, that sales manager cannot be counted on to be highly effective at delegation or follow-up. He or she is most likely not very strong in structuring the work and time of subordinates. On the other hand, such a sales manager is likely to be extremely effective at going in with a salesperson and helping to close tough deals. Of course, one of the things that these highly driven sales managers might have to work on is the tendency to want to do too much themselves. Typically, they have difficulty delegating. Their motivation often is to show the salespeople how to sell by outselling every one of them. In our work with sales managers such as this, we have to get them literally to sit on their drive, if they are to be successful in developing the potential of their sales force.

The second category of sales manager is exemplified by one who possesses strong administrative skills. These managers help plan and structure the work of a sales force, follow up effectively on the work of others and are adept at analysing data. They set goals and objectively evaluate performance. They may possess some sales instincts, but they do not intensely need the close; therefore they are effective delegators. Lacking strong sales instincts, they might not be helpful in closing deals and, in some instances, might even have some problems relating to the highly driven people reporting to them.

By presenting these two broad categories of sales managers, we are trying to highlight the fact that, in order to understand the dynamics of a team, it is essential to start out by understanding the strengths, weaknesses and motivations of the sales manager. A team's productivity can obviously be greatly affected from the top down.

One brief case history on the sales management relationship illustrates this point. We were asked by the vice president of sales for an international computer firm to conduct a team analysis of one of their regional offices in a major city. The primary purpose of this study was to explore the region's strengths and weaknesses, and to make suggestions for improving sales productivity. The executive also wanted us to help increase morale and enthusiasm among managers and other sales personnel.

The region had recently experienced a change in top management. The previous regional manager was held in high regard by the branch managers and sales personnel. After 12 months under a new manager, the organisation continued to grow but not nearly at a level consistent with its previous record. We conducted interviews with the regional management staff and salespeople. During those sessions, Caliper's test findings for each manager and his or her sales staff were reviewed. Suggestions were provided to the managers regarding methods of supervising the people who reported to them.

On the whole there appeared to be strong negative feelings on the part of the region's management team. Part of the problem was solved by comparing the personalities of the old manager with his replacement. The original manager was a strongly driven, dynamic individual who was a classic example of the so-called charismatic leader. On the other hand, his replacement was an individual who was superbly trained in the technical end of the business and possessed the personality dynamics most typical of a technically oriented, highly capable administrator. However, the new regional manager could never have been accused of being charismatic.

Loyalty to the charismatic leader, with the concomitant resentment of his replacement, certainly was part of the problem. More important, however, was the fact that when the old leader set goals or demanded effort, the tendency was to respond positively. On the other hand, the very same demands or goals put forward by the new manager were viewed as unrealistic and were resisted. A negative mentality was established which served to erode confidence in management. If people feel that goals cannot be met, they will not, when push comes to shove, be met. Motivation in this case was a 'top down' activity. In other words, the new regional manager had to embrace his goal with enthusiasm and project his optimism downwards to his staff, which, given his personality, he was not able to do.

What the original manager was able to accomplish through sheer leadership dynamics was to drive the team towards meeting tough quotas tied to compensation. He was also able to cover up, through sheer activity, two fundamental problems which became apparent when the new manager took over; limited formal sales management training for branch managers; and an inefficient developmental programme for the unit sales force.

One of our first suggestions was that the new manager, with the full participation of the managers reporting to him, should re-establish what most people now thought of as unrealistic quotas to a more objectively attainable level. The fact that the old manager could, at least for a short term, drive the team towards the higher goal did not mean that over the long haul that team, led by the new manager, could hope to attain that consistent level of productivity. In interviews, even the strongest supporters of the old manager admitted that some of his projections were optimistic and contained certain inaccurate assumptions that in the long run could prevent those projections from being attained.

Establishing quotas which are realistic from a historical perspective, achievable and, at the same time, challenging is essential to creating a positive, high-energy environment. We strongly recommended that quota-setting activities be carefully reviewed and given sufficient attention so that the goals were challenging, rather than defeating. In addition, we felt that it was important that the new manager recognise his role in creating an environment that was energising, optimistic and results-oriented. Moreover, he must convey these values to his organisation with great concern for the welfare and success of the sales staff, his branch managers and for his own personal gain. Further, as mentioned, by and large we found that the branch managers were poorly prepared for their role as sales managers. None had direct selling experience and formal sales management training had not been provided. It was strongly recommended that all of these managers participate in a formal sales management training programme. By sharing the experience together and acquiring a common language, this activity would facilitate a greater team orientation.

The existing sales force was broken down into three groups organised around individuals' specific areas in need of improvement. Once these targeted training needs were established, trainers were brought in from corporate headquarters to design training geared to the special needs of each group and to implement these specially developed programmes with each of the three groups.

In addition, we developed composite profiles for the most successful sales representatives, which were then used to assist managers in evaluating new applicants. This sales composite helped managers to identify strengths and weaknesses in relationship to successful employees; this improved management's ability to identify applicants who have the greatest chance of success.

As can easily be seen from the above, this sales team needed assistance on every level, starting with the regional manager, who needed specialised assistance in setting realistic goals and motivating his subordinates; to the branch managers, who needed hands-on training in the sales field; to the sales force, who broke up into three groups, with each group receiving training targeted to meet their specific needs.

What can be readily seen from this case is how differently a team will perform, depending on the nature of its leadership. At least in the short run, this particular team was producing as a result of the sheer intensity or dynamism of the leadership provided by the old manager. When that force was removed, however, the real quality of the group found its level. Very different techniques had to be applied and specific solutions to specific problems found, in order to move productivity back up to an acceptable level.

HIRING IN ONE'S OWN IMAGE

One of the most common problems we have encountered in studying sales teams is that they reflect many of their manager's particular strengths, as well as weaknesses. This is because very often people are hired in the image of the manager. The problems stemming from this kind of imbalance can be myriad.

We have seen many situations over the years where a sales force with this kind of imbalance has literally come across to the public as 'a bunch of animals'. There is little or no co-operation among the salespeople themselves. Rather than viewing each other as colleagues, salespeople in such situations view each other as direct competitors. We have seen situations where a salesperson will work harder to pre-empt colleagues — to grab sales out from under them — than to fight the company's competition. The issue of who is first in the month's sales can become more important to the members of the sales team than the level of overall productivity for the company. The manager, in this scenario, is unable to control this jungle atmosphere because he or she is essentially cut from the same mould and so tends to exacerbate the problem rather than cure it.

What finally happens is that people who might tend to balance the group will not come aboard because they do not like the climate, so the people who are brought on tend to be essentially the same personality types, thus compounding the problem.

At the other end of the spectrum are teams we have evaluated where the existing salespeople almost entirely lacked ego-drive. Typically, they survive through good service and ongoing relationship building. In most cases, such companies are well known, so the salespeople are doing business in spite of a total lack of dynamism. Still, half again as much business would result if such companies had real salespeople. The problem is that strongly driven, dynamic salespeople are generally not attracted to teams with such 'sleepy' atmospheres.

The majority of sales forces are not representative of either of these extremes, but consist of people with a range of abilities and personality attributes. Most, however, suffer from some imbalance, and all have to deal with the realities involved in the strengths and weaknesses, motivations and differing personality dynamics of their team members.

USING CHEMISTRY TO BUILD A CHAMPIONSHIP TEAM

Whether the chemistry that exists between management and salespeople, or among the salespeople themselves, is felt to be positive or detrimental relates to top management's vision of where they wish the company to go, how they want it to get there and, most importantly, whether they have the people to accomplish their goals.

There are indeed some companies which see each salesperson as a totally independent island who makes or breaks it for him- or herself with no relationship to other people on the team. If their product is also a small-ticket one involving a quick, hard, one-time close, perhaps their vision would be realised by having a team of 'animals'. There may even be some companies who are so convinced that their only job is that of order takers and servicers that the 'sleepy' climate we discussed would be totally congruent with their vision. Though neither of these extremes normally fits a corporate vision, our point is that it is the vision that must dictate what, if anything, should be done about the existing team. What we suggest, then, is that, first, management meet by themselves or, if needed, with the involvement of an outside consultant, to determine their corporate vision and define their goals. They should ask questions like this.

- How much would we like our team to sell during the next fiscal year and over the next five years?
- Who are the targets for these sales?
- Ideally, how should these sales be made?
- What is the relationship between acquiring brand new business and expanding and maintaining existing accounts?
- Who, ideally, should be charged with each of these responsibilities?
- How much of a gap are we willing to tolerate between the productivity of the top and bottom performers on the sales force?
- Will we earmark funds to further develop our sales team if necessary?
- What kind of climate do we want within the sales team — co-operative, competitive, etc?

Once a corporate vision is defined, a plan can then be developed to reach the goals prescribed by that vision. The next step is to define the tasks needed to achieve these goals, communicate the goals and required tasks, and analyse members of the existing sales team to see if they have the abilities needed to get the job done. Each individual must be looked at to determine whether he or she has the ability to do the job as defined, or whether, through training or a shift in responsibilities, the ability can be developed. The relationship between the sales manager and his or her people has to be understood. Then it has to be determined how that relationship acts positively or negatively towards achieving corporate goals. And, of course, the chemistry of the team itself has to be studied to see how the dynamics of the current team affects the likelihood of reaching those goals.

There are, of course, many tools available to help management move the company forward. Objective measurement of performance geared at developing people in areas of deficiency can go a long way towards increasing productivity and achieving goals. Attitude studies, valid psychological tests, employee productivity workshops and team-building activities are just a few worth noting. Whatever tools are used and, fortunately, there are excellent tools and techniques available today, it is most critical to have a thorough understanding of a company's sales team and how that team meshes with the company's goals, if there is to be any hope of developing a strategy to improve the productivity of that team.

A good example is a study we conducted with a mature company which found it had fallen behind in recent years in new business development and expansion. We started out by examining management's standard job description and making a field evaluation of the sales representative position. We found the primary emphasis was on sales through the existing distribution network — not new business. Through job analysis, we discovered that, essentially, the sales force established relationships with major distributors but paid little attention to direct sales to end users. As a result, competitors were short-circuiting the sales process and thus gaining market shares.

When we analysed the sales force, we uncovered the fact that the vast majority of the sales representatives were, in fact, service-oriented people. Their solid service ability allowed them to retain their accounts since they had extremely good ability to develop long-term relationships. What they lacked as a group was the strong dynamics needed to compete persuasively for new business.

Several additional concerns were identified during the course of this project.

We interviewed a large number of individuals who expressed concern over the company's current methods of tracking and evaluating sales performance. These salespeople and managers stated that the company relied heavily upon the subjective impressions of supervisor ratings. While some attempt had been made by the company to have standardised performance factors evaluated, there was concern that these factors did not actually correspond to real performance. Part of the difficulty in tracking sales representative performance was endemic to sales generated within a distribution environment. To a great extent, the performance of the representatives was tied to the performance of the distributor. Once the sales representative persuaded the distributor to stock the line, the role of the representative became more service than sales oriented. The distributor, in these cases, assumed the active sales role, while the sales representative took the role of technical expert, servicer and factory representative. As a result, tenure was often the most significant factor used to differentiate sales representatives rated successful from those who were rated as unsuccessful. Account maintenance was highly valued and the primary focus of the existing sales force. While distributor retention, volume, expansion and product mix were all extremely important, they could no longer be relied upon as the sole means of evaluating performance. Given the new goals and direction the company wished to pursue, a new performance appraisal system was definitely needed.

Further complicating the firm's performance tracking was the fact that, although sales representatives were responsible for sales calls directly to end users, the company encouraged end users to contact and deal with any authorised distributor within the network system. Thus, despite territory assignments, it was often unclear which sales representative was responsible for making a particular sale. Clearly, this imposed a significant but not unresolvable barrier to developing a more objective performance measurement system. Moreover, it had the effect of discouraging end user sales contacts.

As a result of these findings, we recommended a series of structured sessions, using a focus group/task force approach (which was undertaken) to explore and make recommendations concerning performance tracking options for service and acquisition sales activities. Members of this group included sales representatives, managers, and human resource personnel.

Another major problem that occurred was in the area of communication. Field personnel expressed feelings of isolation from the corporation and an inability to effect change. While their concerns primarily centred around the issues of performance tracking and compensation, there was a general expression of the company's lack of concern for, and recognition of, its field sales staff.

Where possible, we suggested that field sales representatives and managers should be included in forums in which goal setting, strategy development, performance tracking and compensation systems were to be designed. By including employees in the problem solving process, they would be more likely to own the solutions and make the systems work.

As noted earlier, this sales organisation as a group was psychologically more oriented towards service and did not exhibit a strong level of ego-drive. They could not, therefore, derive a strong inner gratification from persuading others. While some individuals might be effective in developing new business, most would focus on retaining existing accounts and providing technical support. If the company wanted to focus, as a primary goal, on the development of new business versus the retention of current business, they would require new people with different personality dynamics, along with a totally restructured performance tracking and incentive plan. While in an ideal world, there might be an abundance of candidates equally suited for both sales and service roles, harsh reality and experience teaches that very few people can do both well. What we strongly suggested was that job differentiation in this specific case would allow for greater flexibility in attaining corporate business objectives.

We recommended establishing separate sales and service roles within the company's structure. Implementation would result in a more strategic approach to hiring, human resource utilisation and the need to hire and motivate a sales force with selling skills matched to specific market requirements.

The study was effective in pointing out characteristics which differentiate a productive service-oriented staff from successful new business developers. The study also pointed out the need to develop a more strategic orientation towards using human resources to accomplish corporate objectives. Our strong bottom-line recommendations to this company were to: (1) redefine sales jobs in terms of sales and service components; (2) develop a performance measurement system which objectively related specifically to sales and service tasks; (3) define a compensation/incentive system that was tied to performance and the motivational characteristics of the sales/service people it covered; and (4) develop a strategic hiring plan that would incorporate overall corporate goals and the individual personality characteristics needed to get the job done.

UPGRADE PRODUCTIVITY

The solutions that our own client companies have found to achieve productivity upgrades are so numerous and so varied that a full description of them would literally be impossible here. Here are just a few of the things our clients have done to upgrade productivity successfully, even before embarking on the hiring of new people.

- Offer developmental programmes, internal or external, in assertiveness training, time management, listening skills, closing techniques, presentation skills, approaches to prospecting and technical training, to name just a few.
- Provide training to enrich the product knowledge (technical know-how) of salespeople.
- Conduct team-building sessions among the salespeople and between salespeople and management to increase morale and productivity.
- Develop a team selling system allowing the strengths of one salesperson to augment the weaknesses of another.
- Reorganise compensation geared to the particular dynamics of the sales team.
- Develop an incentive programme built on group, in addition to individual, productivity.
- Divide sales responsibilities between those capable of new business acquisition and those more suited to maintenance and expansion of existing accounts.
- Reassign salespeople to managers with whom the chemistry would be more effective.
- Counsel and retrain managers as to how to be more effective in working with sales teams, given the dynamics of that team.
- Counsel one-on-one with each salesperson and manager, making them aware of their own strengths and weaknesses, and helping them play more effectively to their strengths and away from their weaknesses.
- Develop a series of one-on-one meetings between individual salespeople and their managers with top management, or perhaps an outside consultant, as a meeting facilitator.
- Install objective performance measurement systems (or review and update old ones to be sure they reflect changes in the company's direction).
- Utilise focus groups to uncover and resolve problem issues.

Which of these activities, or combination of activities, might be appropriate for a particular company again depends on that all-important understanding of the team, and what gaps exist between the team as currently constituted and the company's vision of the future.

CHAPTER 14

THE MARGINAL PRODUCER

When examining salespeople themselves, broadly speaking, they fall into three categories. There are those precious few — typically the 20 per cent of a firm's salespeople that are highly productive — that sell 80 per cent of what is sold. These individuals have precisely what it takes to sell in their sales situation. They can sense the desires of a prospect, are driven by a need to persuade and can bounce back from the rejection that is an inevitable part of their work. They have enough service motivation to meet the requirements of their job, and they possess most of the other qualities needed in their unique situation. They sell effectively and need only be managed in a manner related to their key motivations, and not managed or compensated in any way to de-motivate them. These are the superstars of whom managers will say, 'I just point them in the right direction'.

At the other end of the spectrum are those who fundamentally lack the dynamics to sell or the particular personality attributes required to sell their particular product or service. In all likelihood, these people derive no pleasure from closing a sale, or, if they do, they lack the qualities needed in their specific sales situation. Since you cannot make someone want to sell or feel the gratification that a real salesperson would obtain from successfully closing a sale, it is very unlikely that there is much that can be done to develop this group. Our approach is to ascertain their real basic occupational motivations and, if possible, place them in more appropriate positions within the company, since, after all, they do know the company and its products. If it is at all possible, it is preferable to salvage the investment in them by placing them in a more productive position. In addition, it can obviously be seen that there is a valuable morale factor if this kind of job crossover can occur.

The second action to be taken, where the above is not appropriate or possible, is to replace members of this group as quickly as possible with appropriate and productive new recruits.

It is the middle group in most sales teams into which most salespeople fall. This is the most difficult group to deal with. They produce sales, but not with consistently high performance; they are simply not up to par. Management has already invested time, money and effort in them, so it is important to try to make that investment pay off. The important issue is knowing which specific strategy might be designed for each individual to allow him or her to produce at a higher level, if, indeed, they possess the potential to do so.

There is obviously no single solution or formula. Analysing each individual's strengths and weaknesses within a group and separating the overall group into subgroups with similar weaknesses is the first step in determining management strategies to overcome these limitations. What we typically have found is that one group will need assistance in closing techniques; more often than not, they can greatly benefit from formal assertiveness training. Another group that is not totally lacking in empathy, but is extremely impatient, can be greatly helped by attending a listening skills workshop. Another group may have less-than-average ability in the area of personal organisation. Acquiring tools that will assist these individuals in time management and improve their overall self-starting ability might be all they need to function more productively. The list could go on, but these examples should be sufficient to make the point. Often, these middling producers (people who are just good enough not to be fired, but not really productive enough to meet the needs of the company) can be helped enormously by focusing on one area of weakness and, through targeted training and supervision, helping them work through that weakness and so perform at a substantially higher level. A batsman who is going through a lean patch undertakes extra batting practice. A bowler who is bowling off-line works with his coach to improve his technique. In the same way, the salesperson dragged down by one weakness (if that problem can be uncovered) can be helped by working to improve, at least to some degree, that specific area.

Let us examine why some people, given proper management and training, can succeed, while others, under the same circumstances, will turn up empty handed. *Marginal,* as we will see, turns out to be a very big word.

The key factor is whether an individual's marginal performance relates to his or her fundamental lack of appropriate dynamics, or whether it is limited by some particular personality factor that can be corrected. Finally, it must be determined whether there might be some outside factors which are working to lower productivity in relation to his or her real potential.

Let us look at three individual cases from our files, which exemplify this point.

We assessed the sales potential of a young man (we will call him Phillip) who was working for a large manufacturing company. He had great references, he had impressed the management of the company in the initial interview and he had scored well on our test. Yet, with all of that going for him, and after a good start making three important sales in the first month, he had sunk into a six-month slump.

The sales manager was perplexed. He asked us to review all the facts to see whether there was a better solution than dismissing Phillip, who had seemed so ideal at first.

Psychological testing indicated that Phillip possessed very strong sales dynamics. He was empathic, enjoyed persuading and could deal with rejection. However, he had a strong need for approval, particularly from authority figures.

Realising that, we assessed Phillip's manager. When the personality profiles were placed side by side, the problem became apparent. The manager, who had come up from sales himself, was a hard-driving, extremely aggressive, assertive individual, with adequate empathy. He was an individualist. When dealing with salespeople, his tendency was to leave them alone unless there was an obvious problem or concern that required his attention. He was from the school that believed that performance tells the story. 'When I was in sales', he told us, 'the last thing I wanted was to have a manager looking over my shoulder.'

The problem, as it turned out, was not with the manager, because, after all, he had sold successfully and, in fact, managed a rather productive sales force. Nor was the problem with Phillip, the salesperson, who had the ability to sell. Rather, the problem related to the chemistry between manager and salesperson.

Had the company been small, we would have suggested that the manager try to provide more approval, guidance and ongoing support to help relate better to Phillip and improve his performance. Of course, it is difficult to reprogramme one's particular management approach and technique, but, when possible, behavioural modifications should be made to improve overall effectiveness.

Since the company had offices in other locations, however, a better suggestion was that Phillip be shifted to another office whose manager was the type who characteristically functions in a more supportive, caring way. The shift resulted in an almost immediate turnaround for Phillip, and today he is functioning at the level of production that was expected of him initially. By altering the outside factor — the management approach as related to Phillip's needs — productivity could be substantially improved.

The problem with Holly, a property salesperson, was much simpler to solve. She, like Phillip, had tremendous sales dynamics but was clearly not performing well after having been promoted to a position that called for selling commercial property.

Interestingly, when management first reviewed her application and psychological assessment, she was not being considered for that particular target market. However, after having succeeded at selling moderately priced homes, she asked to be promoted and, fearing they might lose her to a competitor, management complied. She was promoted to a position that called for selling commercial properties.

Holly was impatient, highly driven, somewhat disorganised, and desperately in need of instant gratification. She was a classic short-term, goal-oriented individual who wanted quick and frequent closes. As a result, she simply lacked the patience for long-term follow-up and service.

Obviously, with commercial properties, long-term follow-up and service are as critical to success as the ability to sell. Thus, the job that she was promoted to because of her strong sales ability was precisely the wrong job for her.

At our suggestion, the manager decided to move her into a property securing responsibility. Securing involves the need for a strong close and the kind of immediate yes or no response that Holly's drive and impatience demanded. Property securing therefore made for an ideal job match. The move was made, again with excellent results.

As a footnote, we should mention that management had been rightly concerned that Holly might consider the suggested shift a demotion, since the new position did not carry the prestige of commercial sales. However, the manager had emphasised that many of the buildings Holly would be securing might be highly prestigious commercial properties or homes.

The manager had explained that the only difference would be securing the property for the company, as opposed to going through the long, agonising process of following up. By describing the move in that way, the manager was able to tap into Holly's basic personality attributes and so was able to save an otherwise impossible situation.

The final example relates to Sally, a salesperson for a printing firm, who, unlike Phillip and Holly, was performing adequately. The problem was that she was performing *just* adequately. Her manager felt strongly that, given her presentation, appearance, knowledge of printing and overall manner, her performance should have been near the top of the sales force.

Her good qualities included empathy and the drive to sell effectively, as well as time management skills, excellent service motivation, and the attention to detail and sense of responsibility necessary to follow up and provide the kind of expertise often required in printing sales.

However, she needed approval and was unassertive. She would sometimes hesitate to push strongly enough for the close lest she incur disapproval. Whenever there was some resistance to a possible sale, her tendency was to back off a bit too soon.

Of course, no salesperson, particularly in the printing industry, should be overly pushy or aggressive. Yet there are times when an effective salesperson senses that the prospect is on the verge of making a decision and needs only the slightest push in the right direction. However, when such an opportunity would present itself, Sally's tendency was not to risk that slight push.

The sales she made, therefore, were the automatic ones — jobs that sold themselves or called for only the least bit of soft persuasion. Far too many sales were slipping through her fingers because of her unwillingness to be assertive at the right time.

She attended an assertiveness training programme and a few counselling sessions dealing with her reluctance to risk rejection. The combination proved effective. Although she is still not selling at the very top level of the sales force, she has moved from below average to well above average, and her manager feels that growth will continue.

After gaining an understanding of the key strengths and key weaknesses of these three marginal producers, management was able to substantially upgrade their production by taking actions relating to these strengths and weaknesses. Phillip needed only to be placed under a manager whose style played more effectively to his needs. Holly's job responsibilities had to be shifted from one involving patience and follow-through (of which she was constitutionally incapable) to one playing to her specific strengths: assertive, highly persuasive closing. Sally simply needed some assertiveness training and counselling to overcome a particular weakness, thus freeing her to be far more productive.

By understanding the particular qualities of marginal producers, management can frequently upgrade their performance by making modifications that are sometimes far simpler than the examples we have just presented. We have seen situations in which simply attending a one-day time planning workshop, or having a manager slightly modify his or her approach or building in a modest incentive programme can make all the difference in the world. Sometimes these small modifications can literally convert a salesperson skating on the edge of dismissal into a highly productive contributor. The key, of course, in all of these situations is whether the individual is marginal because of one or another correctable situation, or whether the problem is that the individual is basically, and fundamentally, not suited to the position. In the former case, management will benefit by making every effort to make those corrections, as in the three cases we presented; but in the latter case, as painful as it may be, it is better for management, and in the long run the employee, to make whatever changes are necessary, but not to allow that unsuitable employee to continue frustrating him- or herself and the company through unproductive performance.

CHAPTER 15

TRAINING AND COMPENSATING TO ACHIEVE MAXIMUM PRODUCTIVITY

At a recent corporate management meeting, the tension was palpable. The company's president was angry, and it was clear that someone was about to get a roasting.

'The sales training programme you endorsed fell flat on its face', he said to his top sales executives, 'and I've got the charts here to prove it.'

Sales charts were flashed on to the slide screen, and the president was in no way disposed towards understatement in pointing out the source of his displeasure. After implementing an extensive and costly countrywide sales training programme for which salespeople had been taken out of the field for a full three days, the charts showed only a modest initial sales increase, which almost immediately fell back to the original base figure.

While the sales vice president and the regional sales managers squirmed, the president noted the high costs, both direct and indirect, of the training programme, and demanded an explanation, 'It's obvious that the training failed. Now I want to know why.'

As is typical in situations such as this, both the sales training team and the sales training approach were blamed, but no one doubted that the fault lay somewhere between the trainers themselves and the training curriculum they were using. The automatic assumption, however, that the fault lies with trainers and/or the training programme is simplistic and, as often as not, simply wrong. In fact, in many instances, the fault lies elsewhere; it lies with the sales trainees.

Over the years, we have discussed this problem with many top professional trainers, and most agree that, all too often, valid training programmes fail because they are expected to train people who are simply not capable of doing the work. Most of these pros will affirm that sales training often ignores the most basic reality not only of selling, but of human personality as well: people cannot be trained to do what they are fundamentally not suited to do. Attempting to make someone do what they are not capable of doing will only result in frustration and failure.

Indisputably, every salesperson can benefit from appropriate sales training. The person who is new to selling — the young man or woman in a first job or the converted school teacher, farmer or mechanic — must be oriented to the business of selling and given insights into some of its techniques and requirements, regardless of their inherent abilities. Experienced salespeople can benefit from more advanced training in areas such as the development of proposals and presentation skills. There is a continuing need in many businesses for ongoing product training, particularly now, when rapid change is the norm, not the exception. This training can range from a basic review of product features on simple product lines to detailed scientific indoctrination in advanced technological equipment. In addition, training must precede the introduction of new products into the marketplace.

There is, then, an important place for several varieties of sales training. And with the large investments companies make to build and maintain their sales forces, there are invariably large amounts of money riding on the outcome of sales training programmes.

But when these training programmes do not produce the expected results, there is a predisposition to characterise trainers and sales training programmes as failures. The truth of the matter is that they are often given the impossible task of 'making silk purses out of sows' ears'.

We are convinced that training can succeed only if selection succeeds. Good raw silk must be provided before the training department or consultants can be expected to produce a purse of the requisite quality.

Appropriate training can make the inherently successful salesperson more productive. But people devoid of sales potential — for example, rigid, opinionated and unempathic individuals — rarely respond to training, no matter how thorough and scientifically valid the training may be. People lacking ego-drive, those individuals who gain no personal gratification from the sales process or from closing a sale, are not likely to respond to sales training because the process is simply too much of an effort, and they simply do not enjoy the work. They may go through the motions prescribed by the trainers, but the long-term results are likely to be nil. In addition to attempting to train people who lack basic sales dynamics and so should not be trained, many otherwise excellent training programmes fail because they attempt to provide exactly the same training to an entire group with little or no recognition of individual differences.

Effective training involves the recognition that no two people operate in precisely the same way. The salesperson who is extremely impulsive and ego-driven needs little urging, through training or otherwise, to push for a close. His or her training should more appropriately stress the best techniques for listening and for acquiring insights into the customer's needs and point of view.

In a training class, however, the individual seated near this impulsive, driven salesperson may very well be in need of help in closing. He or she may be extraordinarily empathic when relating to prospective customers but somewhat too hesitant to move towards a close. The training for these two distinct people must obviously have different emphasis. The important point here is that training which does not recognise these individual differences and provide for them will fail one person or the other, or both.

A genuinely successful training programme for 25 people must, in effect, be 25 separate training programmes proceeding simultaneously. Only this approach can show each person how to operate to his or her fullest potential and in accordance with his or her own personality makeup, but even here each of those 25 persons had better have at least some potential to do the job for which they are being trained.

An old friend of ours in the consulting business, on first hearing of this concept, had a natural reaction. He said, 'Why, that idea is just like the aeroplane. Anybody can look at it and tell that it can never get off the ground.'

Indeed, it might appear to be an outline for chaos in the training-room, but this is not the way it works in practice. Such a programme does, however, require somewhat more careful preparation than is usual and certainly precludes the purely canned training programme unless that programme is substantially modified to deal with each unique situation. With knowledge of the specific makeup of the group both in terms of experiential and personality factors, trainers can design role play and other exercises.

Role play and other exercises can be designed to deal with the specific strengths, weaknesses and motivations of the individuals within the training group helping people who need closing assistance to practise their closing, while others can be working on their listening skills, and still others on work and time planning. It is obviously not our purpose here to structure a training programme. We simply want to underscore that if training is to be effective, it must be geared to the individual as opposed to providing an approach that supposedly covers all.

In addition, skilled professional trainers, whether on the company's staff or retained to carry out a specific training project, must acquire knowledge of the company's products, marketing approaches and support systems. Only then can the training be geared to the individual in terms of their personal qualities, as well as to the job function that person must carry out.

It is certainly easier for an on-board training department to develop this kind of awareness, but it is just as vital, though more difficult, for the outside training consultant to do so as well.

If an outside training firm is to be effective, it must overcome the concern that it characteristically works across a broad spectrum of business and industry. The team training insurance sales representatives this week may be training salespeople from a light machinery manufacturing firm next week, and software salespeople the following week. There are certain similarities among selling jobs, but problems differ so vastly from one industry to another and, in fact, from one company within an industry to another that a realistic grasp of the sales situation within the specific company by the trainer is vital for the most effective training. This grasp can best be attained by the trainers spending several days in the field with salespeople and their sales managers, experiencing the selling firsthand, seeing sales resistance and developing successful responses to that resistance.

The above is not to imply that in-house training programmes are superior to outside firms, even though the former may have a better automatic grasp of a company's sales situation. Very often as a practical matter, because of the size of the company or the infrequency with which training programmes are needed, a full-time, in-house training staff may not be advisable or even possible. An outside training firm, when retained, should be as aware of the specific company's situation as would an in-house training operation. The good firms are perfectly capable of reaching this goal.

With prior evaluation of each person to be trained, and with a thorough, first-hand study of the field sales requirements completed, the training group is ready to put together the programme and proceed.

However, there remains the problem of personalising the training for each individual. This can be handled by structuring a training format that allocates minimum time to lectures and maximum time to a combination of intensive individual counselling and group sessions, both small and large.

The individual evaluations are used to structure groups. Individuals possessing intense ego-drive may be put together in a group, while other individuals needing help with personal organisation might be doing other exercises. A group might be made up of ego-driven people and individuals with less ego-drive but outstanding listening skills. In short, prior knowledge of the dynamics of the individuals in the training group allows the trainers to use their strengths and weaknesses as a key part of the training process. It allows for the most ideal training situation, where the trainees will be working to train each other through participating in activities.

Admittedly, the overall approach to training we are describing is more difficult and requires some innovation on the part of the trainers, but it meets the three requirements we consider absolute:

- It offers a thorough picture of each individual's real abilities and personality dynamics.
- It optimises, on the basis of this picture, each individual's potential.
- It deals with a 'real-world' situation; that is, it trains people to sell their particular products in their particular markets, taking into consideration their particular sales problems, in terms of their particular personalities.

There is no single best way to sell to which all can conform. There are no perfect formulae, no magic words that apply to all men and women equally, any more than there is one single way in which all bowlers should bowl cricket balls or all batsmen should hit them.

The same is true of selling. Training should be seen as an approach to help salespeople maximise their own abilities in their own way. Forcing them into another mould simply does not work, and, if anything, it helps to guarantee failure for a person who may have enormous natural potential.

REWARDING THE SALESPERSON

Rewards as a sales motivator have been explored, scrutinised, pondered and analysed by innumerable experts. No reasonably good reference library fails to yield shelves of books detailing 'best methods' of rewarding sales forces. This embarrassment of riches turns out to be of dubious value. A sales force is comprised of individual human beings with broadly varying needs, points of view, self-perceptions and psychological characteristics who cannot be infallibly categorised, measured and punched out to formula. It therefore follows that there is no one best plan for rewarding all of them.

It is safe to make only one generalisation about compensation: the programme that motivates best or, perhaps even better put, that does not serve to demotivate, is one that is geared to the specific needs of each individual. For example, a highly ego-driven salesperson with inordinate self-confidence is likely to be most acutely motivated by a reward system based on incentives, that is, one that offers little base in the form of draw or salary, but that has a steeply graduated top end; this individual would be de-motivated and frustrated by a programme limiting top end potential even if it provided for more security. On the other hand, such a commission-oriented programme can be inappropriate (and, in fact, may have a reverse motivational impact) for a person with less confidence and ego-drive. In all probability, he or she will respond more positively to the higher draw or salary base which his or her associate might find unappealing.

Obviously, one compensation plan cannot have equal motivational effects on both of these individuals. And, just as obviously, a flexible plan that provides both individuals with the kind of compensation to which each will respond best will be most successful. Clearly, there are many firms, particularly smaller ones, that cannot, as a practical matter, have a number of reward plans, a different one for each individual salesperson. Yet, even in these situations, some creativity and imagination could effect subtle differences within basically similar plans to produce a positive impact on individuals. A number of our clients, including some relatively small companies, have prepared three or four plans. They literally sat down and worked with individual salespeople to select the plan with which they were most comfortable. In a small company, where people tend to know each other's business, there is the danger of jealousy where an individual under one reward plan out-earns someone working under a different plan. However, if an open discussion was held and the individual voluntarily chose his or her plan with all the facts (including the earnings potential and the security) laid out, that jealousy would be less likely to occur.

What we are suggesting here, just as we did in our discussion on training, is a far more difficult approach to the issue of reward. It is certainly easier to set up one unified plan that covers the entire sales force, whether a company develops a reward programme itself or brings in outside experts to help them. Yet, as tempting as taking this easier road may be, thought should be given to how much is invested in the sales force and how critical maximum sales productivity is to the success of the company. Thus, if, with a little more effort and a little more creativity, reward systems can be created to help maximise the productivity of each salesperson, isn't that extra work well worth it? A reward plan that speaks to each individual's motivations will not only enhance productivity, but can play an important role in substantially increasing the retention of the most productive salespeople.

Another aspect of reward that should be touched on is the fact that salespeople, regardless of their personality dynamics, are not totally immune to the lure of 'the golden handcuffs'. An attractive pension and retirement package, profit-sharing programme and accumulating bonuses help to develop an identification with the company, a feeling within the salespeople that they are in fact part of a team. We have found that the more an individual feels a sense of participation in the overall success of the firm, the more he or she will be motivated to contribute to that success. This applies across the full range of sales personalities. Security-oriented individuals like bonuses and profit-sharing potential because they can get side benefits without having to run the risks inherent in straight-commission sales. To commission-oriented salespeople, bonuses and profit sharing provide more opportunities to share in the big money and, in addition, to feel that they are working for themselves, which is often the real desire of hard-driving salespeople.

Before completing our discussion of rewards, an important point should be made. As important as money is, and as potentially valuable or inhibiting as a reward plan can be, the key to sales success still remains whether the individual possesses the basic dynamics or motivations, and whether he or she has the other requirements necessary to sell successfully in a specific sales job. It is that inner motivation that drives the salesperson to the next prospect and propels him or her out of the door the next morning. Money helps the successful salesperson keep score. Like a medal in the armed forces, a trip to Hawaii, a pat on the back, or the number one on the sales chart, money is a symbol of success. But it is the inner motivation, the desire to get the yes and the emotional gratification that closing brings that is the force behind the real salesperson's performance.

Obviously, no one can live on emotional gratification alone, but as we have suggested in these pages, it is critical that the financial rewards should be tied closely with the kind of emotional gratification the individual requires.

In concluding this discussion of training and compensation, it is important to re-emphasise the fundamental point that the key to an individual's sales success is the attributes and motivations that exist within the individual. Training will fail if it is not geared to helping a person play to his or her unique strengths and overcome specific weaknesses. In the same way, compensation will fail if it does not enhance each individual's unique attributes. Only with this kind of individualised approach can training and compensation achieve what they are designed to do — enhance, not inhibit, performance.

CHAPTER 16

SOURCES OF SALES TALENT

Despite all that has been said about the importance of maximising the productivity of a company's existing team, there is a point when hiring must be undertaken to meet corporate goals. On the negative side, if too many people are simply inappropriate to do a company's sales job and either leave on their own or are dismissed, some of these people will have to be replaced. On the positive side, the company may be growing and markets may be opening to the degree that additional people are needed to get the job done. Even here, an understanding of a company's existing personnel could provide one of the best sources of new talent before going to the time, expense and risks of hiring from the outside. Many of our insurance company clients find their new producers/salespeople from among their secretaries, underwriters or customer service representatives. Likewise, many car dealers we work with are able to find excellent service salespeople among their mechanics. Many production people in printing firms, given the opportunity, prove to be the company's best salespeople. Some of our largest company clients have been able to recruit top salespeople from their accounting departments, engineers and even factory personnel. So, before turning to the outside, a company should take a hard look at its existing people to see if some of their employees who may be performing in non-sales jobs not fully suited to their abilities might not be the best available candidates to fill any new sales job openings. Obviously, the advantage to the company of knowing the individual and his or her work habits, and having the individual know the company is enormous, if that individual has the ability to fill the job. This does not even include the morale factor to be gained by giving people an opportunity to better themselves within the company instead of being fired because of their inability to do a job for which they were never suited and never should have been hired in the first place.

Whether recruiting from within a company or turning to the outside for new salespeople, a thorough knowledge of the existing sales team is critical to the success of the recruiting and selection process. How a prospective sales-person's personality fits into the climate of the existing sales force, as well as the chemistry between the manager and the potential salesperson, are factors that are just as important to effective hiring as matching the personality to the job itself. Only by knowing the manager's dynamics and taking into account all of the team issues discussed in Chapter 13 can the right hiring decision be made.

After companies have done everything in their power to maximise the productivity of their existing sales team and to recruit sales talent from within their own company, there will invariably come a time when external recruitment of sales talent is required. To use the sports analogy one more time, while a football team can improve markedly through good coaching, practice and team spirit, very often one or more additional players either purchased or traded will turn an average team into a champion. The success of the team often depends a great deal on the effectiveness of the manager's choices. Some team managers somehow seem to avoid drafting superstars, while others have the Midas touch, selecting superstars from Fourth Division or non-league teams.

The business of recruiting and selecting for industry is quite similar. Companies who make selections from good sources of talent will build their winning team, while the others will perpetuate their mediocrity. As a start, let us look at the sources of sales talent and then, in later chapters, discuss the process by which recruits can be selected and turned into effective producers.

It is difficult to explain why the abundance of sales potential surrounding every sales executive so often goes undetected, particularly since the sales and marketing profession is in most other ways one of the most creative, inventive and progressive elements in today's business community, and it has the tools and methodologies available to find and cultivate the required people if it would but use them.

Sales managers and personnel directors work very hard to recruit salespeople. But rarely do they consistently find and hire genuinely successful sales personnel. Obvious sources of good people are frequently ignored, while an incredibly large proportion of recruiting energy and money are misguidedly spent elsewhere.

Earlier on, we said that more than half of the people now working in sales jobs should not be so employed. This incredible statistic tells us that the average company wastes well over half of the money it spends on recruiting, selecting and training its sales force. This amounts to millions of pounds annually.

What makes this all the more remarkable is that while companies spend millions in a vain attempt to create salespeople, they ignore an enormous, but essentially untapped, reservoir of genuine sales talent around them.

In evaluating the widest variety of population segments in this country, we have discovered that one out of every four people has more inherent ability to sell than well over one-half of the people currently attempting to earn their living in sales. Statistically, what this means is that if the entire population, regardless of what people are currently doing, was used as an enormous source of sales talent, with proper selection, one out of four of these people would be found to have excellent sales potential.

So much of the failure in recruiting results from companies searching for sales talent in the wrong places. Companies continue to attempt to attract and steal salespeople from their competitors, feeling that the experience factor will place them way ahead of the game. However, when one accepts the statistical fact that 80 per cent of the salespeople attempting to sell today are either in the wrong job or are attempting to sell the wrong product or service, then one quickly realises that this method is doomed to fail. Companies who steal from their competitors are indulging in the recirculation of mediocrity. More often than not, they have attracted someone to their company who was not successful in the company he or she worked for and will not be successful for them. For, after all, why would a successful person with seniority and experience leave their company? All too often, it is just another case of someone who is in the wrong job. Of course, the individual never blames him- or herself for the lack of success; he or she uses all the old familiar excuses for failure — the manager I worked for is not a professional, the company's reward plan is not equitable etc.

This point was brought home to us when a large manufacturing firm retained us to evaluate their 300-plus sales force for four of their divisions. Our finding was that less than 10 per cent of the salespeople we assessed had potential for selling in their current jobs. When we reported our findings to the firm's management, we were surprised that the results shocked us more than they shocked them. They had known for some time that something was radically wrong, but they did not know what it was or how to cure it. They asked us to uncover the reasons for their extremely poor recruiting and selection results.

We found that their problems lay in (1) their recruiting sources, (2) their hiring criteria and (3) their random assignment of people to sell specific products. Since then we have found that their pattern is hardly atypical of many companies.

Salespeople were recruited by this firm primarily from closely related businesses. They had an ongoing aggressive effort to pirate salespeople from competitive firms, often through luring them with escalated salaries. This method provided the company with a continuing flow of 'experienced' salespeople. Rarely, however, did these experienced people prove to be top-level performers. Although it is true that they started off better than novices, and they certainly required less product training, more often than not, they levelled off at a mediocre plateau after a short time and remained there.

In examining this group, it became quite clear that over 80 per cent lacked the critical characteristics to be successful in sales. The results of recruiting 'experienced' salespeople was to build failure into their recruiting process.

A second source of talent from which the company recruited was recent graduates from engineering colleges. Only individuals whose results were in the top quarter of their class were considered.

Upon interviewing the salespeople who were recruited in this manner, we discovered that, in essence, the job had been misrepresented to them. Most of them had never previously considered selling as a career, but were persuaded to come with the company when told that sales was the best stepping-stone to management and that they would not be selling in any real sense, but, rather, providing technical service and consultation to customers. Thus, people who by predisposition and training were set to be engineers were almost deceived into taking sales positions. It was not surprising to find that the majority did not like or want to sell, and that most lacked the raw ability to do so even if they wanted to.

It was readily apparent to us that this recruiting procedure could hardly be expected to produce a dynamic crop of highly motivated and successful salespeople.

In analysing this college recruitment programme, we wondered why only the top quarter of the class was eligible for consideration. No executive could give us a reasoned answer. We asked whether individuals with 2:2 degrees from the same colleges would not have enough engineering knowledge to sell the products, and the answer was that they would.

We then had our next reasons for recruiting failure.

Paradoxically, the individuals they were recruiting from campuses were the least likely to be top salespeople. They were literally tapping the worst possible sources of sales talent. Typically, those who excl in scientific subjects — those with unusually high degrees of technical orientation — are not 'people oriented' (for lack of a better term). This type of graduate is generally more interested in pursuing research and development activities than in dealing with people. Scientists are inclined to regard sales as an activity somewhat beneath their dignity. The engineer or scientist who does slip into sales usually becomes dissatisfied and is an early candidate for resignation or dismissal.

We are certainly not saying that among these top-grade people there are no individuals who have sales ability or who indeed should be selling. Those individuals certainly exist, and we have evaluated and met a number of them. What we are emphasising, however, is the fact that, from a statistical point of view, limiting a company's recruitment to this source of sales talent unnecessarily reduces that source and actually focuses on a source of talent that is likely to produce lower numbers of sales candidates.

A company selling technical products should, by all means, seek technically educated people to represent them. However, logic and experience dictate seeking those performing in the middle of the graduating class. The reason: a person's grades below the first quarter may not reflect less intelligence or understanding of engineering, but, rather, the kind of personality that goes towards making an excellent salesperson. He or she may have lower grades because they diverted their attention from books to a wide range of extracurricular activities, often at the expense of the top scholastic rating they might otherwise have easily earned.

Technical expertise and understanding is highly desirable in certain kinds of selling. However, sales ability is still more important, and this cannot be taught, whereas product knowledge can. A more valid approach in this type of recruiting is not to ask how much the potential salesperson knows, but how much he or she really has to know in order to sell the product.

The third problem this company had in its overall selection/recruiting process proved more difficult to pinpoint. But finally, after considerable digging, we found that the problem was a failure to 'job match'.

In the past, little thought had been given to which individual, once recruited, should be placed in which sales situation. It was usually assumed that a salesperson should start with the smaller products division and work his or her way up to selling for the large contract division. In looking at the salespeople in the two divisions, we found that at least half of each group would be more effective selling in the other. For example, many possessing the strong ego-drive needed for fast, frequent closes were trapped in selling large contract orders to the government, where the most sales they could hope to close would be a few each year. Others possessing the patience to handle and enjoy the long-term sales situation were trying without success to compete in the hard-closing, highly competitive, small products field.

Once we uncovered this problem, we recommended: (1) massive switching of job assignments; and (2) careful matching of people to jobs in the future.

This was our final, major recommendation. Quite naturally, the firm's management required some convincing when we pointed out the three principal error factors we had uncovered, particularly since the first two had always appeared to be real virtues in recruiting and, in addition, were long-standing and well-accepted practices in the field. However, after we had documented our conclusions, the company's recruiting procedures began to change. Gradually, more adjustments were made than just in these three areas, but the changing of thought beginning at that early point made a significant contribution towards the company's ultimate sales force goals. Over the next few years, the firm assembled one of the finest and most effective sales organisations of any its size in the industry.

It should be emphasised that the error factors in recruiting stemming from tapping the wrong source of talent are in no way an isolated phenomenon. Actually, the mistakes the firm had been making were much less obvious than many. In fact, by seeking talent in very limited areas, a great many business executives with hiring responsibilities appear to turn their backs on the very people they are seeking.

Our experience indicates that the universe of potential salespeople is much greater than most managers realise. An excellent source, for example, is individuals who might now be working in administrative jobs, but who may be frustrated in their jobs and would welcome the opportunity of being in sales. Other hidden talent can be found among the misemployed and the under-employed. For example, capable women returning to work after raising families comprise a huge resource that is all too often overlooked due to industrial reluctance to put women into certain selling jobs. However, those industries which have pioneered in utilising female sales talent, such as property and insurance, have experienced enormously successful results.

In short, people with sales potential are there, waiting for an opportunity to be productive. What is needed is for recruiting and personnel managers to relax outworn notions about where to find them, how to identify them and where to mobilise them.

The range of 'knockout' factors—that is, the automatic disqualifiers many managers apply to job applicants — never ceases to amaze us. A recruiting manager who laughs at the absurdities of another's insistence on job experience may automatically eliminate from consideration all men over 50 and not even bother to see anyone who does not fit his or her preconceived notions as to sex, marital status, job stability and education.

What does this cost? It may spell the difference between success and failure. Our experience shows that a man of 50 may have more open-mindedness and youthful vigour than a man half his age; that women have the same ranges of business talent as men; that race has nothing to do with ability to sell; that being divorced or single; experienced or inexperienced; stable or a 'job-hopper' are never by themselves valid reasons for rejecting an applicant.

Printing companies have discovered outstanding printing salespeople among their factory employees. Dozens of estate agents have discovered that file clerks or secretaries in their offices possessed the ability to outsell their salespeople. Machine repairmen have turned out to be top-notch salespeople of the products they repair. Of course, the mere fact that someone repairs a product, or that he or she works in the factory where it is manufactured, does not automatically mean that they can sell that product. But it is logical to look at talent close to home first since (1) almost invariably some of this talent exists there; and (2) when you find it, you have the important advantages of product and company familiarity and the morale boost that accompanies upgrading from within the organisation.

Another source of talent is the tremendous number of underemployed people in business. We had the opportunity to demonstrate this point dramatically in a programme we conducted. We were asked to administer our test battery to a wide range of clerical workers and others in non-sales positions. By typical standards, this should be an unlikely population to produce sales talent. Yet, after testing 450 of these people, we found that 187 had real sales ability. Interestingly, this proportion is higher than is typical for the general population.

Of the 187 with sales ability, 175 entered a four-week sales training programme we conducted, covering eight three-hour sessions and emphasising personal counselling. At the end of the four weeks, we were able to place 152 of the 175 in good sales jobs, and, in following up one year later, we found that the great majority were still on their jobs and performing well.

All of our experience in this area tends to document our contention that recruiting problems diminish or even disappear when recruiters discard false preconceptions about recruiting sources and hiring criteria, substituting instead the only really relevant question: does he or she have the raw ability to sell?

There is one other source, the most overlooked human resource of all, for prospective talent, and that is the underemployed or even the unemployed.

There is a great paradox that is to be found in every local newspaper. While the pages of the business section feature statistics on unemployment, the classified section carries advertisements for thousands of jobs. The first glance may not be as startling because the condition has become so familiar to most of us that we have long ceased to notice it. But the implications deserve our close attention. To consider the problem in human terms, we have only to reflect upon the impact of life for thousands of people without hope, without dignity, without future and without a sense of fulfilment in normal societal terms. From a thoroughly selfish perspective, as a society we pay a large price, both financially and personally, by perpetuating this gruesome situation. We cannot emphasise enough that in all our studies over the last three decades, we have found that there are thousands of unemployed people who possess the personality dynamics necessary for successfully filling many sales jobs. Although in the past there have been scattered programmes designed to bring this unemployed group into industry, unfortunately, most programmes fail to provide an effective mechanism for real and lasting results. Even to this day, many managers negatively label unemployed people as unmotivated, unskilled, irresponsible and lazy. The result is that, while hundreds of thousands of sales jobs go unfilled, seven times that number of people who could fill them are arbitrarily excluded from consideration.

Meanwhile, because business has failed in so many cases to persuade the unemployed that there are job opportunities for them, fear, failure of confidence and lack of external qualifications effectively bar many of these individuals from applying for most of these jobs.

This unfortunate situation is made more painful by the fact that, recognised or not, the same range of abilities exists among the underemployed or unemployed as among any other segment of the population. Among this group one out of every four persons possesses the ability to sell successfully, given the requisite training and product knowledge. However, cultural factors and the communication gap between business and the unemployed keep these potentially successful salespeople out of the sales profession. Most programmes to bridge the gap between those needing jobs filled and those in dire need of jobs have failed, mainly because there was a tendency to place people in jobs without regard to their basic inner motivations. The failure to consider the individual differences in this group stems back to the labelling we discussed earlier and the assumption that this entire group shares an identical personality.

It is small wonder then that the unemployed have been haphazardly placed in programmes with turnover rates in excess of 60 per cent. Another paradox exists, however, when one considers that the turnover rate which has been accepted for decades by the insurance, property and motor industries is just as high. Yet, when the same turnover rate occurs in this group, it is seen as conclusive evidence of the fundamental individuality of the group.

In the late 1960s we undertook two major programmes which provided conclusive evidence that the unemployed and underemployed are an untapped and exceptionally rich source of talent. Suffice it to say here that, in these two programmes, when people's personalities were job matched to a specific job, people succeeded. People were not only highly productive and remained in their jobs, but many were promoted and moved on to managerial positions.

In all, more than 3,000 people were placed with some 70 companies; nearly half of them filled sales positions and the remainder were placed in more than 50 other job categories. And in a follow-up after two years, it was found that less than 3 per cent had been dismissed because of inability to do the job. To re-emphasise the importance of this figure, few, if any, of these individuals had sold before, or had filled jobs similar to the ones in which they were placed.

What they had was the basic ability to do the job in which they were placed and, of course, they were also given the necessary training in technique and product to do the job.

These programmes put our hypothesis 'that sales ability exists across the population regardless of what individuals have or have not done in the past' to the test. These programmes demonstrated that if the broadest possible source of sales talent is tapped, and effective techniques are used, highly productive people can be brought into the sales profession in sufficient numbers to fill most, if not all, of the sales openings.

What, then, are the sources of sales talent to which management can turn in its effort to recruit productive people? First, as we emphasised earlier, perhaps the best source of talent (certainly the easiest) is a company's existing personnel. Companies of any size are most likely to have people doing non-sales jobs; some of them could potentially be highly productive salespeople. Some of these paradoxes may in fact be individuals who are not doing particularly good work in their current position. Their below-par performance may result simply from the fact that they are not currently doing what they are best suited to do; if they were in sales, they could be outstanding. Management should look at home first, before expending the time, money and effort involved in external recruiting.

Another source of talent can involve people working for competitors, but not necessarily in sales roles. Competitors' secretaries, technical people and production people know the industry, and may have sales potential. Thus, while stealing from one's competitor by hiring away salespeople is likely to result in recirculating mediocrity, finding sales potential from another company's mechanics, technicians or secretaries might indeed prove to be an excellent source of sales talent.

Finally, we suggest primarily that the entire population be thought of as a virtually limitless source of productive talent. Rather than arbitrarily establishing knockout procedures or barriers to limit such sources, management should focus on those few qualities that are really and objectively necessary as limiters. If there is a certain level of prior technical knowledge or special education necessary to do a job, then, of course, those factors should be used as initial screeners. In other words, if there is prior knowledge or background necessary that management really cannot provide to an inexperienced applicant, those factors obviously reduce a company's sources of talent, but only those truly objective requirements should be utilised.

In short, management should try to minimise the reasons for screening out people and emphasise the fact that if an individual has the basic ability he or she is worth providing with all of the training necessary to actualise that ability.

CHAPTER 17

RECRUITING PRODUCTIVE TALENT

In Part 3, we described the job matching approach as an effective alternative to the traditional, tried and untrue selection techniques and criteria that have contributed importantly to sales turnover and to the dreadful fact that only 20 per cent of all salespeople are responsible for 80 per cent of what is sold. To facilitate successful hiring decisions, it is essential that each of the three steps of the job matching process be completed in a thorough, comprehensive manner. Failure to appropriately address any one step could have a serious negative impact on the quality of the final hiring decision.

Before management can concern itself with recruitment issues, the job for which candidates are to be recruited must be thoroughly analysed along the lines discussed in Chapter 9.

These essential steps are the base from which the entire selection process is conducted. Its importance cannot be overemphasised. In order to select the candidate with the greatest likelihood of success in a particular position, the hiring manager must be clear about the specific responsibilities that comprise that job. This sounds simple but it is often the biggest stumbling block in the entire hiring process.

JOB DESCRIPTION

A critical part of analysing and understanding the job for which people are being recruited is the development of an objective, detailed job description. The job description should avoid statements that are too general and do not relate specifically to a performance outcome. If, for example, an insurance agency is hiring a salesperson, it would be important to indicate that the acquisition of new business is a critical expectation of the job over and above simply retaining and expanding an existing book of business. In other words, it is not enough to say, 'Sales for a property and health insurance agency'. Rather, the job description should include management's specific expectations. Some element of performance appraisal — how the new employee will be judged — should also be part of the job description. Similarly, staying with the insurance agency for a moment, instead of simply writing, 'Sells personal insurance', the agency manager should indicate specific lines sold by the agency, for example, 'Sells policies in car, home and life insurance'.

If developed correctly, the job description can serve both as a tool allowing management to view applicants more objectively and as an excellent self-screener allowing potential applicants to screen themselves in or out. If applicants do not really want to do what is objectively described in the job description, it is far better that they know this early on rather than go through the long, time-consuming and expensive selection process only to make that discovery in the end, or worse, to make the disovery after they are on the job.

PROFILING REQUIRED SKILLS

Each task in the job description must be considered in terms of qualifications and skills objectively required to do the job. It is here that a profile of the individual to be hired should be developed. As with the definition of the job itself, the profile should be both comprehensive and realistic with regard to a company's specific expectations. While it is likely that few, if any, candidates will match the profile in every way, it will serve as a yardstick by which 'fit' or job match can be measured and evaluated. What management should try to do here is to judge the kind of motivations, skills and personality strengths that are required to do the job as it is understood and described. If, for example, the insurance agency wants an individual who will be producing a good deal of new business, including outside cold-calling, they would certainly want to include ego-drive and ego-strength as part of the required profile. If, on the other hand, the agency emphasised internal retention and expansion of business, they might want to de-emphasise the level of ego-drive, perhaps not emphasise ego-strength at all, but definitely stress service motivation, detail ability and sense of responsibility. What we are suggesting is that management should go as far as it can, given its hopefully good understanding of the functional requirements of the job, to spell out and describe the kind of individual capable of filling that job.

OTHER FACTORS

In addition to profiling the factors objectively required to do the job, other personal factors relating to an individual applicant's suitability to the specific job need to be outlined in order for the most effective job match to occur. A number of these factors can, broadly speaking, be lumped under 'chemistry'. Some of these personal factors unique to a company include: the relationship between the manager's personality and the applicant; the company's culture or environment; and the strengths and weaknesses of the existing sales team and how the applicant fits into that team. Some of these specific factors, such as how the individual's chemistry meshes with the chemistry of the team, can play as important a role in determining success or failure as the basic match of personality attributes to the job.

There is one more personal factor that should be touched on here — an applicant's career aspirations. Candidates who indicate a strong desire to move up in the organisation will not be well-suited for a role from which there is little or no upward mobility. There are many jobs that need to be done with great skill and professionalism, but which simply do not lead to other higher positions. If that is the case, such should be stated to the applicant. A classic example is the situation in which an individual is applying for a sales job, but clearly wants to use sales as a vehicle towards rapid advancement to management. If such rapid advancement is not realistically possible, or if it is determined that the individual should remain in sales due to a lack of management talent, that individual should probably not be hired. At the very least, an objective, frank discussion should be held where the individual is presented with the realities of the situation. Even then, if the individual continues to express an interest in the job, management has to decide whether the individual is just saying this as a short-term expedient or whether he or she has really come to terms with the fact that upward mobility, at least into a management role, is not a short-term reality.

Be realistic about the career opportunities you have to offer. Honesty will help you avoid hiring a frustrated employee who will leave within a year of employment.

RECRUITING VIABLE CANDIDATES

We have spent a great deal of time bemoaning the fact that so many people attempting to earn a living in sales should not be in sales or, at the least, should not be in the specific sales situation in which they find themselves. What we have said repeatedly, and in the recruiting context it is worth repeating yet again, is that less than one in four people who are currently selling are properly placed in their sales role.

This negative fact, however, provides management with an exciting recruiting opportunity if management has the courage to take advantage of that opportunity. What is just as true is that one in four people in the general population, regardless of what they are currently doing, also have good sales ability. Though it may be a radical thing to say, the truth is that there is just as high a proportion of potentially talented salespeople who are not in sales as there is in the sales profession itself.

The implications of this fact are both obvious and exciting. If management is willing to scrap the old criteria — age, sex, experience etc — and is willing to open up its recruiting efforts to the entire population, providing only realistically necessary knockout requirements, the potential resources from which sales talent can be tapped are literally limitless. Thus, the first step in recruiting salespeople should involve putting out the broadest possible net designed not arbitrarily to limit applicants, but to attract as many applicants as possible who might possess the potential to do the job. Of course, the use of such a broad net has to include management's willingness to provide product knowledge and sales training, since many of the applicants willing to enter the company lack these tools, but as we have said, you can teach product and you can teach sales technique but you cannot teach the raw, basic ability — the motivation to sell.

To risk stating the obvious, if there are objective requirements without which an individual cannot be considered, those requirements should certainly be included, but one should always ask, 'Is this really a requirement or, if we find the person with the right ability, can we teach it?'

The key to tapping this broad net is a comprehensive recruiting plan. A multi-faceted approach to attracting applicants is ideal, particularly if there is any urgency, and if numbers of positions are in need of filling.

Newspaper ads are, of course, the first and most obvious means of recruiting candidates, but radio, television, school and college careers offices and employment agencies could all play an important role in an integrated, effective recruitment effort. Whether we are talking about a newspaper or radio ad, a job posted on a school bulletin board or given to an employment agency, it is critical that the ad should sell the company. Include whatever limiting requirements realistically exist. But, if management really wants to tap the available talent pool, it must stress that 'we care far more about what you are than what you might happen to be doing or what you might have done in the past'. This sentiment should only be expressed if it is truly meant, because it will create substantial numbers of applicants. People are afraid to apply for jobs for which, on the surface, they are not qualified, but as we have said repeatedly, these may include some of the very best applicants, and a company's advertising approach must invite these people to step forward and apply. Some of our clients have placed recruitment ads outside of the sales category. They have been concerned that some of those people without sales experience would not look under the sales category for a job. They placed their ads under 'new opportunities' and had very good results. It is not sufficient to use terms like 'equal opportunity employer', or even 'no experience necessary'. If management really wants people with potential but without obvious qualifications to apply, it must ask such people to do so in a very aggressive, direct, unambiguous way.

Referrals

Beyond the broad brush approach to recruiting, which newspapers, radio and even offering jobs to employment agencies and schools involve, there is an additional, and exceptionally effective, approach. Just as job seekers must network to identify leads, hiring managers must communicate their staffing needs and objectives to as broad a range of contacts as possible. Employees, fellow members of the chamber of commerce or professional and trade associations, and even friends, neighbours and members at your golf club all possess the potential to know just that individual who is right for the job. Companies have offered employees bonuses for recommending individuals who are hired, and this is certainly a positive way of involving people on a company's current team in the process of improving that team.

Career night programmes

We have worked with a number of our client companies in helping them to develop what we have termed a career night programme. This approach works with a company seeking to fill multiple openings for a specific job, and can also work where a group of companies can get together in a joint hiring effort. For example, city car dealer groups, insurance agencies in a particular area, or a group of estate agencies can pool their efforts to put together a career night programme that might not be appropriate for any of them but, when combined, might work extremely well.

Whether a career night is sponsored by one company or by a group, the aim is to get a maximum number of candidates into a room at the same time. A representative of the company or the group can tell the company or the industry story and describe the job, including details about requirements, performance expectations, difficulties and opportunities. If numbers permit, they could even start the screening-in process by having each individual speak for 30 to 60 seconds, during which time some judgements could be made about their ability to articulate, their appearance and the like. During the same evening, people could be asked to fill out application forms if they still want to be considered after the job has been described, to hand in a cv and to complete psychological tests if these are involved in the screening process. What the career night can achieve, simply, is to do with several dozen people at the same time what management might otherwise have to do with one applicant at a time — describe the job, answer questions, hand out application forms, administer tests etc. There are obviously many variations on the career night theme. But the concept of this kind of group screening has worked well for many of our clients and, where applicable, can be an efficient and rapid means of filling multiple positions.

Banking of applicants

A major source of talent from which to recruit can be found among individuals who have at one time or another applied for a position with a company. Each company should establish its own 'applicant bank' in which are filed cvs, background letters and/or application forms filled out by applicants who were not chosen for past job openings but who might be suited to future openings. This applicant bank should also include unsolicited cvs and any applications that companies invariably receive through the year. To make this applicant bank most effective, each applicant should receive a letter indicating that the company has sufficient interest in them to bank them for future consideration. This contact can make the applicant's response to a future offer of an interview a far more positive one.

When developing an applicant bank, one should remember the one or two excellent candidates for a past opening who were beaten to the job by somebody just a bit better. Also, there may be many applicants for non-sales positions who might be suited to a company's next sales opening. Thus, their applications should be immediately available for review at the start of the recruiting process.

In conclusion, effective recruitment should begin by tapping into the enormous pool of talent that exists across the population. Knockout requirements should be kept to an objective, realistic minimum, and recruitment should be aimed at finding individuals with the raw ability to do the job, regardless of what they may or may not have done in the past. Such a broad-brush approach, using all of the techniques we discussed, will produce large numbers of applicants, many of whom obviously will not be suited to the job, but there will also be many who are well suited, many of whom would be screened out if you were using the old approaches. If proper screening is conducted and proper selection techniques employed, substantial progress will be made in finding and hiring salespeople who will be productive, and who will remain with the company because they are simply too successful not to do so.

CHAPTER 18

SCREENING OUT THE INAPPROPRIATE

If the recruiting process discussed in the last chapter is as successful as it should be, there will be large numbers of applicants expressing interest in your vacant position, about 25 per cent of whom are likely to have good sales ability. If the recruiting approach was appropriate, some of these will be well-suited to the specific sales position for which the recruiting programme was undertaken. Yet, though every recruiting programme aims to recruit large numbers of applicants from which to choose, the existence of those large numbers creates certain problems. Thus, what we are suggesting is a pyramid approach to the selection process, starting with the broadest base of applicants that can be created by good recruiting, and then narrowing, step by step, to the peak of the pyramid from which the finalists are studied, and the individual or individuals selected to fill the position.

Broadly speaking, this pyramid process is divided into a screening-out segment narrowing the base to manageable numbers, and then a final screening-in process designed to make the best possible selection from among those still under consideration. In this chapter, we will look at the process by which inappropriate people are screened out, while the next chapters will deal in depth with each component by which the screening in takes place, and the final hiring decision is made.

REVIEW OF CV

The first step in screening out the obviously inappropriate is the CV review. This typically can be done quickly and yet can accomplish a great deal towards reducing the sheer numbers of applicants with whom time must be taken. We should insert a word of warning here which applies to any step in the screening-out process. In order to deal with the practical necessity of screening out large numbers of people, a few diamonds in the rough could be screened out with the group. This should be kept in mind as the cvs are reviewed so that where there is some doubt, if numbers permit, the benefit of that doubt should go to the applicant, at least carrying him or her on to the next step. Obviously, numbers dictate how much that benefit of doubt can be given to how many people, and there is some risk of a diamond in the rough being washed out.

Cvs should be reviewed in order to ascertain the degree to which applicants possess the essential job requirements. To this end, applicants who have submitted cvs can be separated into three distinct groups: those having most of the requirements; those possessing some of the important requirements; and those clearly not qualified to assume the job responsibilities.

The third group will obviously be screened out immediately, but in doing this management should be certain that it is not screening out on the basis of invalid criteria, but that it really is screening out on the basis of clear, objective facts which would preclude the individual from being effective on the job. In this connection, judgement should not be swayed by the writing style or appearance of the cv. Content should be the main concern. Professional cv writers can enhance the appearance and style of a cv, but, if that cv is properly examined, it is far more difficult for them to 'doctor' its contents. This being said, we have nevertheless seen situations in which professional cv preparers can even, without specifically lying, write a cv in such a way that it comes across as better than it really is after analysis. On the other side of the coin, individuals who do not have the money or the sophistication to use the professionals may not sell themselves nearly as well in the cv but, of course, may still possess excellent potential to do the job. So, while it is absolutely necessary as a practical matter to screen out people on the basis of their cvs, some care should be taken to avoid being trapped in superficials. In reviewing the cv, it is important to get an overview to ascertain an applicant's complete job history. Then read between the lines to assess not only what is stated on the cv, but the story behind job changes, periods of unemployment, seeming inconsistencies in dates or other information etc.

On the positive side, above and beyond sales experience, which, as we have repeatedly emphasised, may be totally irrelevant except in certain, very specific situations, management should look for job experience that indicates specific accomplishments and the overcoming of obstacles. Ideally, these accomplishments should be measurable, and should involve clear, hands-on experience. In other words, since sales is so much an individual activity, some evidence that the applicant has accomplished something individually, whether in sales or not, is certainly a positive.

Another obvious positive is a pattern of job changes, all of which move in the direction of enhancing the individual's career. On the negative side of that coin is the job hopper who explains each change by indicating poor environment, little opportunity etc. Also, the job hopper who appears to be at most running parallel or, at worst, cycling down from job to job could present an important red flag. Job hopping, *per se*, should not be a knockout, as it all too often is, but the reasons for those changes and the kind of changes might be. What should always be borne in mind is the enormous number of people in the wrong jobs. Individuals with the kind of strong personality a company might wish to hire might be just the people who will not tolerate boredom or a job that obviously does not meet their needs. So, in some instances, and we have seen many examples of this, the very people who are penalised by the automatic knockout as job hoppers, can be the very people that the company might really want. Again, knock people out if the job hopping is evaluated as obviously negative, but do not let job hopping itself be the knockout factor.

Another positive element relates to an individual's community involvement — memberships in community organisations, volunteer work etc. This may be particularly pertinent where experience is lacking. Many women, for example, who have been out of the workforce for 10 or 15 years raising a family may not bring pertinent experience to their applications, but may make up for this by presenting evidence of their effective work in the community. Successful volunteer work for the NSPCC may be as indicative of sales potential as many paid positions, and perhaps more indicative than most.

Additional red flags might include unexplained gaps in the chronology of the cv; focusing on myriad trivial details, which often can be a means of taking up space to cover up the lack of real substance in the cv; and the overuse of phrases such as 'familiarity with', 'knowledge of' or 'participated in the development of'. If people have strong knowledge of a product or service, or have really developed a programme or product, they will say so and in fact emphasise it in their cv. Equivocal words such as these are often set up to suggest the applicant is qualified for a particular position. Use of these words is certainly not a knockout but should be viewed with at least some suspicion.

The review of the cv, then, permits management to eliminate obviously inappropriate people from further consideration, but in no sense allows management to make a positive hiring decision. All that a review of a cv can be expected to do is to narrow the pyramid, and to point to those individuals who are worth further exploration in the next step.

THE TELEPHONE SCREEN

While there can be no doubt that an in-person interview will yield more data than a telephone conversation, again, as a practical matter, if the number of applicants demands it, the telephone screen becomes a valuable tool as a less time-consuming next step in the screening-out process. What we are suggesting is that those individuals grouped in the first category of cv review — those having most of the requirements — should be telephoned. Most often, this telephone call can be limited to between five and ten minutes, because its purpose is not to make a positive hiring decision, but simply to screen out clearly inappropriate people. If, for example, someone's voice is absolutely atrocious, and the manager who telephones knows perfectly well that this person could not be exposed to customers, that knowledge becomes available after only a few seconds; a polite two or three minute conversation can serve to screen out that applicant.

What the telephone interview is designed to do is simply to determine whether or not the applicant is worth pursuing further. To accomplish this, the interview should serve to straighten out any discrepancies in the cv, briefly explain the job, including its negatives, answer the applicant's questions and permit the applicant to sell him- or herself as a viable candidate. Though appearance and other important factors cannot be evaluated over the telephone, it is amazing how much good judgement can be made from this brief five or ten-minute telephone interview. This is even more true depending on how much telephone work the person will be doing for a firm; telephone sales are accelerating rapidly and will continue to do so. So, while this method is not foolproof, if an individual fails to sell the hiring manager on the telephone, this could be a good indication that the screening process for that individual should stop right there.

If the decision is made that an applicant should be brought to the next step, a *brief* initial interview should be scheduled. If the manager is not certain (perhaps he or she wants to screen other applicants before deciding who to bring in) or has definitely decided not to pursue the particular applicant, the statement can simply be made that they will be contacted shortly as to the next step. We do suggest that, in situations where there is not a next step, a polite letter be sent indicating that there are simply too many highly qualified applicants at this time, but that their cv will be kept on file should future opportunities occur. This is simply good personnel policy and good public relations for the company.

THE BRIEF INITIAL INTERVIEW

This initial in-person interview should, again, be brief, hopefully no more than 10 to 15 minutes. It is most important that the brevity of the interview is spelled out on the telephone when that interview is being scheduled. Management does not want an applicant to feel that he or she is being pushed out in too short a time, particularly if it wants to continue looking at that applicant for possible hire. Even where the initial interview serves to screen out the applicant, good personnel policy still demands courtesy and so defining the brevity of the interview in advance is essential.

Just as with the telephone interview, the in-person interview is not designed to produce a positive hiring decision. In our view, management simply does not have enough information, nor can it, at this stage to make a good judgement. What happens all too often is that the initial interview becomes the hiring interview, and the only way it can be this is if management uses the superficials — experience, appearance, markets, age etc — as the criteria for hiring or not hiring the applicant. If the real job match decision is to be made, data which can only be gathered in the screening-in process will be needed. What this brief interview is designed to do, then, is simply to examine additional factors in a little more depth to permit screening out still more people. Just as the atrocious voice might allow screening out on the telephone, grossly inappropriate appearance might permit the same decision in the interview. The interview should also be used to review the application form, which the applicant should have been asked to fill out before the interview, and to review the cv together with the applicant to clarify definitions, resolve discrepancies, explain gaps etc and allow the applicant a brief opportunity to sell him- or herself to the manager. As we will discuss in more depth in a later chapter, the interview is severely limited as a means of gaining objective information, but much of what the interview can provide to management can be obtained in those first 10 or 15 minutes as readily as in a prolonged, one-hour 'dance'. A screen-out can be as simple as 'I do not like this person' or 'I do not feel comfortable with this person' or 'I do not think I would enjoy working with this person'. Here, as in any other screening-out process, a manager might not enjoy working with an individual who has great potential to do the job, so someone valuable might be lost. However, since the manager is the fixture, that risk must sometimes be taken because if the manager does not want to work with the person, that individual's objective potential might not be realised.

So, like the initial review of cvs and the telephone screen, the initial interview should serve to screen out still more individuals who, in the manager's judgement, are not likely to be appropriate for the position. These individuals who are screened out should simply be told that they will be contacted and, of course, they should receive the same letter explaining that there were simply too many better-qualified applicants for the position. On the other hand, those individuals management wishes to pursue further should be asked to provide a minimum of two business references before they leave the interview. If these are readily offered, a number of managers have used the technique of asking for two more to try to get references that might not be ideal in the mind of the applicant. Also, while the individual is there, it might be wise to schedule him or her for psychological testing even, if convenient, immediately following the interview. We will discuss the role of psychological testing later, but suffice it to say here that if an individual takes the test the same day and is then screened out in the next step (the reference check), that test need not be evaluated and so will not cost the company any money or any time.

REFERENCE CHECKS

Though many managers downplay the value of reference checking for many good reasons, this step should nevertheless be taken as the final part of the screening-out process. Though there are some obvious weaknesses, and though the feedback received from the reference checks has to be viewed with some cynicism, if done correctly, reference checking can provide enough value to be well worth the effort.

While we strongly suggest that reference checks be done, it is still important to review their weaknesses, in order to suggest how these weaknesses can be overcome and how the most possible value can be derived from the exercise.

First, the applicant is certainly going to provide references with which he or she is totally comfortable. No one will knowingly give a potential employer names of people who will say negative things about them. That is why it is important, as we suggested above, to ask for two references beyond the initial two so that, hopefully, the applicant can be pushed into providing names with which they are at least one degree less happy. The second problem relates to a pervasive guilt that exists among managers who have fired people. If the references are from a company from which the applicant was fired, that manager is very likely to give the most glowing references possible as a means of alleviating his or her own guilt. A manager recently told us, 'Yes, I gave that idiot a terrific reference, but I sure did not want his starving family on my conscience.' Though managers will only rarely express such thoughts that directly, the sentiment exists. Therefore, references must be viewed with some suspicion.

Thirdly, without knowing precisely what the applicant did in his or her previous job, it could be very difficult to get the reference, even if they want to be forthcoming, to relate the applicant's performance to the hiring company's position.

After all of this, why bother with the process at all? How can any value be derived from a process so replete with problems? The answer is that, if done correctly, as we said earlier, some value and perhaps some important value, can still be derived from reference checking; it could help eliminate some people and move others into the final screening-in process with more confidence.

The first important thing to do is to have the hiring manager make the reference calls him- or herself. We emphasise here 'make the call'. When silly form letters are sent to referees we can guarantee that they will receive silly form letters in reply, stating the dates of employment, but providing nothing in terms of valuable information. Letters may be acceptable for employment verification, but they certainly are not acceptable as a valid means of checking references.

When the hiring manager makes the call, it is important to tune in carefully to the tone of the person called as well as the content of what is said. If the hiring manager uses his or her empathy, pauses, inflections and things that are not said can often provide more valuable information than the glib words that might be expected. If a company cares about who is hired, the responsible manager should make the call and should use all his or her listening skills in doing so.

In this connection, who is accepted as a referee and who is telephoned is also important. A former supervisor is obviously ideal, and former peers or even subordinates could be acceptable. In any event, wherever possible the referees should be related to a job or jobs that the applicant has done, and again where possible, these jobs should be as close to the prospective job as possible. This does not necessarily mean that the former job had to be one in sales, but if there is a reference where the individual worked in a community relations, in advertising, in public relations or even in providing a key service, these would obviously be better references and more related to the job for which the applicant is being considered than, say a foreman on a construction site. Yet, that foreman, if he or she supervised the applicant for a period of time and knows something of his or her work habits and attitudes, could be a much better reference than someone who says, 'Yes, so and so sold me my house, and she was very good.'

There may be times when business referees are not available. We are thinking particularly of the women who is returning to the workforce after a period of years, or the college student seeking his or her first job or an individual who has been ill for a long period of time. Judgement calls have to be made here, and referees providing as much information as possible might have to be accepted, even though they are not specifically job related.

The key to the actual discussion with the referee is to find ways to give that referee 'permission' to say negative things. Ways must be found to alleviate the fear of litigation and to allow the referee to indicate negatives without feeling that they are hurting the applicant. One of the first things that can be done is to preface your questions with a compliment or to reflect something complimentary said by the referee. For example, 'I found Joe to be extremely personable, but have you ever noticed that he is somewhat impatient?' or, 'It is great that he is such a terrific closer, but are there any areas in his sales approach with which he might need close supervision or some additional training?' or, 'From our interviews, and from other references, we certainly agree with you about his presentation skills, but this job involves a minimum of four solid hours on the phone every day. If he is uncomfortable with that he will fail in a week. How do you feel he will react to that, and what do you think we can do to help him?'

A summary kind of probing question could be something like this, 'I am really pleased to hear all of these things, and frankly I am not surprised because she comes across as a very impressive person. Now that I have told you something about the job, can you suggest ways that we can help her? Do you think she needs any kind of training, supervision or whatever? What I am asking is, how can we help her achieve her top potential?'

What you are doing here in asking for these suggestions is allowing the former manager at least to touch on some possible weaknesses that the referee would never state as such if asked directly, 'What are her weaknesses?' We might add, incidentally, that at the very end of an interview, it might not be a bad idea to ask just that. 'That is great; now can you tell me what her weaknesses are, so that we can do our best to help her work through them?' This is not likely to get you as far as the more indirect kinds of questions, but at the very end of the interview, there is little to lose and perhaps some information to be gained.

The reference check should also, of course, include a review of the job functions performed by the applicant. Before even discussing the strengths and weaknesses of the applicant, it is important to know exactly what he or she did on the job. The more the manager knows about the job function, and whether or not the job title was similar to the one for which the applicant is being considered, the more the manager can make a judgement as to the relationship between satisfactory or unsatisfactory function on the prior job and functional expectations of the new one. In this area, the hiring manager is likely to get some fairly objective information because the former employer can describe the job and the requirements for doing the job well, without getting into the individual's performance on that job. What is interesting here is that often in talking about the referee's company, and the job which the applicant held, subtle information can emerge relating very specifically to the applicant. Here again, careful listening is important but what is said or not said in describing the job can reflect, one way or the other, on the applicant; this can be furthered by a subtle, probing question where appropriate.

With all its weaknesses, careful, well-executed reference checks can provide enough information to help screen out additional people, which is important because it is in the screening-in process that a company must properly invest time, money and effort. Thus, the more inappropriate people that can be screened out, the more effective will be the screening-in process, and so the more effective can be the final hiring decision. What is being sought in the reference checks is just a few additional facts, some confirmations of cv and interview data, and some overall feel, subjective though it may be, as to whether the candidate continues to be a valid applicant.

At the end of the reference check, management will have screened out, in all probability, a substantial majority of the broad base of applicants that their recruiting process had brought in. True, as we have said before, a few potentially good people might be screened out, but as a practical matter, this narrowing pyramid process has to take place if management is not to spend literally all of its time screening-in applicants. Although this is not a perfect process, hopefully, at least in the vast majority of cases, inappropriate people have been eliminated and now those who have a legitimate chance to be selected remain. They will be put through what we call the screening-in process, leading to the final hiring decision.

The next three chapters will deal with that screening-in process, leading, hopefully, to the hiring of the successful, productive, professional salesperson.

CHAPTER 19

PSYCHOLOGICAL TESTING: THE PROVIDER OF OBJECTIVE INSIGHTS

In the last chapter, we dealt with means by which individuals can be screened out. We stressed, and this is worth repeating, that neither the cv review, the telephone interview, the short, initial in-person interview nor the reference checks can or should serve to make a positive hiring decision. Each of these steps is designed to trigger red flags that allow management to narrow the applicant pool to a manageable degree. In other words, by the time we have reached the screening-in-process, we should be dealing with candidates who are worthy of in-depth consideration, and hopefully so few of them as to make that in-depth evaluation both possible and economically feasible.

The reason that a positive hiring decision cannot be made on the basis of the earlier steps is simple. All of these steps involve subjective, not objective, feedback. The cv, as we discussed, may be professionally prepared and may or may not reflect what the applicant has done, and rarely, even at best, will it involve an objective presentation of how well the applicant performed in the past. The telephone interview can at most provide management with a subjective impression, which may be good enough to screen out people but is certainly not sufficient to make the enormous commitment involved in offering someone a job. Similarly, the in-person interview can create impressions which, if sufficiently negative, could knock out someone, but still does not provide objective input into the dynamics of the individual. And, finally, reference checking has so many built-in flaws, and even when properly conducted is still so subjective, that only negative factors might be usable, but certainly all the praise in the world could not, or at least should not, convince management to make a job offer. After all of these subjective knockouts have reduced the applicant pyramid to a manageable size, what is needed is objective information about the individual obtained through use of a valid psychological test and the confirmatory input of an in-depth interview.

The need for this objective input has, in a large sense, been recognised by the industry at least since the end of the Second World War. By the late 1950s, when our work really began, tests, structured interview guides and demographic scales had proliferated. As we mentioned earlier, this proliferation actually began our involvement in the business of testing and evaluating personnel, since we were asked to review many of these then-available assessment instruments to help a company decide the most effective way to reduce its sales turnover. Even back in the 1950s, companies would state emphatically how capable they were of hiring 'eyeball to eyeball' while groping for some objectivity to help them make a more balanced, sound and hopefully correct hiring decision. In their attempt to reach for this objectivity, they would set up arbitrary cut-off scores on invalid tests, use tests developed for one purpose for a totally unrelated purpose and, in short, flounder through the jungle of available instruments and procedures, often making matters worse instead of infusing the objectivity they sought into their hiring.

While we emphatically state that the use of *valid* psychological testing is critical to effective hiring, we should begin our discussion of testing by examining why, despite millions of pounds, and more than four decades of work involving thousands of PhDs, so many of the tests offered are totally invalid, inappropriate and ineffective as an aid to management in making objective hiring decisions. It was our in-depth four-year study of why so many tests misfired which led us to the development of our own testing instruments.

WHY TESTS MISFIRE

There are an unlucky seven basic reasons that most tests fail to produce the accurate results which industry seeks.

1.   Tests have been looking for interest, not ability

The concept that a person's interest can be equated with their ability is an important cause of test failure. Tests have been developed by asking questions of successful applicants, with the assumption that if an applicant expresses the same kind of interest pattern as a successful performer, he or she too would be a successful performer.

This assumption is wrong on its face. Psychologically, interest does not equal aptitude, and this is quite simple to illustrate. Someone may have exactly the same interests as Steve Cram, Linford Christie and John Regis, but may be entirely lacking in their athletic skills. By the same token, an individual might have the same interest pattern as a successful salesperson or manager, but have little talent for selling or managing. Even if he or she wanted to sell or manage, it does not mean that they could.

2.   Tests have been eminently 'fakeable'

Anyone applying for a job will attempt to give the answers he or she thinks the potential employer wants to hear. The intelligent applicant knows enough to say that he or she would 'rather be a manager of people than a librarian', 'rather be with people than at home reading a book', 'rather lead a group discussion than be a forest ranger', or that he or she 'prefers talking at a public meeting to listening to good music'.

Much has been written on how to beat aptitude tests, but, even without such help, a person of average intelligence can soon see what is being sought and then give the tester what the tester wants. Thus, the tests may only succeed in screening out the notably unintelligent or the notably naïve. The perceptive interviewer, however, is likely to notice blatant stupidity more quickly than tests do, and the individual who may be too naïve to fabricate answers could conceivably be the applicant with the best real potential.

3.   Tests have favoured group conformity, not individual creativity

Recent critics of psychological testing decry testers who seek conformist and standardised approaches for judging salespeople, managers and other applicants. This criticism is all too valid. The creative thinker, the impulsive free spirit, the original, imaginative, hard-driving individual is often screened out by tests which demand rigid adherence to convention — an adherence, in fact, that borders on passive acceptance of authority and a fear of anything that might upset the bureaucratic apple cart. Paradoxically, while this fearful, cautious authoritarian conformist might make a good civil servant, a reasonably effective controller or a rule-book executive, he or she would never be a successful salesperson, a dynamic sales manager or an assertive administrator.

Many of these tests not only fail to select good salespeople or managers, but possibly screen out the really top producers because of their creativity, impulsiveness or originality — characteristics which most tests downgrade as evidence of strangeness, weakness or even instability.

4.   Tests have tried to isolate fractional traits rather than reveal the whole dynamics of the person

Most personality and aptitude tests, in their construction and approach, see personality as a series or bundle of piecemeal traits. Thus, someone might be high in sociability, while being low in self-sufficiency and dominance. Someone else might be high in personal relations, but low in co-operativeness. Somehow, the whole got lost. The dynamic interaction that is personality, as viewed by most modern-day psychologists, is buried in a series of fractionalised, separable traits.

It is said that the salesperson, like the boy scout, should be very sociable, dominant, friendly, responsible, honest and loyal. The totality—the dynamics within the person that will permit him or her to sell successfully—is lost sight of. Clearly, someone might be sociable, responsible and so on, but still be a poor salesperson or manager.

5. Tests have depended heavily on past experience as a prime qualification

We have emphasised that four out of five people currently earning their living in sales should not be or, at least, certainly should not be in their specific sales job. We also mentioned that it is these inappropriately placed salespeople who constitute the 80 per cent who sell only 20 per cent of what is sold. Given this fact, any test that favours persons already holding sales jobs can only serve to perpetuate inappropriate typecasting.

Some sales aptitude tests use vocabulary and/or the understanding of sales or management situations to measure an applicant's potential sales or management ability. These techniques seek to ascertain experience rather than real ability. Anyone who has ever sold or who has been exposed to selling, even academically, may do well in most tests, whether or not he or she has any inherent sales ability. Terms such as 'close', 'cold canvass' and 'prospecting' will be familiar. The testee will be able to rattle off appropriate responses, even if his or her dynamics guarantees him or her far better prospects as an engineer or manager than as a salesperson. On the other hand, the inexperienced, but potentially strong, salesperson is not likely to know these terms. If judged by experience-oriented techniques, his or her appraisal will be unfavourable. By the same token, an individual who has served as a manager for a number of years would be extremely familiar with such terms as 'line versus staff', 'management by objectives' and 'strategic planning' and, as a result, would have an unfair advantage over an inexperienced person applying for a managerial position.

6. Many tests are used for purposes for which they were not originally designed

A very well-known test that dates back to the late 1930s in its original form was designed to study the psychotic behaviour of inmates at mental hospitals. The test was developed using the inmates of hospitals as the study group and people visiting them as the control group against which the study group could be compared, item by item. This test, like a number of others in this category, has value in clinical use, but goes completely astray when it is inappropriately used for personnel evaluation and selection. The reason is simple; it goes back to the fakeability issue, but more importantly to the motivation to fake.

We like to cite the example of an individual applying for a large life insurance policy. Can one imagine the applicant, while being examined by the life insurance company's doctor, pointing to a place on her chest and saying, 'Doctor, can you tell me if this lump might be a problem?' Or, can one imagine a 50-year old man saying to the insurance doctor, 'I have these sticky pains in my chest. Do you think they are a problem?' Obviously, the applicant will not do anything of the sort, but, rather, will hope that the insurance doctor discovers nothing, and clears him or her for the policy. Perhaps the very next day those individuals might go to their own doctor; at that time they certainly will point out the lump or talk about the chest pain. The difference here is exactly what the difference is when a test designed for purely clinical purposes is used for a sales or management selection. When someone is in psychological pain or looking for vocational guidance, they will answer a test truthfully or reveal themselves as fully as they can within their own personal limitations in an interview, in order to get the help they seek. On the other hand, when that individual is applying for a job, looking for a promotion or in any way taking a test for their company, they are going to cover up their weaknesses and work to sell their strengths just as surely as the two-packets-a-day smoker will present him- or herself to the life insurance company as a non-smoker, or the woman with the lump or the man with the pain will reveal nothing of the sort to the company's doctor. Thus, a test may be perfectly useful when a fundamental assumption can be made that people will, at least as far as they can, attempt to tell the truth, and yet be totally invalid as an instrument designed really to uncover an individual's sales potential. Yet, since many of these tests have famous names and have been around for a long time, and were studied by psychologists in school, they are often used as part of a company's selection procedures with the negative results that we have discussed throughout this book.

7. Many tests produce general results without relating to the specific job match

Some tests may, with some validity, describe the personality of an individual. These are among the relatively few that have avoided all of the pitfalls we have just discussed. Yet, even some of these fail to provide management with the in-depth information it needs to make the hiring decision. The key to this problem is the job match. Even if a test accurately describes the level of assertiveness, dominance, or sociability possessed by an individual, the question still remains as to how those levels relate to the specific requirements of the job in question. It is certainly easy to say that the management wants the most assertive person possible, or the most social, but, as we have seen, there definitely can be too much of a quality — even ego-drive — for a specific job, and balances of many qualities are required for other jobs. These tests, which are often spat out by computers, with the results presented in a neat graph, fail in any sense to relate their results to the functional requirements of the specific company's job. It is really left to the manager to decide if the particular applicant is assertive enough, energetic enough or driven enough, to do the job and, although this data can be useful, it often falls short in providing the precise information the manager really needs to make the best hiring decision.

If tests in this category are indeed accurate in their description of an individual's traits, this provides an important plus in that it offers management input that it can get in no other way. However, the potential misuse, misunderstanding and failure to job match that data can lead to incorrect and costly hiring decisions.

Over the years, companies have used tests which were invalid for one or more of the reasons we discussed and have often been badly burned by such tests. When we speak to potential clients, we experience the most difficulty with those who have attempted to use psychological testing because, while they recognise the need for such testing, they have found the results to be less than satisfactory. Our sales job, then, is not only to persuade them as to the importance of psychological testing, but also to persuade them that there are indeed tests, including our own testing instrument, that avoid the seven pitfalls and can really provide the accurate information they need.

Despite all of the failures of psychological testing, it is clear that valid, job-related psychological testing must be a critical part of any effective hiring programme. What is clearly needed is an objective method of penetrating the superficials and the façade presented in the cv, in the interview and even through the references. Given today's technology, the best means of doing this is through a valid, in-depth psychological test.

Such a test, if constructed to avoid the seven pitfalls, can penetrate the façade that individuals work hard to build. Such a valid test can assess the basic strengths, weaknesses and motivations of an individual, even if that individual worked very hard to use the test as another way of constructing the façade. An effective test literally uses the means by which an individual fakes as a means of understanding who that individual really is. An effective test, in the hands of business-oriented individuals capable of proper evaluation, can help management directly determine not only the strengths, weaknesses and motivations of an individual on staff, or an applicant, but also can relate that data to the specific functional requirements of the job; they can use the test to help determine whether or not there is a job match. The test can help them determine whether the central qualities and motivations of the individual match the functional requirements of the job, while also helping to determine whether the individual has a fatal flaw that might preclude him or her from doing the job, even with their strengths.

But how can management select a valid test? Literally thousands of tests are on the market, ranging from score-it-yourself versions costing a few pounds to batteries of tests in assessment centres costing thousands of pounds. As we have said, a vast majority of these tests, regardless of price, are not job-related, valid predictors of success. Thus, as important as the use of a psychological test is to the selection process, it is even more important for management to be certain that the test is valid and effectively assesses the particular qualities needed to succeed on the job.

With thousands of tests available, many looking quite similar, how can a test be selected that is legal and will help predict whether an applicant can really do a specific job? Without extensive research into each test, it is extremely difficult to make this choice. Yet, this choice is of critical importance.

Making the right hiring decision is too vital not to use the best input available. That input definitely includes the data that can be provided by a valid psychological test. Using the wrong test, however, can be costly.

First, there can be serious legal implications if a test is discriminatory and not provably predictive. This also means that the test must be provably predictive for the job for which the test is used.

In other words, if a test is used to select a salesperson, that test should predict sales success with good statistical accuracy.

Using the wrong test could be even more costly if it is inaccurate. It could influence management to hire the wrong person and perhaps prevent the hiring of potentially productive people. The cost of such a mistake is enormous.

Therefore, in order to reduce the problem of test selection to a manageable level, we have developed a series of questions that management should ask about any test before deciding to use it. If the answer provided by the test publisher to any of these questions is no or is noncommital, that test should not be used under any circumstances.

1. Is the test specifically job related? Does it measure qualities required for your particular job?
2. Does the publisher of the test provide published proof that the test does not discriminate against individuals by sex, age, race, colour, religion or national origin?

3. Does the publisher provide published proof that the test has a high level of predictive validity across the industry and specifically in a situation at least closely related to the position for which the test is being given? Is there proof that people actually do perform as the test predicts they will?
4. Is the database from which the test is developed, and on which the test's reliability and validity is measured, large enough and compiled over enough years to provide dependable evidence of its reliability and validity? In other words, has the test publisher tested enough people and followed actual performance over enough years to prove that the test works?
5. Does the publisher provide you with a list of customers you can contact who have used the test long enough to judge the results?
6. Are the test results related specifically to a company, or are they generalised results? The key here is whether the test is evaluated against a company's particular requirements, ie job description.
7. Are results of the test provided promptly so that management will not lose good applicants as a result of waiting?
8. Does the company provide a trained test evaluator who is a specialist in your field? Will the evaluator discuss the test results with you and provide assistance in relating those results to other steps of the assessment process?
9. Will the testing company provide ongoing help if problems or questions arise relating to poor initial performance, slumps, future promotions, training and management issues?
10. Are the qualities measured by the test those that are essential to performance in the job for which the test is to be used? If, for example, the test does not measure ego-drive (persuasive motivation) it probably would not be appropriate for use in sales selection. It is important that the test clearly measures exactly those qualities that management wants to assess in its developmental, promotion or hiring decisions.

There are other admonitions relating to the use of even the best psychological tests. The test should be simple enough to administer in a company's office. As a practical matter, except in the selection of the highest level executive, it is not effective to have potential candidates travel great distances to a testing office or to have test administrators travel the country to visit the company.

Under no circumstances should an individual be allowed to take a test at home. Even the best test will be distorted and become invalid if the responses are a group product or the product of someone other than the individual who is supposed to be taking the test. If there is lying, or faking, to be done, it had better be the lies or fakes of the person being evaluated. We remember a graphic case that makes this point rather dramatically. A couple of years ago we evaluated an applicant for a good client. We spoke rhapsodically about the virtues of the individual being evaluated, including making such statements as, 'This is one of the most assertive, driven and yet empathic people we have ever had the pleasure of looking at, and we certainly feel that he can make a real contribution to your sales force.' Everyone has had the experience of having said something and knowing, with deadly certainty, that they have somehow made a colossal blunder. The silence on the other end of the phone after our comment conveyed precisely that message. When the client was able to speak, he said that we had described an individual who was exactly the opposite of his employee. He added, with great intensity, that if the employee had ego-drive, he, our client, was an astronaut on the way to Mars.

Though we readily admit that no method, including our own testing, is 100 per cent accurate, rarely do we make a mistake as colossal as this one. Thus, purely out of self-defence, we probed the situation and found out that indeed our applicant had taken the test home. It took only a bit more exploration, and our client's questioning of his employee, to discover that his wife, who was also well known to our client, had actually 'helped' her husband. She, of course, as we are certain the reader now realises, was the assertive, driven, empathic individual we described, and so we were able to maintain our relationship with a very good client.

Naturally, most situations are not quite this dramatic, but the danger of invalidating even the best test by having someone take it home and allow one or more persons to contribute to it is a serious one, and should be avoided whenever humanly possible.

WHAT CAN A VALID TEST DO?

A valid psychological test that uncovers an individual's basic occupational motivations can go a long way towards reducing costly mistakes. It is capable of accurately assessing dozens of attributes and integrating those attributes to describe a human being's strengths, weaknesses and key motivations. It should also be capable of integrating these qualities with the job requirements to make the job match.

A valid test should be able to penetrate an individual's façade and provide management with objective insights into his or her basic personality and motivations. By way of example, our psychological test can provide answers to such questions as the following.

- Does the individual have persuasive motivation?
- Can he or she listen effectively?

- Can he or she take rejection?
- Does the individual have service motivation?
- Is the individual assertive enough to ask for an order and tenacious enough to follow through?
- Is the individual a good self-starter?
- Can the individual organise his or her work and time, and follow up on the work of others?
- Can he or she make decisions?
- Does the individual have the potential to grow on the job or can he or she only be expected to perform at the entry level?
- Is he or she intensely competitive or laid back?
- Can the individual cope with detail sufficiently?
- Is the individual shrewd in judging situations as well as people?
- Is the individual an original, innovative, creative thinker, or is he or she bound by tradition?

There are, of course, many more questions. But whether we talk about our test or any other valid test that may be used for the evaluation of sales and sales management personnel, these questions and many others related to the sales job should be answered reliably. The right test can provide data that in no way can be objectively provided by the earlier steps in the screening process. This data can really only be provided by penetrating the individual's façade and getting at the reality of who the individual is; that is best done by a test which meets all of the criteria we have discussed.

In addition to being a vital part of the decision-making process, the test results can also play an important role in structuring the final step of the process — the in-depth interview. By integrating the data provided by all of the earlier steps with the insights provided by the test, the interviewer can structure that interview in such a way so as to probe discrepancies and apparent weaknesses, and to move the interview away from the superficial and toward specifics. For example, if the test shows the applicant to be rigid and opinionated, this fact might be presented in the interview, and the applicant's reaction studied carefully. In short, the test results, as well as all of the previous data, form the basis for a more effective interview with the potential to produce more valid results.

In addition to its use in the selection process, an in-depth psychological test can be used to develop appropriate prescriptive training programmes designed to strengthen an individual in areas where he or she is weak. Rather than waste valuable training funds, management can use the test results to pinpoint specific areas in which training is most needed and gear supervision towards providing the specific support the salesperson requires.

Similarly, a test should provide important insights on how to manage effectively each individual currently on the staff. It can provide important direction as to who might be promotable and into what positions.

A valid test, in short, is vital as part of an effective selection process, and can be equally important as a tool in upgrading the productivity of an entire organisation.

CHAPTER 20

THE IN-DEPTH INTERVIEW: THE FINAL STEP

After receiving the evaluations of the psychological test, management will probably have eliminated some additional candidates, now narrowing the pyramid to those very few who should be brought to the last stage of the selection process — the in-depth interview. It is at this point that an interview should be as long as necessary and that interviews with several executives should be employed where appropriate. If company policy dictates, spouse interviews and even second or third interviews with the candidate may all be proper in helping to make that all-important final hiring decision. All that could have been done has been done to eliminate people who are clearly inappropriate for the investment of this kind of time. The use of the valid psychological test should give some clear indications that the remaining people have some of the important attributes making for a potentially good job match; there should be no indication that they have a non-trainable fatal flaw which would preclude them from doing the job effectively. What remains now is to bring together all of the data that has been gathered by all the steps in the screening process, to use the in-depth interview or interviews to integrate that data, and to use every technique available to confirm, in as absolute way as possible, the efficacy of the hiring decision.

A further purpose of this in-depth interview is to make certain not only that management wants to hire the candidate, but that the candidate fully knows and understands the opportunities that the job offers and is also aware of all of its negatives. This way both parties enter the relationship with all of the facts in hand and all of the potential problems presented up front so that any concerns can be worked out jointly. To state the obvious, it is far better, for example, to know that the amount of travel involved would create an impossible burden on a salesperson's family life before the hiring decision is made than to find this out a month or two later after time, money and effort have been invested in the individual. It is not management's job to sell the position to the applicant.

Rather, management should arrive, with the applicant, at the best joint decision — whether negative or positive. If the proper screening has been carried through, by the time you reach the stage of the final in-depth interview you are dealing with people who clearly possess the potential to do the job, and now it is everyone's responsibility to see if that potential is a practical, on-the-job reality. That is why an oversell, or a lack of honesty in presenting all aspects of the job, can serve to defeat all of the work that has gone before and ultimately contribute to an inappropriate decision.

Like every other stage of the selection process, the in-depth interview, while of great importance as the final step in making the hiring decision, is still flawed; its flaws must be thoroughly understood and worked through in order to get the most out of this step. Just as a review of cvs leaves much to be desired, a telephone screen can easily fool the interviewer, reference checks have serious problems and even the best psychological tests are not perfect, similarly, the in-depth interview has many built-in problems.

As we have indicated, the final in-depth interview is critical in that, despite all the flaws we will be discussing, it can provide valuable input into the hiring process. If not dealt with carefully, however, this input could confuse as much as it clarifies. How often after hiring someone who does not work out has a manager thought to him- or herself, 'But they looked so good in the interview'?

Part of the problem is the inherent limitation of interviews. Very few of us can interview with the skill, depth and finesse of a Brian Walden. And even if we could, that would not completely solve the problem.

More often than not, instead of lending insight, interviews become a form of theatre in which all of the actors are tripping over one another, trying to put their best feet forward. The employers are busy trying to create a favourable impression of themselves and their company, while the applicants are trying to mould themselves into whatever they perceive is desired.

Meanwhile, it must be kept in mind that any bookshop worth its salt has a shelf full of guides for playing this game to the hilt. Anyone serious about applying for a job has read at least one of these guides.

So, job interviews are replete with people trying to leave the best first impression. The result, all too often, is what we call 'interview stars', those individuals whose best performance occurs during the interview.

These stars are able to convey a favourable first impression, but that impression bears no relationship to their eventual performance. Even for a sales position it must be kept in mind that, just because someone can sell themselves in an interview, it does not necessarily imply an ability to sell a product or a service.

The interview star is overly concerned with making a favourable impression. It is fundamental to such an individual's sense of well-being to be liked, appreciated and perceived in favourable terms. An individual with this motivation will work very hard to make a good impression in an interview and, with the help of a few guides, will probably succeed. Yet, while this motivation to be well-liked is important for many jobs and can be helpful in many sales jobs, it will not, in and of itself, assure success in sales. Sometimes, in fact, as in the case presented by our account executive, (see page 41) too much of a need to be liked can work against an individual's ability to make difficult decisions, let alone to risk rejection when the situation calls for it.

A tip-off provided by this case can also be helpful. The applicant did not try to get the employer to move a little closer towards offering her the job. One can suspect a definite lack of assertiveness and view the existence of ego-drive with suspicion if an applicant does not say something towards the end of the interview such as, 'I like what I have heard. I am extremely interested in being part of your organisation. Will you give me an opportunity?' Even if these or similar words are said, this is by no means proof that the individual is really assertive and/or ego-driven, but certainly their absence, if not creating a red flag, provides a warning blinker light. Here is a good example of how test results and this kind of interview feedback can be integrated. If the test, for example, indicated borderline ego-drive and gave some cause for concern about the applicant's assertiveness, the failure to make this minimum move towards closing the sale (or getting the job) would reinforce the doubts created by the test results. On the other hand, given this same marginal test result, a strong push on the part of the applicant might tip the balance towards the applicant. In any event, there cannot be a simple assumption that because the right words are said in this context the individual is going to be effective. Again, too many instructions on how to interview tell the interviewee that such words are expected and should be employed.

It is in the process of penetrating the façade created by the interviewee that the data produced by the psychological test is of maximum value. The data provided by the test can be used to confirm impressions, explain them or deny them; whatever the case, the interview can be carried forward more effectively with this information. Later, we will discuss some specifics about how the information provided by the test can be used more effectively to structure the interview, but suffice it to say here that every impression gained in the interview should be evaluated against not only the data provided by the test, but also the information provided by all other steps in the screening process. The interview, in short, is the integrator, the sifter and the final arbiter as to what data is real, doubtful, or totally incorrect.

Before turning to a few specific 'how-to's, it might be useful to look at how not to. The following interview is admittedly extreme. We strongly suspect that few interviewers will really conduct such a totally incorrect interview, but we equally strongly suspect that many interviewers make at least some of these mistakes. By being extreme, we hope we are able to make a number of points that mere words or admonitions might not achieve quite as well.

THE INTERVIEW

'Good morning, Ms Moore,' you say. 'It's a pleasure to meet you.'

She says the pleasure is all hers, then comments on the attractive view from your window. While you settle behind your desk, the applicant sits across from you. A friendly smile offsets her intense eyes.

'First off' you say, scanning some papers on your desk, 'I was very impressed with your cv. It was clear and concise. And your background is particularly well suited to this new opening we have in our sales department. In fact, this is an exciting time to be coming on board with us, because things are really booming. But more on that later.' You quickly add, 'I took the liberty of checking some of the references you provided me with and they were all glowing.' Actually, some digging revealed that she was dismissed from one position under curious circumstances, but you decide to wait until later to delve into that.

'Enough of me talking about you,' you add. 'Why don't you tell me about yourself. Let's see, how long ago did you start your current position?'

'The exact date is on my cv, but it has been over two years.' She goes on to say that she's been selling advertising space for a local newspaper, which she likes, but finds limiting. Though the job has enabled her to meet various clients in numerous settings, she would like to find a job that would enable her to be on the road more, with one-to-one contact.

'I'm sorry. I didn't realise you had somebody in your office,' one of your salespeople says, sticking his head inside the door you left slightly ajar. 'I'll check back later. Please excuse the interruption.'

'That's all right,' you say. 'Now, where were we? Oh, yes. Well, I'm sure you have a lot of questions about the company and the job. Let me try to anticipate some of them for you. Since the company was founded a little over a decade ago, we've been on the right track and that road is now smoother than ever. Of course, the owners keep their hands on things, which can get a little difficult at times. As a matter of fact — well, let me just tell you this one quick story to illustrate what I mean,' you say, leaning across your desk, lowering your voice in confidence. 'It happened just the other day, so it's still fresh in my mind, but it's a classic example of what I go through. I had been after the three owners to get an estimate out to a prospective client for the last two weeks. Because they must have their imprint on everything that goes out of here, the estimate was getting delayed for this reason, then for that reason. Yesterday, when I asked about it, I was told it was being reviewed. So I had to do handsprings to get all three of the owners to drop everything else they were doing and concentrate on this proposal. Not only was it aggravating, but it cost us a bundle to get it to its destination on time.

'But that wouldn't be a concern of yours should you come on board,' you quickly insert. 'But, enough of me talking; you must have some questions.'

'As a matter of fact, I was wondering if you could describe this sales position to me in more detail. If I accept this position, what would I be doing on a day-to-day basis?'

Pausing, you say, 'As far as your job is concerned, you'll be constantly selling. Our product is known in the marketplace and highly regarded. So, you'll have a solid base upon which to approach prospects. It depends upon how adept you are at persuading. But, then, I wouldn't be overly concerned about that if I were you. I've always believed that if you can sell, you can sell. Excuse me,' you apologise, as the phone rings. 'No, I'm in the middle of an interview now. Tell her I'll get back in touch with her as soon as I can.'

You continue, 'One thing I wanted to ask you about was Harlequin. I see from your cv you used to work there. Do you remember a guy names Johnson, Robert Johnson?'

'Yes, he used to work in accounting, I believe. I didn't get a chance to know him well,' she says.

'Oh, Bob and I go way back. We were at university together. Those were some times. The things I could tell you about him then. He was crazy on the rugby field and even crazier off,' you say, laughing at the memory. Realising that Ms Moore isn't laughing with you, you quickly change the subject.

'One thing you'll realise if you come on board with us, Ms Moore, and all of our salespeople will confirm this, is that as far as money is concerned, the sky is the limit. Since we work on a commission basis, after your brief training period, your income is only limited by your ability.'

'That was something I was meaning to ask you. Just to give me an idea of where I might stand, what is the average take-home pay for a salesperson on your force?'

'Oh, the average is nothing you should concern yourself with, Ms Moore, since I'm sure you'll do much better than average.' Smiling, you remember another question you wanted to ask. 'One thing I always like to ask is what is the one thing you like least about your current job?'

'That's a rough question,' she says. 'I mean, I don't want to incriminate myself. But, let's see. I'd have to say that the job is needlessly bogged down in detail. I understand the importance of detail, but there is a tendency to waste salespeople's time with paperwork that could be completed more efficiently by someone in a clerical position.'

'I'm sorry to hear you say that,' you say. 'Too many salespeople think of detail as something that simply slows them down in the achievement of their goals. That impatience can be fatal when it comes to satisfying customers. That's the very attitude that can erode that success we've worked so long to build here.' Leaning back in your chair, you stare at the applicant, searching for her response to one of your steadfast beliefs.

Recoiling slightly, she says, 'I don't believe I have any problems handling detail. It's just that I think the operation where I'm currently working could be run more smoothly if salespeople could concentrate more on meeting clients, following up on prospects and the other, more essential parts of selling.'

You could pursue this train of thought, but, glancing at your watch, you realise you're already late for an important session with the owners of the company. 'I'm sorry. The time has just shot right by. I wish we could talk longer, but I'm already late for a meeting, and the owners will probably have my head.' Rising from your seat and gathering a few papers from your desk, you add, 'Listen, it was really a pleasure. I'm not sure how long it will take us to come to a final decision about the job, but it shouldn't be more than a few weeks or so. If you have any questions concerning anything we didn't cover, please don't hesitate to call.' Opening the door to your office, you add, 'My secretary will be glad to direct you to the car park. Thanks again.'

THE TEN ERRORS

The ten basic interviewing errors are as follows.

1. Don't oversell your company

Early in the interview, the interviewer makes his first mistake by bragging about how things are booming, while not giving specifics to back up his claim. He follows this up with pat phrases like 'since its founding, the company has been on the right track and the road is now smoother.' An adept interviewer will lay out the strengths and weaknesses of the firm, putting them in perspective. Do not paint an unrealistic picture of your company in order to lure an applicant on board.

2. Don't be afraid to ask tough questions
The second mistake occurred almost immediately, when the interviewer did not pursue why the applicant was dismissed from a previous job. If you uncover anything during the reference checking or employment history review process that warrants tough questioning, do not be afraid to ask about it during the interview. It is important that you begin your relationship with an applicant on a frank basis.

3. Don't ask for information you already have
The interviewer asked, 'Why don't you tell me about yourself? How long ago did you start your current position?' This shows a lack of interest in the candidate, since this information was obtained earlier. The interview should be used to obtain new information or to confirm or reject tentative information already acquired.

4. Don't allow yourself to be interrupted unless there is an emergency
The interview is interrupted, first by a salesperson sticking his head in the door, and then by a telephone call. Too many interviewers allow the interview to become disjointed by not taking steps to prevent interruptions. Your office door should be closed. Put calls and messages on hold.

5. Don't talk too much
The interviewer then told the applicant, 'Well, I'm sure you have a lot of questions about the company and the job. Let me try to anticipate some of them for you.' This is a classic case of the interviewer who loves to hear his or her own voice. At the most, an interviewer should say one word for every four spoken by the person being interviewed.

6. Don't use the interview as your therapy
As part of his need to hear himself talk, the interviewer told a confidential story about some of the problems he encounters in his position. Too many interviewers use their sessions to spout out their concerns about the company. When an interviewer vents emotions in an interview, he or she may feel better, but may lose a prospective employee in the bargain.

7. Don't be afraid to spell out in detail the requirements of the position

When the applicant got a word in edgeways and asked about the specific requirements of the job and what her compensation would be, she was brushed off with the pat answer, 'The sky is the limit. But then, I wouldn't be concerned about that if I were you. I've always believed that if you can sell, you can sell.' It is imperative that people know what is required of them before beginning a job. The interview is the time to outline the job's requirements, as well as your criteria for evaluating success in the role.

8. Don't gossip or swap war stories

Many interviewers try to find familiar ground they can tread over with the applicant. Though this might seem like a comfortable way to get an interview under way, inquiring about friends and relatives can get things sidetracked, wasting a huge amount of time. The interview should be devoted to obtaining as much information as possible in order to make a sound hiring decision.

9. Don't put the applicant on the defensive

If the job on offer is not stress laden, there really is no point in creating unnecessary tension during the interview. Knowing an applicant's personality strengths and weaknesses is vital to making the best hiring decision. Openly discussing Ms Moore's statement about detail on her former job might provide valuable insight, particularly if the test results provided evidence that there was indeed a sufficiently strong dislike of detail to create concern. A speech embodying a long-held philosophy is inappropriate, but a frank discussion of the role detail plays in the job, and how Ms Moore might deal with the detail aspect of the job, would be constructive and would allow both people to make a more reasoned decision.

10. Don't be afraid to make the interview as long, or as short, as you deem necessary

The final mistake was that the interview was concluded in an unnecessary rush. As the interviewer noticed the time, he realised he was late for another appointment and excused himself hurriedly. To be effective, the interview should make the fullest use of everyone's valuable time. There are no set guidelines on length, so long as you spell out clearly the anticipated length of the interview, and the time is spent wisely.

ADDITIONAL MISTAKES TO AVOID

It may be difficult after reviewing this atrocious interview to imagine that there are other common mistakes, which somehow were not included in the interview.

Here are a few additional mistakes to avoid.

Don't ask questions that can be answered by a simple yes or no. Try whenever possible to ask questions that must be answered at some length and with some explanation. The key to a good question is not only to get a specific answer but to get that answer by listening to the interviewee's response.

Don't simply indulge in generalised conversation as though nothing had occurred prior to the interview. Though this was done to some degree in the interview of Ms Moore, the point should be further elaborated here. The interviewer should have a great deal of information in hand relating to the applicant's past experience, feedback from references, early impressions from the telephone and in-person interview and, of course, the data provided by the psychological test. All of these impressions should be checked throughout the interview and conflicts should be resolved. If, for example, the cv speaks about a previous position as 'a division manager' and the reference checks reveal that the applicant managed no one and the title was simply another name for a salesperson with a territory, that apparent discrepancy should be discussed. 'Tell me specifically what you did on the job. Do the best you can to tell me how you functioned literally hour by hour and day by day.' If after this explanation the discrepancy is still not resolved, the manager should not hesitate to confront the applicant with the evident discrepancy and ask the applicant to discuss it. Obviously, this discrepancy might be more or less important, depending on the nature of the job for which the applicant is being considered.

Similarly, if the applicant described his or her previous job as involving hard, frequent closes and the test indicates some doubt as to their level of ego-drive, questions could be raised about the discrepancy, giving the applicant plenty of opportunity to sell the interviewer on the fact that he or she was able to close despite what the test says, and hopefully getting the applicant to explain precisely how he or she accomplished this. What we are saying here is try to avoid general conversations, and home in as precisely as possible on the specifics.

Don't ramble. Although there is no precise ideal length of an interview, it is important to show the interviewee that there is a respect for time, not only the time of the manager, but the time of the interviewee as well. While being friendly, stay to the point, and keep the interview moving in a clearly defined direction. Finally, unless the individual has been ruled out by the end of the interview, he or she should not be left with a generalised 'we will be in touch'. Rather, it is important to spell out what the next steps may be even if those steps simply involve a management discussion and notification of the applicant. If future interviews are going to be requested, these should be indicated, and if group interviews, spouse interviews and the like are to be part of the process, these should be spelled out as well. In other words, the applicant should leave the interview knowing, with relative precision, when a decision is going to be made, on what basis it might be made and what other steps, if any, may be required in the decision-making process.

STRUCTURING THE INTERVIEW: THE INTERVIEW STRATEGY

As we said earlier, all too often the intermiew is, by its very nature, a form of theatre with the participants performing an adversarial dance. The applicant is trying to make the best impression, and in that effort is working to psyche out the interviewer, looking to say precisely what the interviewer wants to hear. Similarly, the interviewer is trying to penetrate the façade of the applicant to ascertain what is really there, what are their real motives and the like.

In this ritual, the interviewer does begin with some important advantages, which all too often are not taken advantage of. First, and of most importance, the interviewer enters the situation armed with a good deal of knowledge about the applicant. As subjective as some of this knowledge is, it still provides a body of data upon which a strategy for the interview can be laid out. Add to this the more objective input of the test and potential discrepancies between various elements of information produced prior to the interview, and the interviewer really has tools with which to probe the façade with good effectiveness. Using these tools, however, does require planning. Thus, before the interview begins, the interviewer should have firmly in mind, or even in writing, a series of answers that are being sought. The final interview is not simply another place in which to gain an impression, but, rather, should be the mechanism by which everything else in the process is confirmed, denied or left ambiguous. Thus, these discrepancies, problems and/or doubts created by any prior part of the process must be probed in the interview, along the lines we discussed. But such probing must be well-planned and strategy for such probing developed. If the applicant has survived through all of the steps in the screening process, the odds are that there are not too many weaknesses or discrepancies, but those that exist must be dealt with if the proper decision is to be made.

Apropos of this point, and also to be fair to both the applicant and the company, it is really important at one stage or another in this interview to describe the job fully in terms of its functional requirements, performance expectations and potential upward mobility. Such a description should be laid out in fairness to the applicant, but such a description can also serve as an important final screen for the company. If elements of the job expectation, whether involving day-to-day performance appraisal, or potential, happen to fly in the face of certain motivations or weaknesses of the applicant, being aware of them could lead the applicant towards making a negative decision, which in the long run, would be positive for the company. It is better for everyone concerned that the job be presented honestly, with its opportunities and problems, so that the interviewer and the applicant can face the issues, discuss the problems, and together arrive at the most intelligent and mutually beneficial employment decision.

In short, if most of the pitfalls we have outlined can be avoided, and if you are certain and clear about the information you want to obtain, the interview can be extremely important in the final hiring decision.

CHAPTER 21

THE FINAL DECISION

We have been focusing on how a company should best go about the job of building a winning sales team. It is our purpose in this chapter to wrap up and summarise our suggested pyramid process of recruiting, screening and selecting productive salespeople. It is also our purpose, however, to deal to some degree with the other side of the decision-making process — the applicant who has to make his or her decision.

As we look at the final decision and attempt to summarise how it is made, let us understand that the decision is not, or certainly should not be, a unidirectional one. The right decision must be a joint decision by the company and the applicant. There cannot be a winner and a loser in the hiring decision. If the hiring decision is a correct one, it must be a positive one for both the applicant and the employer.

THE COMPANY'S DECISION

Let us bring together all the various facets of the hiring process. To quickly review, the recruiting and screening processes have now been completed. The company has conducted an effective search among its existing employees to determine whether some of its salespeople could be made more productive and to see whether there may be hidden sales talent among individuals doing other, non-sales jobs for the company. After completing this at-home talent search, the company has put out the broadest possible net, tapping every available potential source of talent. It has screened out only those people who clearly lack educational or background factors absolutely and objectively essential to selling the company's product or service, and which realistically could not be provided through a company training proramme. This broad net approach should have brought in a large number of applicants, establishing a large base for what is a pyramid approach to hiring. This base is then narrowed, first through a review of cvs, which eliminates some obviously inappropriate people and then through a brief telephone interview, which can reduce the number of applicants to be considered still further. A brief, in-person interview reduces the valid applicant pool still further and, finally, a reference check completes the screening-out process. By this time, obviously inappropriate people have been eliminated, although at the risk, in some instances, of eliminating an individual with hidden potential. All of these eliminated candidates have been knocked out on the basis of subjective input, eg voice, background, appearance, other people's opinions etc.

It is at this point that the remaining candidates should be few enough in number to permit the company to focus a great deal of attention on them in order to make that final, all-important hiring decision. The first step in the screening-in process is the use of a valid psychological test to uncover an individual's real potential, his or her strengths, weaknesses and motivations, and to provide the data needed to do the final job match. The test should not only serve to help determine whether or not the individual can do the job, but also whether his or her personality integrates properly with the manager's and with the overall chemistry of the sales team. The test should also be used to help plan training and supervisory approaches, should the individual be hired, and the data provided by the test should also play an important part in structuring the in-depth interview to follow.

In all probability, some additional individuals will have been screened out after the test data is reviewed, leaving the final few to be involved in the in-depth interview leading to the final decision.

With all the weaknesses of the interview process, the final interview is still the step that integrates all of the other steps, paving the way for the most effective possible final decision. It is during the final interview that discrepancies in data provided by all the other steps can be reconciled, final impressions confirmed and doubts alleviated. It is here that no effort is too great, no length of interview too long and no further checks too detailed, given the importance of that final hiring decision.

We are certainly not saying that, even with all of these admonitions and even if this pyramid approach is followed meticulously, there will be no hiring mistakes. The process of recruitment and selection still remains as much an art as a science, and when it comes down to it, still depends a good deal on the skill of the individual doing the recruitment and selection. A good, skilled interviewer, no matter how scientific the approach and no matter how good the test, will still produce a better hiring batting average than a less skilled individual. However, even the most skilled interviewer, using the finest, most valid, most reliable and most job-related psychological test and checking references in the most meticulous way, will still make hiring mistakes just as the best sports team will still hire individuals who do not live up to the team's high expectations. This being said, however, it should be emphasised that there is as enormous a difference between the batting average of hiring decisions made in the way we suggest, and those made in the old, haphazard way, as there is between the batting average of a top scorer and a tail ender. Neither is perfect, but if you were a manager of a cricket team, which would you prefer?

THE CANDIDATE'S DECISION

Most managers tend to forget that the candidate is involved in an equally difficult decision-making process. It is as critical for the individual as it is for the company to make a valid, objective decision.

We have not offered an easy '20 questions that candidates can ask themselves to decide whether or not to be in sales'. What we can suggest, rather, is that this pyramid recruitment and selection process, which we recommend companies use, also provides the potential salesperson with help to make a decision.

We hope that after reading this book many people who are not in sales, or have never even considered being in sales, might look towards the profession as an important opportunity. As people, whether in sales or not, explore the various personality attributes which it takes to succeed in sales, they can look at themselves and at least begin the process of self-appraisal. They, at least initially, could ask themselves if they would be happy in an occupation in which persuasion is central to success.

A yes obviously does not mean the individual really has sales potential, but at least a yes might provide a signal that sales might be an opportunity worth further exploration.

If the individual chooses to explore sales, the pyramid selection process used by the company affords that individual, as we said, a step-by-step opportunity not only to persuade the company to continue considering them, but to decide for themselves whether they want to continue to be considered.

Each step, then, in the pyramid process can be thought of by the candidate as part of his or her own information-gathering process. The telephone is a two-way device. The short telephone interview should not be viewed simply as the company's opportunity to ask questions and draw out data from the applicant, but also the applicant's opportunity to find out more from the company. A few probing questions can help the individual determine whether he or she would want to sell that product or service. Parenthetically, if that phone interview and, for that matter, the follow-up in-person interview is projected by the interviewee as a process for mutual data gathering, that very projection lends weight and credibility to the individual's application.

The individual while, of course, trying to sell him- or herself to the company, first in the phone interview and then in person, should also be gathering enough information to decide whether the job would be 'fun', because if a sales job is not fun to an individual, he or she does not have what it takes to succeed in selling.

If the process has gone that far, the final interview should also be used by the applicant to help make the final decision. There is nothing wrong with asking the employer to reveal something about the test results and to talk openly with the employer about how the weaknesses revealed by the test, or in other steps of the process might be worked through on the job. There is nothing wrong, for example, for an individual who has poor time planning skills, which has been revealed by the test and of which the individual is fully aware, to find out whether the company can offer any help in overcoming this problem either through management support, training, or both. If not, perhaps that sales job is not for the particular applicant, and even if the job is offered, it might be better for the applicant to say no.

THE CRITICAL DECISION

What we are saying, in short, is that the hiring decision is an extremely critical one. We have spoken in earlier chapters about the enormous costs of hiring mistakes, and we will focus in the next part on these costs as related to specific industries. Suffice it to say here that the costs to industry are far too great to permit anything but the best techniques to be used in making the hiring decision. At the same time, the applicant must not only sell him- or herself, but must also use every bit of knowledge they can mobilise to help them determine whether or not the opportunity is really for them. As we have said in the first chapter of this book, sales provides a brilliant, unique opportunity to the right person, but the high rate of turnover and the very fact that only 20 per cent of people sell 80 per cent of what is sold proves beyond question that that opportunity is only a good one for the 'right' person.

We are convinced, and we have seen in our work with thousands of clients, that when a company and an individual together make an effort to determine whether a match exists between the individual and the job, both profit enormously. Sometimes the best thing that can happen to an individual is to be turned down for a sales job for which he or she is not appropriate; conversely, some of the greatest sales success stories we have come across are people who never dreamed of sales, but who are now numbered among the sales superstars. The opportunities are exciting, the final decision critical. But, if done systematically, the final decision can be the right one for the company and the individual.

PART 5

MATCHING SALES DYNAMICS TO SPECIFIC INDUSTRIES

When sales professionals discuss what it takes to succeed in sales, they invariably fall into one of two camps. One group asserts that individuals who have what it takes to sell can sell virtually anything. Provide them with someone who can sell and they will gladly teach them the technical aspects of their product or service. The other group insists that a set of unique qualities is needed to sell in their industry and very definitely in their company.

Actually, both groups are right — or, at least, partially. People who possess the basic central dynamics of empathy, ego-drive, ego-strength and service motivation will be able to succeed in some kind of sales. The question is: what kind? To a certain degree, the people in the first camp are right: an individual must begin by having the four essential qualities in order to sell. The second camp is correct, however, in that the varying degrees of these central dynamics, plus the possession of numerous other motivational factors, determine an individual's likelihood to succeed in a specific sales job.

While we have provided a fundamental overview of sales in general up to this point, we are now going to focus on specific industries in depth to demonstrate the nuances of the job matching approach.

In reading the following chapters, it will become readily apparent that there are many more differences within each industry, in terms of definitions and requirements of specific sales roles, than there are between the industries. Since it is obviously impossible to give this kind of in-depth examination to dozens of industries, it is our hope that the six case studies presented will cover the spectrum sufficiently to allow managers to understand better some of the unique factors which distinguish their industry, and to allow individuals to look at industries to see if their own personality attributes match the requirements being sought. We apologise in advance for some redundancy in this section, but we hope that this very redundancy will help to underscore the subtle differences which account for why an individual can have a difficult time in one particular sales situation and be extremely successful in another.

CHAPTER 22

AN AGENCY'S PEOPLE: THE BOTTOM LINE ADVANTAGE

The independent property and health insurance agency, and, in fact, the entire independent agency system, offers an excellent example of the value of capitalism in its purest sense. We say this for a number of reasons, which we will discuss below.

First of all, the independent agency, unlike so many mammoth companies, remains, in most instances, a pure example of entrepreneurism. Typically, an agency is started by one or two individuals who have come up through the independent agency system, and often the agency is perpetuated through generations. Even where mergers or acquisitions have occurred, these are, more often than not, mergers of two or more entrepreneurial enterprises or acquisitions of an entrepreneurial agency by a larger group that certainly started out as, and perhaps even today continues as, an essentially entrepreneurial operation.

Even though notice must be taken of the increasingly large role of national and regional conglomerate agencies, the small entrepreneurial agency is still very present in the independent agency system and can still be profitable in today's marketplace.

The second reason we see the independent agency system as so representative of capitalism at its best relates to the very nature of the system itself. Unlike the individual companies, the independent agency represents many companies, which must compete for that agency's placement of business. Similarly, the agency is competing both with other agencies and with individual companies, and even with banks and life insurance companies, for the consumer's property and health insurance money. They must compete by offering the consumer the best value, which means meeting the consumer's needs through products offered by one or a combination of the companies they represent. Also, they must compete by providing the insurance customer with the kind of support and active representation that is unique to the independent agent. No matter how good the salesperson or how honest the claims department of an individual company may be, they still represent that individual company, and only that individual company. The independent agency, however, while it must represent the companies effectively, must also, equally effectively, represent the insurance customer. In a claim situation, that agency had better support the customer, or the customer will cease to be one rather quickly. A good agency will effectively do so without offending or misrepresenting the companies.

As strong as the argument that only the independent agency continues to represent the insurance buyer may be, that argument often fails to sell the customer. A few pounds in premium savings and/or heavy advertising programmes very often lead the customer to the individual company. The reason is simple. Consumers may be exposed to the name and advertising power of the individual company, but no one may ever have told them persuasively about the advantages of working with an independent agent. If consumers know that they can save a few pounds through an individual company and do not know any counter-arguments, their choice is obvious.

We should hasten to add here that we are not in any way attributing negative characteristics to the individual insurance companies. Many of them are fine, have excellent and fair claims departments, and indeed do an outstanding job for their insurance customers. What we are saying, however, is that if the independent agent fails to sell its advantages, the individual company increasingly becomes the only one to which the consumer is exposed. The fair competition as to their mutual advantages fails to occur, and the individual company wins by default.

To return to the independent agent and capitalism, it should be clear that to really compete effectively the independent agent *must*, more than many companies, have people within the agency who are capable of competing. The independent agency, moreover, must have people all through it, regardless of definition of responsibilities, that are capable of dealing with people on a competitive sales level. Often, the way the receptionist answers the phone, and how that receptionist processes the calls, can make as much difference as to whether or not a prospect becomes a customer as the producer and the customer service representative themselves. The agency, certainly more than any large company, is thought of by the consumer as being that individual within the agency with whom the customer has come in contact — be it the receptionist, a customer service representative or a salesperson; often that first impression remains with the prospect, for good or ill. To succeed, therefore, the independent agent must look at selling, not only in terms of its sales force — its producers — but, really, at all of its agency staff, from receptionist, to underwriters, to claims people, to producers and event to the agency head, as critical parts of the agency's ability to compete for the insurance pound.

There was a time not that long ago when an agency, particularly in a small town, could survive by reminding people that their car or home insurance renewal premiums were due and by simply taking orders. If you needed insurance, everybody knew to call 'Charlie' or 'Joe' and he would write it up for you. Today, even in the smallest areas, and even where 'Charlie' or 'Joe' may have sold insurance for 40 years, that approach is most likely to lead to disaster, because 'Harry' or 'Jill' may well sell it cheaper, and with broader coverage.

Because the total agency must be thought of as a salesperson, we want to make a slight departure from our discussion of what it takes to succeed in sales in its purest sense. What it takes to succeed in sales in the independent agency system is a good agency head, effective producers, strong customer service representatives and even, as we mentioned earlier, an excellent receptionist, underwriters and claims people. In order fully to understand what it takes to succeed in sales in the independent agency system, we must really understand what it takes to succeed in each of these roles, because it is only through an integration of effectiveness within these roles that success can be achieved. Let us then take a brief look at each of these critical agency roles and see how they tie in to overall agency productivity.

THE AGENCY HEAD

There is no neat way to define the personality of the effective agency head. What it is important to point out, however, is that no agency head, no matter how talented, can or should attempt to do all the jobs of the agency. Of course, in a one-person agency, the ideal often cannot be achieved. But wherever possible, the agency head should not attempt to be all things to all people. Simply put, people who try to do everything end up doing very little well.

At minimum, even in the smallest agency, we suggest that the office manager or secretary should possess personality attributes that complement those of the agency head. Only in this way can a proper team be formed, one in which the agent can concentrate on those things for which he or she is best suited.

This being said, there is nevertheless, the key need, whatever the agent's particular strengths and weaknesses, for the head of an agency to be a leader. It is the agency head who sets the tone for the agency and, of course, it is the agency head who is the primary determinant of the quality of the people in the agency.

Thus, while we re-emphasise that no one can or should be everything, there are at least three qualities that the head of an agency should possess if he or she hopes to run an effective organisation: decisiveness; the ability to delegate; and leadership.

Decisiveness

In an average working day, the agency head must be a willing, effective decision-maker. By this we mean that she or he must be willing to make quick decisions, even at the risk of making an occasional error. But this decisiveness must be balanced with responsibility and intelligence in order to make these decisions with judgement and thought.

An effective agency head can neither be too impulsive—too precipitous—nor so overcautious that he or she would fail to act. Balance is the key word here.

Delegation

If agency heads are not to do everything themselves, they obviously must delegate responsibilities to others. The quality with which the agency head delegates, both in terms of willingness to delegate and judgements as to which duties to delegate to whom, can often make or break the agency.

The ability to delegate involves the willingness to delegate, which means not needing to do everything themselves, the patience to take the time to explain the job being delegated, and the empathy and intelligence to determine to whom to delegate what—to judge accurately the abilities and motivations of subordinates.

Leadership

Leadership, of course, is really the all-encompassing term embodying effective management. Good leadership certainly includes the ability to make decisions and the ability to delegate.

But by defining it a bit more narrowly as a separate attribute, we look at leadership as the ability that enables an individual to get other people to do willingly what they have the ability to do but might not spontaneously do on their own.

Leadership involves the assertiveness to lead strongly, yet with the empathy to be sensitive to the needs and abilities of those being led. It is the overall ability to get the job done through maximising the abilities and work of the entire team.

And more

Even if the agency principal possesses all of the above attributes in abundance, human nature being what it is, he or she will have particular strengths and weaknesses that point to the need to emphasise particular functions in the agency. For instance, some agents have come up through the sales route. Having formerly been effective salespeople, this means they possess three essential personality attributes: ego-drive (persuasive motivation); empathy (ability to get feedback from a customer or prospect); and ego-strength (ability to take the rejection inevitably involved in sales).

Such an agent, even in his or her executive position, should continue to be involved in the sales and marketing aspects of the agency. It does not make sense for someone with that sales talent not to be out there selling, but to be wasting time handling administrative detail, which may be the weakest aspect of his or her personality.

What often happens in such cases is that the agency loses its exceptional sales productivity, only to gain a mediocre or worse administrator.

On the other hand, individuals who have come up through the underwriting or administrative route, and whose abilities are primarily administrative, should not attempt to force themselves into a sales role. Rather, such individuals should make their maximum contribution to the agency through administering and running that agency. What we are suggesting is that, instead of attempting to do everything, agency heads should focus on the things they do best — the functions that are most in tune with their personality — and hire a number-two person whose strengths lie in the agency head's weaker areas.

The powerful salesperson must have a strong administrator as number two, while the administrator needs a driven, empathic vice president of sales and marketing.

The agent who tries to do everything him- or herself will probably do nothing very well. The best agents we have worked with know themselves very well. Rather than trying to fit into a prescribed mould, they are keenly aware of their unique strengths and limitations. They structure their agency in a way that allows their strengths to thrive.

PRODUCER

The term *producer* is one of the more confusing in the agency lexicon of position titles.

One agency head will tell us that he or she wants the producer to do one thing: close sales, bring in new business. 'Once a salesperson brings an account in, our customer service staff take good care of it,' they will say, adding, 'we don't want a producer to touch a customer once they are brought on board.'

Other agency heads will define the position entirely differently. The producer they are looking for will inherit a large book of business and his or her primary job will be to service and expand that business, while hopefully getting some referrals out of that business. Rather than cold calling, they expect their producers to build ongoing relationships with large accounts.

Yet another agent may describe producers as doing primarily cold calling. 'Selling is still selling,' as one told us. 'Still, our producers are also responsible for maintaining the accounts once they are on board. We insist that our salespeople follow up "x" dating and continue to work on the growth and maintenance of the accounts they bring in.'

So, when helping an agency select producers, what do we do?

Define the term

The first thing we do is ask agents to define the term *producer* as the role exists in their agency. Then we go about identifying the type of individual who would enjoy and could succeed in that particular job.

In the final analysis, there is no absolute definition of the individual who fits the producer's role. Rather, there are three or more definitions, depending upon the specific situation.

Bringing in new business

In the instance where the producer is primarily responsible for bringing in new business, the personality requirements become very clear-cut. Such a salesperson must possess three central qualities. They are as follows.

Empathy The ability to sense the reactions of other persons accurately and to recognise the clues and cues they provide allows a salesperson to relate effectively to prospects. The salesperson with excellent empathy is not hemmed in by prepared sales tracts but can sense the prospect's reactions and make creative modifications to a presentation when necessary.

Ego-drive This is the inner need to persuade another individual as a means of gaining personal gratification. An ego-driven individual needs to persuade others for the feeling of satisfaction that comes from the victory.

Ego-strength   Salespeople need resiliency to bounce back from rejection and be even more motivated on the next attempt. Essentially, the degree of self-acceptance becomes a key to sales success.

A lack of any one of these three characteristics can guarantee sales failure. But success could hinge on other factors, depending upon the particular sales situation.

For instance, when new business production is the prime responsibility, we can forgive impulsiveness or impatience, even lack of fine detail ability. In some cases, we can even forgive lack of good time-planning skills if the agency is structured in such a way that management can help them with co-ordinating their work. In other situations, however, where people are out on their own without the opportunity to be closely managed, the lack of time-planning skills could be a serious drawback. Again, the situation defines the proper person.

The agent must not make the mistake, however, of looking for a good, purely new business producer and still demand certain service skills. These are unnecessary, and often this demand may deny the agent the benefit of a tremendous salesperson.

Servicing a book of accounts

On the opposite extreme is the so-called producer whose job really is to service a book of accounts. Such individuals should not be called upon to possess particularly strong ego-drive. They are not asked to close new business, so why demand the ability to do so?

What this producer, who really is a senior customer service representative, must possess is the fine empathy needed by all salespeople, plus the exceptional personal organisational skills and the service motivation needed to retain and expand ongoing relationships. Certainly a little bit of persuasive motivation cannot hurt when this producer is suggesting an expansion of business at a point of 'x' dating or asking for a referral and the like. But basically, what is needed is the ability to relate effectively to customers, to meet their needs through providing information and effective service, and through the assertiveness to put the facts in front of the customer. As a matter of fact, where maintenance is the primary responsibility, too much ego-drive can actually get in the way because individuals with enormous ego-drive want the thrill of the close, which they will not experience in a maintenance situation. With too much ego-drive, the person whose basic responsibility is maintenance is going to become restless and will probably, in the long run, leave the agency either on his or her own, or at the agent's request.

New business and maintenance

Probably the most difficult person to find is the producer whose responsibilities include both the aggressive seeking of new business and the maintenance of existing accounts. What is needed here is an individual who has sufficient persuasive motivation — ego-drive — to close sales. Yet, that ego-drive cannot be so strong that the producer loses patience with the maintenance aspect of the role. The right balance of enough drive to close sales, and yet not too much, must be found. Of course, this producer must have excellent empathy and requires the same degree of ego-strength as does the pure new business producer. Yet, he or she also requires many of the attributes of the pure maintenance person. This combination producer must have enough service motivation, personal organisation, detail ability and patience to produce the steady, ongoing work involved in maintaining accounts.

Though this combination of attributes is hard to find in one person, people with these attributes do exist and, in fact, provide an excellent source of future management talent. It is really many of these same attributes that make for the effective sales manager.

From the above, it should be clear that it is terribly important that the agent should determine precisely what responsibilities he or she wishes the producer to undertake. In other words, only through a clear definition of what the producer's role is, can the people be found whose abilities properly match that role.

CUSTOMER SERVICE REPRESENTATIVE

The term *customer service representative* can cover a relatively wide range of differing responsibilities. In some agencies, the customer service representative, or, as some call them, senior customer service representative, is virtually indistinguishable in responsibilities from the producer who is primarily responsible for maintenance of business. This customer service representative, like that producer, is essentially given the responsibility of maintaining existing business. It is often this customer service representative who takes over when the new business producer closes a sale. Thus, the personality attributes needed for this role are virtually identical to those of a producer as defined by some agencies.

Such a customer service representative, like the producer primarily responsible for maintaining and expanding existing business, should have a fair degree of the four key sales dynamics — empathy, ego-drive, service motivation and ego-strength — since sales remains art of the job responsibility.

The senior customer service representative, however, again like the producer with similar responsibilities, probably should not have extremely intense ego-drive. Also, he or she can probably get away with somewhat less ego-strength than can the producer. The reason is that the customer service representative, even if he or she has some expansion of business responsibilities, is still essentially filling that responsibility through servicing an existing customer. Thus, the sale, whether it be a cross-sell or coverage expansion, must, of necessity, be a soft one and, again, one in a service context.

Thus, the likelihood of rejection is much smaller. It is also much easier to avoid rejection by stepping back than it would be in a cold contact situation where a step back often means never seeing the prospect again. As a matter of fact, it is very easy for the customer service representative to step back where resistance is encountered and brief a producer as to the potential business expansion, if more raw servicing ability is needed to accomplish this.

Thus, while the senior customer service representative should clearly possess a sufficient degree of ego-drive and ego-strength, and as much empathy and service motivation as possible, some compromise can be made in the first two areas if the other key customer service attributes are really strong.

For the more junior-level customer service representative, however, there is a real difference in the requirements. In such a case, the job becomes largely clerical. The customer service representative must answer questions, provide information and is sometimes even given minor underwriting responsibilities. However, he or she is rarely, if ever, held responsible for following up on an account, keeping tabs of 'x' dating, or playing other roles in which sales ability or assertiveness is really necessary. This customer service representative must possess, first and foremost, a strong service motivation. What we mean is that the individual must be strongly motivated to be liked. It must be important for them to please someone, and so they will work hard to ingratiate themselves with the customers they are servicing. They want to do a good job because they want to be appreciated for doing that job; they want to be thought of as coming through.

Tied in with this motivation is patience, thoroughness, a strong sense of responsibility and strong inner controls. They must be self-motivated; they must have a taskmaster within themselves, pushing them to work hard so that they can receive the approval which they crave.

Of course, the customer service representative must have the kind of detail ability and organisation skills to allow him or her to do the needed detail work, and he or she must possess sufficient language, maths and underwriting skills to do that work and communicate properly with the customer. Most often, such customer service representatives are not particularly assertive, and tend to be, if anything, overcautious, they are not quick decision makers and certainly, more often than not, do not possess strong ego-drive. For the role, however, these weaknesses are not real drawbacks. The customer service representative does not typically need to be strongly assertive, although some assertiveness is certainly helpful, and their responsibilities do not call for a great deal of decision making on their own. Thus, the over-cautiousness that is a serious drawback in a salesperson, or in a manager and perhaps even in a senior customer service representative, is not a problem in the customer service representative's role and, if anything, some agents might prefer it.

Ego-drive, moreover, could be a drawback because if there is too much need to persuade, the patience to perform the customer service representative role would be likely not to be there. In effect, pleasing customers must be the primary motivation of customer service representatives.

Getting back to assertiveness for a moment, that quality could be extremely important to the customer service representative and, perhaps in addition to the possibility of some sales dynamics, could mark the difference between the individual who could move into a senior position and those who must stay at the junior level. In a senior service role, it is sometimes important to be assertive enough to say no to a customer. If a customer demands a decision so promptly that there is no real likelihood of having it in time, it is far better to say no and assertively explain why than to promise that decision in an attempt to please the customer, only to disappoint that customer later. It is important that the senior customer service representative should be assertive enough to shine the light of reality on a situation so that he or she can really come through as promised, and not offer the 'pie in the sky', which, in the long run, does great damage.

UNDERWRITER

In viewing the underwriter's role, most people would ask, 'What on earth does underwriting have to do with sales?' Unfortunately, in selecting underwriters the response of 'nothing' to that question all too often determines who is hired for the position. The reality is, however, that sales should be an important part of the underwriter's role. Of course, the underwriter must have outstanding detail ability, extraordinarily good self-discipline and personal organisation, and financial competence. But, if we only look at these qualities, how would the underwriter be differentiated from the actuary, the statistician or, for that matter, the junior accountant?

The difference is that an underwriter must be assertive and should possess at least some degree of the central sales dynamics. This should be understood by simply recounting the underwriter's role in an agency. The underwriter takes an order produced by the salesperson and works to fill that order by placing it with one or a combination of companies with which the agency is working. As part of the underwriter's role, however, he or she is frequently faced with the need to say to the producer, 'No, that cannot be placed in that way,' or, 'No, this person cannot get a non-smoker's rate,' or 'With this individual's driving record, it would be impossible to place the policy with any of our companies. It has to be placed in assigned risk.'

Thus, very often the producer and the underwriter are in adversarial positions, even though, theoretically, they are both working toward the same end — producing business for the agency.

On the other side of the coin, it really is the underwriter's job to try, when realistically possible, to place business with their companies. It really is not, or should not be, the underwriter's role to find reasons why not to do business. Rather, he or she should be on the producer's side and try to find ways to place the business, even in the face of some difficulties.

From this description it should be evident that the underwriter must be assertive enough to say no to the producer when no is the only realistic answer, and he or she must also be assertive enough to push their companies when that push could mean placing an important piece of business with a potentially important account. Anyone can write the simple policy, but only the really effective agency can write the creative ones, and the underwriter must play a key role in doing so.

Both of these functions also require, in addition to assertiveness, plain and simple sales ability. The underwriter could simply say no to the producer, and begin a pattern of ongoing warfare with that producer. On the other hand, by saying no and successfully persuading the producer, however much the producer may not like it, that no is indeed the only realistic answer, the two can work together more effectively and essentially pull in the same direction, which is critical to agency success. Similarly, though agencies can sometimes use assertive muscle with a company, it is much better if they can persuade the company that it is in their interest to place this unusual business, and that persuasion essentially must be carried through, at least in many instances, by the underwriter.

In short, the underwriter must possess all the obvious qualities — detail ability, thoroughness, personal organisation and financial competence — but also must have the toughness and the assertiveness to negotiate, and the basic sales ability to persuade if that underwriter is to carry through their responsibilities at the highest level. If an underwriter in an agency lacks the sales dynamics, he or she should at least have the courage to involve the agency head or some other appropriate manager if the underwriter is simply not suited for the kind of tough negotiation or push necessary.

CLAIMS

When viewing the claims department of an agency, we can say virtually the same thing as we did for the underwriter, and virtually the same qualities are required. Perhaps the single biggest differences might relate to the degree of empathy needed and to the level of service motivation that is essential. The claim is, after all, the reason why the insurance was purchased in the first place. Every customer is convinced that their highest possible claim is fully justified and that that claim should be met virtually without question. The claims person must deal with that perception, must please the customer and, yet, again given the dual representation of the agency, must also be fair to the company the agency represents. That balance does indeed require outstanding empathy in relating to the customer, and outstanding service motivation so that the claim will be actively processed and fairly met. Still, an underwriter must have enough ego-drive and ego-strength to persuade customers if they are being at all unreasonable and, of course, to persuade the company when persuasion is required. An effective claims person can often mean the difference between a customer being lost or saved by the agency, and perhaps even more important, the difference between a quickly satisfied claim and costly, dragged-out litigation. The claims person, simply put, should not simply be someone who writes up the paperwork on a claim, but should be an effective functionary who handles the claim for the claimant and the company, and hopefully resolves it to everyone's satisfaction. As in underwriting, to accomplish this often means plain and simple selling.

We began by expressing our view that the independent agent and independent agency system present a fine example of capitalism working at its best. The best elements of capitalism — the opportunity for the entrepreneur, the need to compete effectively in order to survive and the need to produce in order to compete effectively — are all present in the independent agency system. We have worked with literally thousands of agents and with national and state organisations of agents, and have found the leadership in the industry indeed represents all of these fine elements. We hope that we have made the point, however, that there are many highly effective organisations competing very successfully for new business and also working very hard to take agents' existing business away from them. Thus, to compete, the agency must be certain that every person in every position we touched on here is effective enough to be the one person with whom the insurance customer has come in contact. As we have said, to the prospect or customer, the agency is that one individual with whom the person has had an experience. If the experience is good, sales can be made and customers kept. If, however, the experience is with an individual inappropriate to his or her job, thus producing a negative situation, the result is both a non-sale, a potential loss to the independent agency system itself and a customer who is ready to be taken away at the first temptation. An agency's people, regardless of how good a story the agency itself has to tell, must indeed be its bottom line advantage.

CHAPTER 23

WHAT IT TAKES TO SUCCEED IN LIFE INSURANCE SALES

The life insurance industry of today can no longer be thought of, in its pure sense, as an industry unto itself. The life insurance industry positions itself correctly as one involved in overall financial and estate planning. With the existing tax laws, it is difficult to think of a proper estate plan that does not in some way integrate life insurance as a key part, if for no other reason than to avoid substantial estate taxes. We know of few, if any, benefit packages offered by industry that do not include life insurance and, of course, accident and health insurance. Increasing numbers of business use life insurance to insure perpetuation and business continuity, and as important cornerstones of their pension and/or profit sharing plans. The life insurance industry has been progressive and creative in developing products such as 'minimum deposit' and 'universal life' to meet the consumer's changing needs and to fit better into its increasing role as part of a broad financial picture. The industry has also moved aggressively towards reducing overall life insurance costs, adjusting these costs to the changing mortality table.

With all this, the life insurance agent of today is, or at least should be, a key player in helping both the consumer and business to develop an integrated financial plan. The life insurance agent is, or, again, should be, an ultimate example of consultative selling.

Yet, with all of the progressive changes made by the industry, and with the objective importance of life insurance as it exists today, there is still an enormous gap, perhaps as wide as it was three decades ago, between what the life insurance agent should be and the perception of what the life insurance agent is.

The gap is perhaps best exemplified in Woody Allen's film, *Sleeper*. After being frozen as a medical experiment, Woody Allen awakens centuries later to a drastically changed world. The curious scientists ask, 'What was it like to be dead for several centuries?' After pausing, he answers, 'It was kind of like spending an evening with an insurance salesman.'

It was, in fact, a life insurance company which in early 1958 asked us to do the research study that eventually led to the development of our psychological test, and to the founding of our company. The insurance company had been suffering a 55 to 60 per cent turnover of agents during their first year, and an 85 to 90 per cent turnover over the first three years. They indicated that, despite all of their efforts, that turnover figure had not changed in more than two decades.

Now, more than three decades later, the industry turnover rate continues to be 55 to 60 per cent in one year and 85 to 90 per cent in three years.

With the enormous progress over the past 30 plus years in technology and the major advances that the industry has made in the quality and diversity of products it offers, how can the absolute failure to reduce turnover be explained?

We can offer three possible explanations. First, the life insurance industry continues to cling to the belief that if a person has the proper connections — markets — and, of course, is given good training and has the desire to succeed, that person can sell life insurance.

Secondly, some companies convey to the applicant their need to sell the applicant, even those possessing the most superficial qualifications, on joining the life insurance company, rather than, as in most industries, having the applicant work to sell themselves to the company.

And, thirdly, many life insurance executives feel, and often state openly, that high turnover in life insurance sales is endemic to the industry and that such turnover must be accepted as an unavoidable cost of doing business.

Let us take a closer look at the three reasons, which, in our view, go far to explain why the insurance industry has such a difficult time reducing turnover and increasing productivity and professionalism.

MARKETS

A simplistic view of what we now call 'markets' is the old notion that if an agent sold his or her grandmother, aunt, or first cousin a policy, and bought a policy him- or herself, that would be reason enough to be hired. Of course, today companies do not admit to this posture, but they still use the term *markets* as a good reason for hiring. If an individual is a member of a golf club or comes from an old, respected and influential family in the town, the assumption is that their contacts can be converted into life insurance sales. If that were so, and given the enormous income potential in the life insurance industry, why have companies simply not been able to hire people with such a market and permanently eliminate the turnover and productivity problem? The answer is, as it is in so many of life's situations, that when the right person is given an opportunity, he or she will cash in on it, while others, theoretically having the same opportunity, will have nothing to show for it. When an individual has the ability to sell, there is certainly an enormous advantage in having those ready markets to whom to sell. Without that sales ability, however, the markets become an unfulfilling tease, and the non-salesperson rapidly begins to be viewed as a pain in the neck, a leech or a cipher, rather than as a respected member of the community that theoretically was his or her market.

We recall the case of a man who had completed 20 years in the military. He retired with a colonel's rank and so was able to live on a fairly adequate retirement pension. This gentleman, whom we will call 'Mr Townsend', was very much part of the 'old boy network'. He was a graduate of the *right* school and college, was a member of all the *right* clubs and was friendly with all the key business and political leaders in the area. He, in fact, had a perfect market. Naturally, he was an excellent target for recruiting by several life insurance companies, one of which hired him.

Mr Townsend was introduced to us by one of our clients, who asked if we could work with him to determine why, despite all his obvious advantages, he was not succeeding in life insurance sales. After testing and interviewing him in depth, we were able to determine that he clearly lacked the dynamics of a salesperson. He was an excellent leader, but was not a persuader. As a colonel in the army, he could tell people what to do, but as a life insurance agent, he had to sell them on what to do and that simply was not him.

Mr Townsend was not selling, and he also was losing friends and influence in the process. People began thinking of him as being interested in them only because he wanted to sell them something, and that is obviously the quickest way to alienate people *en masse*.

When we explored other possibilities with Mr Townsend, the fact that he had bought and sold stocks quite successfully for many years emerged. He had family money to invest and did so most successfully. His personality, moreover, was very much that of an effective money manager. He enjoyed following stocks and loved the trading game, and again, both on paper and in practice, was very good at it. It was decided that he would leave life insurance sales and seek a position as a portfolio manager, which he did, and in which to this day he is very successful. We might add that he has recovered most, though not all of his friends.

It is important to re-emphasise here that markets are certainly of value. Everything else being equal, which it rarely is, we would certainly suggest to all of our life insurance clients that they should hire an effective agent *with* a market rather than one without one. However, we would suggest even more strongly that if the choice is between a non-salesperson with a market, and an individual with tremendous sales talent, but lacking a market, we would urge the hiring of the second individual without any hesitation.

SELLING THE APPLICANT ON THE INDUSTRY

A feeling of inferiority pervades some life insurance companies, leading them to seek individuals who may possess only the most superficial qualifications but who would be willing to work for them. The idea is that if they are too selective, they simply will not have enough people to fill the positions. Given the potential income of successful life insurance agents, this feeling is, to say the least, ludicrous and extremely costly.

Many successful life insurance salespeople become millionaires. Many others earn an exceptionally good income, and that income typically grows over the years. The life insurance agent, even more than most salespeople, is able to run his or her own show, work his or her own hours, and really be an independent businessperson without many of the inventory and other obligations that it normally takes to start and run a business and, again, often with far better rewards than the hardworking businessperson can dream of receiving.

The very fact that a life insurance policy not only produces excellent income at the sale, but continues to produce income for the agent over ten years, or even a lifetime, makes the industry unique. With all of this going for it, why should the life insurance industry have to persuade someone to join them? The opposite should be true. People should be knocking on the doors of life insurance companies trying to break into an élite field of high earners. The reality, however, is that they are not, and the industry is forced continually to look for large numbers of people who might be pursuaded to try to sell life insurance.

The reason goes back to the question of image. The very people who the life insurance industry would like to attract are likely to resist being tarred by the same brush as the old insurance instalment collector. Yes, the income potential may be great in theory, they reason, but, 'How can I imagine "so and so" (a life insurance salesperson they know) making that kind of income?' In other words, the income potential and the image do not go together, and so people resist the industry. Another reason for resistance relates to the very ease with which an individual can become a life insurance agent in some companies. 'If the job is so easy to get, and the life insurance company is so eager to get me, how good could the job possibly be?'

IS HIGH TURNOVER ENDEMIC?

Our research indicates that the high turnover in life insurance sales is not endemic to the industry. In fact, with proper selection, the life insurance industry, given its potential for high income, can substantially reduce its turnover rate and greatly increase its productivity. The costs of the ghastly revolving door are all too well-known, though rarely are they openly quantified. According to an industry report, it costs high productivity companies with high turnover (approximately 83 per cent after three years) £112,000 per retained agent. On the other hand, for high productivity companies with better retention (66 per cent turnover or 34 per cent of the agents retained after three years), the cost is reduced to £53,000 per retained agent. In other words, the cost of that additional 19 per cent turnover is £60,000 per retained agent over a three-year period, and these figures do not include interest costs.

In addition to these measurable costs are the hidden, but all-important, costs of burnt territory and destroyed image that result from the public's exposure to life insurance agents who should not be. The image of the debit life insurance collector coming to the door each week is as negatively vivid to an entire generation as is that of the tyre-kicking, fast-talking used car salesman. Even today, as often as not, life insurance agents choose to call themselves financial consultants or financial planners rather than accepting the label of 'life insurance salespersons'.

What is unfortunate about the image is that life insurance should indeed play a key role in nearly everyone's financial planning, as we said earlier. The life insurance industry provides an enormous service, the proper use of which could make the difference between financial stability and catastrophe to millions of people. As the industry develops increasingly sophisticated products, and as the mortality tables permit lower and lower percentages of the premium to go into the coverage of mortality costs, life insurance products become more and more a part of living and not simply a hedge against dying. Given this fact, and the key role that life insurance must play in estate planning and pensions, why should the life insurance agent not be at least as well respected as the accountant, the lawyer and the professional who manages to be called 'the financial planner'? The answer is that, indeed, the life insurance agent should earn that level of respect, but too many do not deserve it and so do not get it.

To us, there is a great irony here. Of all the industries we have studied, life insurance in theory should have one of the lowest turnover rates. The very structure of compensation within the industry works to avoid turnover. Given the normal contract, the agent makes a percentage of the first-year premium and then receives a renewal each year that the policy remains in force. It is these renewals that build income that often exceeds, after a number of years, the income produced by first sales. When an agent leaves the company, these renewals are generally lost. Thus, unlike most jobs, when you leave, you are giving up not only money you earned through working but also guaranteed income in which you are vested because of your past work. This is a classic golden handcuffs situation, and yet the turnover rate is catastrophic. It is obvious that those golden handcuffs cannot be on very tight if the turnover is that high. It is as simple as the fact that the people hired are so unproductive that the few pounds earned in renewals makes no difference as an incentive to continue. It is the good salespeople who are locked into the golden handcuffs because they produce the sales that produce the high renewals and, of course, it is they who represent 15 per cent who stay on, earn the big money, and become the professional career life insurance agents.

WHAT IS THE SOLUTION?

The cure in each of these three cases is the same. The industry must hire more selectively, and must hire people, not because they have the markets, but because they have the ability to be effective life insurance salespeople. If they hire more selectively, the job will immediately become more desirable. If they hire more effective professionals, the image will slowly turn around, and people will be more willing and even anxious to be identified with the industry. And if they hire more productive people, they will earn the kind of income that will lock them into the industry and automatically reduce the ghastly waste that is the life insurance industry's revolving door.

HOW TO DO IT

Life insurance companies, like all of the sales industry, have to begin by scrapping both the notion of hiring on the basis only of superficial qualifications — the warm body approach — and, even where they want to be more selective, the old, invalid hiring criteria: age, sex, race, experience, education and markets. They have to replace these incorrect approaches to hiring with a selective process based on whether or not an individual possesses the real potential to sell life insurance packages in a consultative way for the specific company, given their specific markets, and given their specific product mix.

THE BASIC DYNAMICS

As in all sales situations, the life insurance agent must start by possessing four key personality attributes if he or she hopes to succeed. They must have the empathy that allows them to read a prospect and to judge what their real needs are that might be met by one or a combination of the products the agent has to offer. Particularly when dealing with life insurance, those needs can involve a multitude of hidden agendas. Fear of death is one of the great obstacles and working around that fear to meet the clients' needs requires great empathy as well as great sensitivity. Getting the right sense of the client's real purpose and real needs, regardless of what is actually said, can, in life insurance sales more than in most, make the difference between the beginning of a long-term relationship with an important customer and total failure. In today's market, a canned approach is virtually out, while the empathic response is the ultimate key.

Yet, again, as in many sales situations, empathy is not enough. Once the agent has picked up the cues and clues, and fully understands the hidden agendas and the prospect's real motives, he or she still must have the persuasive motivation (ego-drive) to use the feedback as a tool for persuasion. Understanding can develop friendships, but ego-drive makes sales. Yet, there could be many situations in which too much ego-drive could be counterproductive. Again you are dealing with very important feelings, fears and needs that the potential customer may not even recognise. Too hard a push at the wrong time or too much of a demand for an immediate decision could succeed in alienation rather than closure. What is needed is the right balance of ego-drive and empathy, depending on the customer and the product mix.

As life insurance products become more and more complex, and as they become more and more integrated into an overall financial plan, consultative skills and service motivation become increasingly critical elements for success in life insurance sales. The need to do a good job, the desire to come through and the strong sense of responsibility, along with the need to be appreciated, which are all involved in service motivation, can make the difference between success and failure. The life insurance salesperson cannot close a sale and leave because he or she is often viewed as the consultant who solves problems, looks at programmes and plays an ongoing, continuing role in the financial life of the customer. This is of enormous value because it provides the salesperson with continual opportunities to cross-sell, to sell increasing amounts of a product or to add other products into the customer's product mix. Yet, the salesperson cannot be an individual who is only talking to the customer with an eye towards another immediate sale. He or she has genuinely to convey to the customer and be assured that the customer most often reads this, that the agent wants to be of service. Successful agents enjoy doing a good job for the customer and being appreciated for the help they provide, as much as they enjoy closing a sale in the first place. That combination, together with empathy, is certainly not the old insurance salesperson image, but provides the kind of consultative image that the successful representative of the life insurance industry must convey today.

As for ego-strength, the fourth of the critical central dynamics, there can be no lack in this area, even with an abundance of the other three qualities. Again, we are dealing with enormous sensitivities and fears relating to death. Thus, regardless of the need for the product and regardless of the ability of the life insurance agent, rejection is going to be a fact of life. There are precious few life insurance agents who can honestly say they close one in two contacts, and we include the insurance superstars in that statement. So, along with the sensitivity and empathy, the drive and the service motivation, the life insurance agent had better be able to take the rejection, deal with it for what it is, and go on to the next presentation with increased motivation to close that sale.

The first thing life insurance companies must do if they are to close the vicious revolving door — the vicious cycle of non-productivity — is to seek people with these central dynamics, again, regardless of their markets or experience. Then companies should look for individuals among those people who have the other qualities necessary to sell their particular products. The possession of those additional qualities can make as much of a difference to success or failure as the possession of the central dynamics themselves.

One of our life insurance company clients provides a good example of the need for these additional qualities. As a training ground, their new agents were assigned the after-5pm business. In that market, the possession of empathy, ego-drive and ego-strength alone could mean success, since in most of these sales situations, the sale is made or not made on the first contact. However, a problem developed in the third year, when the company began to lose large numbers of previously effective people. We found that the key to this loss lay in the change of responsibilities at the end of the second year.

What occurred was that, after two years, the company would take their most successful salespeople — that is, successful in the small product market — and move them into what they termed full career agent status with the responsibility of selling estate planning, pension plans etc from 9am to 5pm.

What was clearly the problem, as confirmed by our research and testing of the people attempting to make the transition, was that though they invariably possessed the empathy, ego-drive and go-strength to sell the small policy buyer and get quick closes, many lacked the other vital attributes required in the consultative sell involved in the larger product, business market. So they soon dropped off.

Our research indicates that, as life insurance products become more complex and integrated with other financial products, the need for consultative selling will increase. Consultative selling involves the selling of solutions, not mere products. The facts are that the old rules of selling no longer spell success in the life insurance industry.

The successful life insurance salesperson will have to be that unique individual who has the technical knowledge to understand the product's possibilities, the conceptual ability to interpret the client's needs, and the drive and wherewithal to seize opportunities. The prototype of a life insurance salesperson, the quick closer of the past who needs instant grafitication, cannot be successful today. What is needed, in addition to the four dynamics discussed, are excellent personal organisational skills and good detail ability, a strong sense of personality responsibility, and a high level of conceptual intelligence and persistence, along with a strong desire to solve the customer's problem and to provide service. Serious deficiencies in any of these qualities can be as disastrous to success in today's life insurance environment as the lack of empathy, ego-drive and ego-strength themselves.

THE JOB MATCHING SOLUTION

We have said in the strongest possible terms that the life insurance industry can reduce turnover, increase per-agent productivity, and sustantially upgrade the industry's image by replacing its current hiring approaches with one involving the hiring of people possessing the personality attributes to sell successfully in the company. In other words, the old haphazard hiring approaches should be replaced by one which we term *job matching*.

We have compared the productivity and turnover of people hired the old way with that of people who have been hired using the job matching approach. As we present these comparisons, keep the industry norm in mind — 55 to 60 per cent turnover in one year and 85 to 90 per cent turnover in three. Also keep in mind the fact that across the industry, and even probably more true of the life insurance industry, 20 per cent of the people sell 80 per cent of what is sold. With this as background, here are the comparisons: of those individuals hired using the job matching approach — their personality effectively matched to the company and to the products being sold — 61 per cent are in the top half of their sales force after 14 months on the job, while, of those hired the old way, only 7 per cent are that successful. Looking at turnover, 28 per cent of the job matched individuals are no longer with their company after 14 months, though many of these remain in the industry but with another company. Of the individuals hired the old way, on the other hand, there is a very typical 57 per cent turnover rate at the end of 14 months, with a vast majority of these leaving the industry because of poor productivity.

It should be clear that it takes a very special human being to succeed selling life insurance in today's market. If the industry continues hiring thousands of people on the basis of its inappropriate criteria, or no criteria, the results will be increasingly negative, given the needs in today's market and with today's products. At the very least, it can safely be said that if the approach to hiring does not change, the problem of the revolving door will continue to be discussed 25 years from now. On the other hand, if the industry is willing to institute objective, sound and proper job matching methods, a major impact on turnover and agent productivity can be achieved.

CHAPTER 24

LOCKING THE PROPERTY REVOLVING DOOR

The turnover rate in the property industry is as high today as it was 30 years ago. Each year, 55 per cent of all property salespeople continue to leave their companies, either to go with other property firms or to leave the industry entirely. Over the course of three years, more than 85 per cent of sales associates are no longer with their original company. This incredibly high turnover rate continues to exist, primarily because of what we have termed the warm body approach to recruitment and selection.

Many owners and managers of estate agencies have been lulled into erroneously believing that a high turnover rate costs them little or nothing. They argue, 'If we contract salespeople, and we do not have to pay them a salary, we have nothing to lose. We simply provide them with a desk and a telephone. So if they sell even one property, we are that much ahead of the game.' Those who believe this myth simply fill spaces with bodies and feel they have recruited successfully if every desk for which space is available is filled by one of these bodies.

There is another fallacy that relates to this fill-all-the-desks-with-warm-bodies concept. It is a fallacy that is perpetuated by the industry and bought by many individuals. It goes something like this: 'Everybody has had the experience of buying homes, and there is a literally limitless supply of people buying and selling homes, land etc. So, if someone is fairly intelligent, and is presentable and interested in a good career, even part-time, they could and should sell property.'

This fallacy is an open invitation to the dabbler and creates an endless drain on the time and effort of an estate agency's principals or managers.

This anyone-can-sell-property myth, which has characterised the industry too long, must be shattered. Managers should recruit selectively. That is, they should choose only those salespeople who possess personality characteristics that match the requirements of the position and who are capable of achieving maximum productivity. The hidden costs of indiscriminate recruiting and selecting are just too high.

COUNTING THE COSTS

To begin assessing the costs, consider the results of our studies of more than 15,000 corporate clients, including nearly 3,000 estate agencies. These studies prove that more than four out of five people attempting to sell in the property industry seriously lack the appropriate personality dynamics to indicate that they would have any chance for real success in the industry. Why does this matter if they do not cost the company anything, anyway?

First, consider advertising. When managers are asked why they advertise, they invariably answer, 'To make the phone ring.' Advertising, by itself, rarely sells a property. Successful advertising creates enough interest to cause prospects to call your company. Then the ball is in the salesperson's court.

So what happens when that precious prospect, produced at great expense, contacts one of the four out of five salespeople who are unsuited for selling property? The odds are that the prospect will not become a buyer. To see the evidence in clear numerical terms, apply the formula below to your company. First, fill in the volume sold by your best producer during the past year. Next, enter the number of salespeople who worked for your company during the same period. Multiply those two figures and subtract the actual volume sold by your company during the past year from the product. The result is the minimum amount of money your company lost because all your prospects did not contact your best producer.

(A) Volume in £ sold by best producer during the past year   ———
(B) Number of salespeople working for company during past year   ———
(C) Multiply (A) × (B)   ———
(D) Volume sold by company during past year   ———
(E) Subtract (D) from (C)   ———

The fact that your top salesperson sells that many properties, and that volume in £, given your economic conditions, competition and so on, means that every salesperson in your company could generate that sales volume. It could be done, because it has been done. Consider the possibility that your less capable salespeople are driving away the prospects who contact them, thereby losing business that could be converted into profit by true professionals. The telephones and desks you provide the 'no cost' salespeople are actually costing you a great deal.

In addition to this cost, assess the cost or profitability, of each salesperson by examining his or her conversion ratio. That is, compare the number of calls to which a salesperson responds with the number of sales he or she closes. A good conversion ratio means hard money for the estate agency.

In fact, the cost of unproductive salespeople may be even greater than these numbers indicate. Your salespeople convey an overall impression of your company to prospective buyers and sellers. To the average consumer, your company is the salesperson with whom he or she has contact. If the experience with the salesperson is good, a sale is more likely and your company will probably also gain referrals and the intangible benefit of a good reputation. However, an unpleasant experience can create a negative ripple effect that extends far beyond one lost sale and can adversely affect your company and the entire industry.

Ultimately, what is sold in the property industry is professionalism. If consumers fail to encounter true property professionals, it is easy for them to say to themselves, 'I'd rather buy or sell a house myself than deal with someone like that.'

If you agree that every salesperson should represent your company in the most professional way possible, and should have the potential to achieve a high conversion ratio, it stands to reason that you should stop believing that people 'cost you nothing'. If your company and the property industry are to move forward as you would like, the notion of the no-cost associate must be scrapped. We have told many property groups that, in our view, the lack of salary perhaps creates one of the great disservices to the industry, because it makes the hiring decision so easy and, again, the costs are so great. What we suggest is replacing this haphazard filling of desks by these costly 'free' warm bodies with real selectivity. Bear in mind that the property salesperson is selling the largest item that virtually anyone ever purchases on the residential side and, on the commercial side, is often dealing with high-powered people who must respect the salesperson; otherwise it is unlikely they will ever do business with that person or that company again. Thus, in this industry more than in many, careful selection of the people capable of doing the job is key, and must be instituted if the profession is to reach the level of respect its importance deserves.

HOW TO DO IT

As we have suggested for all sales jobs across the industry, the key to selecting productive people in the property industry involves matching the personality strengths and weaknesses of an individual to the functional requirements of the specific property job. In this chapter we cannot possibly deal with all the permutations and combinations involved in selling property. To match an individual to a job you must look at the size of the property firm, its geographic location, its management structure, the level of property sold — flats, country properties and so on — whether it has both a commercial and residential branch, and much more. With these enormous variations in mind, however, what we can do here is look at the three major categories of property sales: advertisement, residential and commercial sales. If we understand that within these categories the variations are enormous, an overview, at least, could prove helpful to understanding how job matching can bring more effective people into the industry. There is not doubt that if firms hire or contract with an individual who is suited to residential sales (if that is the position) or is suited to advertisement sales and so forth, a huge step forward can be taken. Let us look at these broad categories, in the hope that this can be a start and the refinements can follow.

Securing property

The very nature of the work involved in securing property clearly defines the personality attributes required to do the job. The securer is the closest thing in the property business to the pure salesperson. The job involves the persuasion of a seller, not only to convince the seller to allow a firm to sell their property with the intended 2 or 3 per cent commission (a loss of profit to the seller), but also to allow the salesperson's firm to have an exclusive on the property for a specified period of time. Thus, not only does the securer have to convince the seller that it is worth paying 2 or 3 per cent, but also to persuade the seller that his or her firm is the best one to do the job of selling the property at the best possible price and in the most prompt manner possible.

What is clearly indicated by the nature of this task is that the listing salesperson must have a good deal of ego-drive — the inner motivation to persuade and convince as a key means of gaining personal gratification — if she or he is to have any hope of securing their share of listings. Such salespersons are very likely to have one opportunity to close the prospect, and if they do not succeed, the likelihood of eventually making the sale reduces substantially. Yet, as much as they need the strong drive to close, they must also have good empathy to temper that drive. If they do not have the ability to sense the reactions of the prospect, and so to deal with those reactions sensitively, they are likely, if they have ego-drive, to barge ahead and be thought of by the prospect as some kind of a pushy bulldozer with whom the seller would not think of doing business. Such bulldozers, though they might secure an occasional sale, are not likely to secure the majority of them and may burn permanent territory for their firm by offending the prospect.

Thus, what is needed in property securing is an individual who can sense the reactions of other people and use the feedback he or she receives as a tool with which their ego-drive — their persuasive ability — can be used most effectively. Such individuals must also have sufficient ego-strength — a good sense of self — to deal calmly with the inevitable rejections. They must not personalise those rejections and, even when rejected, must be stable enough to leave the prospect with a good feeling, with enough openness that they may become a prospect again at some later time.

Finally, the securer has to be assertive enough, all of the sensitivity issues notwithstanding, to ask for the order, and where appropriate, he or she has to be persistent enough and personally well-organised enough to follow up. Though they may be in the minority, there are situations where a second or third call could be appropriate. Sometimes, with proper follow-up, a property securer could notice the same ad for a private sale three months later and use that opportunity again to contact the prospect who has not as yet sold their property, to see if they might now be more open to talk to them. Again, this requires sensitivity, but it also requires sufficient tenacity and personal organisation to enable the salesperson to be aware of that ad.

Residential sales

The residential salesperson, by contrast, does not require the same level of ego-drive as does the property securer. In fact, there is some evidence that too much ego-drive — an overly strong need for the immediate close — could constitute a negative in many residential sales situations. People normally cannot be sold a house in any manner even resembling hard sell. The process is really that of presenting the property to the prospect, although it should quickly be added that salesmanship still plays a vital role in achieving the end result.

Given the fact that selling plays a role, there definitely is a need for ego-drive on the part of the successful residential salesperson, but this ego-drive should ideally be moderately strong, not of the intense variety needed by the property securer. The residential salesperson should enjoy the close, but should also be motivated in other important ways as well, particularly towards providing service.

What the residential salesperson must possess is an exceptionally high level of empathy. Buying a property, whether it is a piece of land or a house, is an enormously important and emotionally charged process for buyers. They are most often making the largest single purchase that they have ever made and, beyond the money, are ordinarily making an enormous commitment to that purchase. They are not only buying a home, they are also buying an area, a town, a school system, a transportation system, local council tax rates and much more. Thus, empathy on the part of the residential salesperson is critical if he or she is to read the needs and requirements of the prospect and present the products that really meet those needs. We have had enough experiences as property consumers to attest to the fact that all too often people are shown properties that are totally irrelevant to their real needs, and often even opposite to their expressed requirements. What has happened to us, and to many people we know, is that property salespeople trot out their inventory, trying to push properties that they happen to have exclusives on, instead of focusing on the prospect's requirements. This not only fails to sell a property, but often so offends the prospect, and literally tires them out, that even when they are shown a more appropriate property, they tend to resist it and probably will not buy. Thus, residential salespeople as has been said, must have outstanding empathy along with at least moderate drive, but they must also have extremely strong service motivation. At least as much as they may want to close, they must be motivated to receive the 'Thank you' 'You did a good job' or 'I appreciate that'. In other words, to go along with their need to sell, they must, if they are to be successful, have an extremely strong need to please the prospect.

Regardless of the selection offered, however, the prospect is still not necessarily going to buy the first or second property presented to them. Thus, the salesperson must have extraordinary patience, persistence and the ability not only to stay with a prospect but also to show them properties in a systematic, organised, efficient manner designed to maximise his or her time and to respect the time of the prospect. Again, we have seen property salespeople make prospects wait around for a key, criss-cross town inefficiently, spending more time in the car than viewing properties, and in general waste an inordinate quantity of time. Such inefficiency can be just as destructive to the sale as all of the other areas we have just discussed.

Another critical personality quality that many residential salespeople should have is conceptual ability. This does not mean that the salesperson has to be an architect or an interior designer, but they should have sufficient creative and conceptual skill to be able to talk with the prospect in these areas, and help them visualise the potential of the property. Along the same lines, though they need not be local experts, they must have sufficient detail ability and, of course, knowledge to deal with local questions, since these issues frequently occur.

Finally the salesperson probably does not need the same level of ego-strength as does the property securer who is exposed to frequent rejections because he or she is trying to make a quick sale. The residential salesperson with the empathy and other abilities we just discussed is really providing a service requested by the buyer. The prospect wants to find a house or a piece of land, and so the salesperson is perceived by that prospect as providing an important service. Even when the prospect does not buy the particular property shown to them, it is the property that is not exactly right as opposed to the salesperson being rejected. Thus, though obviously residential salespeople must have some ego-strength — they cannot be totally down on themselves — they can probably get away with a little less ego-strength than can the ad seller who is exposed to constant rejection.

Commercial sales

In this era of computers, industry is constantly consulting statistics to guide the development of management policy. One of the most important, yet rarely used, statistics is what we referred to earlier as the conversion ratio. This is the percentage of contacted prospects that are converted to customers. This conversion ratio is critical at all times, in that the company has invested enormous time, money and effort to develop prospects. Lost prospects represent wasted time, money and effort, and, of even greater importance, business permanently lost to the company. In these highly competitive times, the conversion ratio is even more critical.

In commercial as well as residential property, advertising rarely sells the product. Successful advertising creates prospects. However, it is the salesperson representing the company and dealing directly with the created prospect that creates the sale. It is critical, then, that the individual responsible for converting prospects possesses the ability to do just that. For a start, the commercial property salesperson must possess the three personality qualities essential to sales success: empathy; ego-drive; and ego-strength. Yet, in commercial property sales, more than in many other fields, other qualities can be as important to success as the possession of these central dynamics. Perhaps the primary one among these is detail ability.

If an individual possesses the three critical dynamics, but is unable to cope with detail, success in commercial property is unlikely. The commercial salesperson must be able to cope with detail and use data as an integral part of the sales presentation. Details, ranging from the simple, 'How much per square foot?' to the complexities of write-offs on partitions in an open space environment, are part and parcel of the commercial property sale. If the salesperson's ability to utilise detail is anything but top-notch, all the sales ability in the world is not likely to result in a sale.

On the other hand, many commercial salespeople rely totally on the shuffling of data but forget, largely because of their lack of ego-drive, that the data still has to be presented persuasively in order to demonstrate its benefits to the potential customer. Thus, just as the person with good sales dynamics but little detail ability cannot succeed in commercial property, neither can the detail-oriented individual succeed without the basic dynamics of empathy, ego-drive and ego-strength. Unfortunately, too many commercial property salespeople rely purely on details, and thus perform poorly. Being enmeshed in detail, and so focusing on detail for its own sake, can be as negative to the sale as total lack of detail ability. When detail ability is integrated with the basic sales dynamics, the details involved in the situation can be used as a tool to help make the sale; it is through that integration that commercial property can be sold.

The commercial property salesperson must be shrewd in order to judge or have insight into a situation. He or she must be a tough negotiator, be personally well-organised, be assertive in interpersonal relationships, have good conceptual ability and be able to think on his or her feet. The individual must be persistent, patient, thorough and a good communicator. Also, in comparison to many listing or residential situations, commercial sales are unique in that the commercial salesperson must be comfortable dealing with people on the highest levels. This is a characteristic lacking in many people, including many salespeople. Some people may have strong sales dynamics but can be in awe of people in positions of power. We have seen many individuals who have empathy and ego-drive totally freeze when confronting the managing director of a company or a public official in high office. They no longer see the person; they are swept away by the aura of the position. This power block cannot exist in effective commercial salespeople. They must deal with the chairman of the board of a large corporation as comfortably as with an office manager, and that comfort must be real and not feigned. People read discomfort very accurately and do not respect it. Typically, buyers in positions of power will not want to do business with someone who stands in awe of them, but they will want to do business with a peer in a relationship of mutual respect. Thus, that ability to be a peer, regardless of the position of the individual, is critical.

Of course, many of these qualities are helpful and even necessary in many sales situations, but all of them are really essential if an individual hopes to sell commercial property successfully and particularly if the individual hopes to sell at a high level.

FINDING QUALIFIED PEOPLE

The question could be asked, 'Where might these highly qualified people be found?' Do these paragons, capable of selling advertisements, making residential sales, or selling commercial property, or, even more problematic, a combination of these, really exist?

The answer is that people with the ability to do the job exist in some abundance. The problem is that property firms do not look for these people in the right places. Typically, estate agents will try to pirate a competitor's salesperson or manager. Rarely do they ask themselves why these people wish to change companies. If they were really successful with a competitor, why would they be willing to change jobs? The answer might be that they were not really that successful. They may have blamed lack of success on everything but their own ability and be joining you to find some elusive pot of gold at the end of a non-existent rainbow. The result of pirating in this industry, as in many others, is the recirculation of mediocrity.

As we said earlier, many property firms use the warm body approach, literally hiring or contracting with anyone. Others, particularly many of the commercial estate agency firms, continue to use the old criteria, particularly age and experience, which all of our studies have proven have no validity as predictors of success.

The reality is that, while only some 20 per cent of people now selling in the property industry have the ability to sell, one out of four individuals walking or driving by your office also possess that ability, regardless of what they are currently doing. A good percentage of them possess the ability to sell property, whether advertisements, residential property or commercial sales. What this provides is a virtually limitless source of talent, if the old preconceptions can be scrapped. There is no question that, if an individual possesses the dynamics suiting her or him to the appropriate sales job and, of course, is given appropriate training and supervision, he or she will succeed.

The answer, then, to recruiting and selecting effective people for the property industry, people who will provide the professionalism that the industry needs and deserves, is to open up the recruiting efforts to the broadest possible population. Select carefully from that broad population those one in four who have the ability to sell, and select from among those the individuals who have the ability to sell a particular property product for a specific property firm. If training and effective supervision are provided to those appropriate individuals, the property revolving door will indeed begin to be locked and your advertising budget will begin to pay off far better because of the increasingly higher conversion ratio produced by an increasingly higher level of professionals.

CHAPTER 25

CAR SALES: THEN AND NOW

While it was a life insurance company that asked us to do the research that led to the founding of Caliper in 1961, it was the car industry that provided us with the first opportunity to put our theories into actual practice. A large manufacturer contracted for a study utilising 30 of its dealerships across the country. The results of that study were published in the *Journal of Psychology*, July/August 1964 issue, and were written about less formally in other publications such as *Automotive News* and *Sales and Marketing Magazine*.

It was, in fact, the work we did with those 30 dealerships and the referrals stemming from that work that effectively launched our company. This work also convinced us, if we still had any lingering doubts, that sales success could be accurately predicted using the test we developed and utilising the job matching process as a replacement for the old, haphazard hiring criteria that industry typically used. Parenthetically, all too often these same haphazard, invalid criteria continue to be used today.

Since the publication of this initial study, we have worked with literally thousands of car dealerships and this work, together with projects with a number of manufacturers, has, we hope, allowed us both to know the industry well and to chart its evolution, at least from a sales and management personnel perspective, over three decades.

From the perspective of what it takes to succeed in sales, the car industry, second only perhaps to banking, has changed most markedly. Any discussion of what it *really* takes to succeed in car sales today would read very differently from the same discussion in 1961.

This difference can be summarised rather simply, though the implications of this difference are enormous. When we wrote about the car industry in the early 1960s, we were able to discuss sales success in the car industry quite accurately, primarily in terms of an individual possessing empathy and ego-drive. If an individual was able to get good feedback from a prospect, was able to really sense their needs and reactions (empathy) and was motivated to use that feedback as a persuasive tool (ego-drive), by and large, that individual would succeed in car sales. Even then there were some regional and product differences and some differences related to the dealer's system, but fundamentally the possession of these two qualities made for success, and the lack of the same allowed a confident prediction of sales failure.

Today, a discussion of what it takes to succeed in car sales would centre more on consultative sales than the very comfortable, simplistic realities of the early 1960s.

The reason for this evolution, or perhaps revolution might even be the better term, relates largely to the enormous change of attitude of the buying public. Through the 1960s and into the early 1970s the public's love affair with the car flourished. Perhaps the deprivations of the Second World War, when new cars were totally unavailable, still lingered in the hearts of the car consumer. Perhaps the car was the one symbol of success, of freedom, of status that could be grasped by many people with modest means. We could speculate forever as to the cause, but, for whatever reason, the car was indeed the passion and the pride of millions of people.

The result of this love affair provided the car industry with the happy situation of prospects entering a dealership really wanting to buy a car. The sale still had to be made, as evidenced by the gross failure of salespeople lacking empathy and ego-drive, but the sale was made easier by the fact that the prospect wanted to be a customer if he or she could be properly sold. Also, the issues involved in the sale were frequently as simple as the appearance and/or power of the car and its affordability. What also made it easier for the industry and, of course, for the salesperson, was the two-year mentality. A customer today could very easily become a customer again, two or three years from today, when they are ready to trade the car for the new, beautiful styles of 1967, or again the new model just brought out in 1969. Newness and disposability made for a nearly endless supply of customers and, again, the desire to buy made for relatively easy sales, at least for a good salesperson.

Some car experts began talking about changes in the late 1960s and early 1970s, and spoke long and loud about the need for the industry to change some of its thinking to get ready for these changes. Their voices, by and large, were cries in the wilderness, and it was not until the trauma of the Arab oil embargo that the reality of the need for change was brought home to the industry and to the buying public. That change totally altered, probably for ever, the nature of what it would take to succeed in car sales.

THE OIL CRISIS

So much has been written about the impact of the Arab oil embargo of 1974 that a great deal need not be reiterated here. Suffice it to say that for the first time in the post-war world, people had to begin thinking about the practicalities of driving. Whether dealing with petrol queues or the rapidly accelerating price of petrol, the car-buying public had to view their vehicles in a very different way. Suddenly mpg became more meaningful than chrome, and efficiency, rather than power became the key selling point. Add to all of this the increasing complexity of car technology, including on-board computers and other components, previously thought of only for aeroplanes, and certainly not for cars, and you end up with a product that is sold or not sold based on a multiplicity of often complex issues.

The sales situation was made still more difficult by the rapid attitudinal change away from the notion of a new car every two years. People became very interested in how many Volvos were still on the road with a million miles on the clock, or how many ten-year-old plus Volkswagens were still running around. This interest in durability with a concomitant sales value, in long warranties and 24-hour road service has been accelerating as the price of the car has increased exponentially.

The major impact of these factors also relates very much to the question of what it takes to succeed in sales in this industry. Many dealers, primarily marginally successful dealers or very small dealers, have either gone out of business or have been acquired by or merged with bigger, more successful operations. The megadealer, the chain and the multiple brand showroom increasingly are becoming the name of the car retail game, and the small dealership, unless run with great skill, will have a great deal of trouble surviving.

CAR SALES IN THE 1990s AND BEYOND

What, then, does it take to succeed in car sales today, and how has the industry responded to the changed requirements?

As we said earlier, the profile of what it takes to succeed in car sales today much more closely resembles the profile of the consultative salesperson than it does that of the successful car salesperson of the 1960s. More than ever, the car salesperson is selling the consumer the second largest ticket item he or she will ever buy. What is being sold is not only transportation, but also status, and what is included is economy, financing, high degrees of technology, warranties, lease programmes and so much more that we will not bore the reader with listing them all here. The car salesperson has to be competent to deal with all of these components and to provide the kind of consultative sale that meets the customer's needs through a balanced integration of components focused on their specific needs. Of course, empathy and ego-drive are still essential because, as in any other kind of sale, the word *sale* is still the essence, and without empathy and ego-drive, few people can succeed in any kind of sale. Today, however, ego-strength becomes a far more important component, because, with all the complexities and the enormous multiplicity of alternative product options, the potential for rejection is greater than ever. Just as the salesperson has to use empathy to understand the customer's needs, and to try to meet those needs with one or another of the products that he or she is offering, salespeople must also have the ego-strength to understand that, despite all of their best efforts, the customer could say no. If that no is too devastating to the salesperson's sense of wellbeing, he or she is simply not going to be ready for the next customer who, if approached properly, would be ready to say yes.

Where the car salesperson used to be typical of the hard-driving, detail-hating salesperson, today he or she must have at least a decent tolerance of detail to succeed. Of course, no one can be everything, and so, more often than not, an individual with enough ego-drive to close effectively does not really like handling detail. Yet, like it or not, the car salesperson, particularly as you go upscale, had better be able to handle detail with effectiveness. These salespersons must, at least, be able to deal with warranty issues, put together a lease package and discuss details of the technology of the car. Of course, they can bring in help when issues get beyond their capability, but they had better be able to go to a certain point with the customer, if they are not to lose credibility with that increasingly sophisticated customer.

Similarly, while so many sales could earlier be generated by in-showroom traffic — people wanting to have the experience of buying a new car — so much today must be generated, as in so many other industries, through customer follow-up, referrals and the process of literally going out prospecting. Obviously, the less automatically the prospect is created, the more the salesperson must generate that prospect. This, of course, varies enormously from region to region and even from big city to rural area. But the overall reality that prospect generation is a much more important component of car sales than it ever was cannot be denied. In order to generate these prospects, the salesperson cannot simply stay in the showroom waiting for the inevitable flow of traffic, but must be a sufficiently good self-starter to go after the prospects, and sufficiently well-organised to keep records, follow up on customers, and ask for and follow up referrals, if real success is to be achieved. Again, while this is far more important in rural areas where traffic density is less, it is becoming increasingly important even in the urban areas, where traffic flow can be expected to be better. The sheer complexity of what is being sold also often necessitates a team approach to sales. Even if the salesperson possesses enough detail ability, self-starting ability and personal organisation to do the bulk of the work, there are still going to be many situations in which other people will have to be brought in to put a particular deal together. Being able to work with a team to bring in resources and to gather information when necessary is probably as critical to today's car sale as anything we have discussed. Nobody can be everything and know everything, and so long as the salesperson can bring matters to a certain point and not look incompetent to the buyer, bringing in expert help, for example, in constructing a lease, looks good to customers because they know they are dealing with an organisation and not simply a salesperson. This component of being a good team player is often lacking in the typical hard-driving salesperson, and certainly was lacking in many of the star car salespeople of the 1960s.

Communication skills are another important area of difference. Obviously, to sell anything, some ability to communicate is necessary. But today in car sales, it is not enough just to know the technology and financing and have a desire to sell them. Rather, it is critical to be able to communicate this knowledge intelligently, but in a way that is comprehensible to the prospect. The best way to offend and drive away customers is to make them feel inept or incompetent by talking over their heads.

Communication is also critical in another respect. As prospects have to be generated, it becomes more and more important for the car salesperson, like the insurance agent, property person and banker, to become an integral part of their community. Being in the Rotary Club or local chamber of commerce and taking other leadership roles in the community becomes very important. To achieve this in a positive way, communicative skills and, for that matter, some leadership ability must play an important part.

We can add to this recipe such obvious elements as intelligence, flexibility, shrewdness and the ability to think on one's feet, and we are still only beginning to describe the kind of person who will be truly successful in today's complex car market.

DIFFERENCES WITHIN THE MARKET

After having said this, it is still important to emphasise that enormous differences still exist within the industry in terms of who will or will not be successful in a given situation. Since no one can be everything, matching the right person to the job still becomes a key to predicting whether or not an individual will succeed in a particular dealership. There is still no doubt that an individual in a large urban dealership who possesses empathy, ego-drive and ego-strength can probably get by with somewhat less of the other elements than he or she could if in a relatively small dealership in a rural area where virtually no in-house traffic could be counted upon. The need to be a participant in the community is obviously more critical in a small to medium-sized town than it is in a large city where such participation would hardly be noticed. The need to be fully skilled in all of the complex areas of the car sale is far more critical in the small dealership than it would be in the larger dealership blessed with lease specialists and the like. The need for fine intellect, sophistication and outstanding presentation skills is still probably greater when selling high price cars than when selling at lower price levels and, similarly, the need for referrals and the ability to obtain them are probably greater at these higher levels as well. We will not take the time here, nor could we, to fully break down the subtle differences in what it takes to succeed in selling Vauxhalls or Rolls-Royces, Volkswagens or Mercedes, Ladas or Porsches. We hope a few of these more general comments convey the concept, but, as you look at individual salespeople and how they fit into a specific dealership, you must also look at product, region, dealership size, sales system, organisational structure and more to determine how that individual salesperson might fit into that dealership and to which level of success he or she might aspire in that context.

Before leaving this issue, one other element should be touched on again as a dealer and a prospective salesperson attempt to make a decision as to whether or not they are well matched. That is the sales system employed by the dealership. There are, of course, many such systems and variations within each of these, but suffice it to say here that there is a critical difference between a system that fundamentally expects the salesperson to carry through a deal from beginning to end, including all of the paperwork, and other systems in which the salesperson brings the sale to a certain point and then automatically involves other people, typically an assistant sales manager or a sales manager. There are also important differences between systems where each salesperson takes his or her turn as prospects come in the door and other more *laissez-faire* systems where every customer is up for grabs. Similarly, the dealership must make up its mind as to what percentage of time an individual is in the showroom or is expected to be outside, prospecting. All these elements obviously relate to the personality required for success. If, for example, a salesperson is not really expected to close, but is expected to bring a prospect to a certain point after which the sales manager really closes the sale, one could give up some ego-drive in assessing the potential effectiveness of that salesperson, but would probably not compromise on empathy, presentation skills and even assertiveness. Similarly, that sales manager should have a great deal of ego-drive, in addition to other attributes. Also, if there is a regulated system, super-aggressiveness might not be necessary, because the salesperson has his or her turn with the customer, but in a *laissez-faire* situation, survival could depend on that very aggressiveness. In a final example, where the system primarily calls for showroom activity, one could probably compromise in the area of self-starting or personal organisation, but, again, this is becoming less and less realistic. On the other hand, where prospecting is key, no compromise can be made in these areas.

SERVICE AND PARTS

Before discussing how the industry has dealt with the increasingly complex nature of the car salesperson, let us look at two frequently neglected areas involving sales productivity: service and parts.

Service

When customers bring their cars in for service, unless it is purely routine maintenance service, it is tantamount to going to the dentist. You know you need to go to the dentist, but you certainly do not do it because you want to. Similarly, your car needs service, and so you go for that service but it is really the last thing you want to do. Who in their right mind enjoys paying money simply to keep their car going properly? What makes it worse, not only are you paying money, but your car is unavailable for a period of time, and, of course, you have to invest your own time, money and effort to get it to and from the dealership. So, when a customer meets the service administrator, there is an immediate built-in hostility. At least when the customer pays money for a new car, he or she is deriving a desired benefit. But service is a troublesome annoyance, a painful necessity in the mind of the customer. The question then is how does the service administrator deal with that problematic relationship? Certainly, they can, as they often do, simply say, 'What is wrong with your car?', write down what the customer says, and give a completion date. What this does, of course, is leaves the relationship on this disgruntled level and results in, at most, selling the customer only what the customer thinks he or she needs. How much better it would be if the service administrator, or what we hope is the service salesperson, probed a problem with a customer. How much better for the overall relationship betwen dealership and customer it would be if the service salesperson asked how long the problem had existed, asked questions about other functions that might be related to the problem, explored with the customer whether somehow the problem might be placed under warranty, and generally looked at problem solving rather than at simply writing up the order. Most sophisticated dealers will state emphatically that this kind of approach by a service salesperson can not only turn an adversarial relationship into a positive one, but can also frequently result in increased sales by the service department.

What we are suggesting is that a service salesperson should have all of the dynamics necessary to function in a good service role, but must also be sufficiently sales oriented to view each service contact as a potential sales opportunity. If that service salesperson possesses the right dynamics, he or she might even contact every new buyer after a certain period of time to make certain that the car is running well, to remind them of their 1,000-mile service and, perhaps near the end of a year, remind them that their time in which they might buy the extended five-year warranty has nearly expired. These are all sales, whether the word service is attached to them or not, and so sales dynamics should be part of the service salesperson's makeup. Obviously the single most important dynamic that a service salesperson must possess is empathy. Only with empathy can a service person understand why customers might be angry, what their needs are and how to meet those needs sufficiently to alleviate any anger. On the other hand, you probably would not want a service salesperson with overly intense ego-drive. Yes, they must have enough persuasive motivation to look for sales opportunities and for that matter to close. But service motivation must still be the more dominant force within their dynamics. They must want to make a sale, but even more importantly they must want to please the customer. As a key means of gaining personal gratification, they must need to hear, 'Thank you', 'You did a good job', or 'I appreciate that'.

Along with these qualities, the service salesperson must be reasonably assertive, which is the dynamic most often lacking in service administrators we have evaluated in hundreds of dealerships. The customer is going to demand same-day delivery or insist that a particular job is covered under warranty even though it expired three years ago. In such cases, the service salesperson must be sufficiently assertive kindly and sensitively, but still firmly, to say no. As in any other service situation, the unkept promise is the worst negative, and so the ability to say no with reason, empathy and ego-drive, is critical. The service salesperson further has to have all the other attributes of the service person — good sense of responsibility, excellent detail ability, and sufficient co-ordinative and follow-up skills — to process a service order and see to it that the service department does their job in doing quality work in a timely manner. In other words, the service salesperson must deliver as promised. What successful dealers realise is that after the sale is made the dealership is not the salesperson, and is rarely if ever the dealer him- or herself, but rather is almost entirely the service administrator and/or service manager. The quality of the relationship between the service salesperson and the customer more often than not can make the difference between the potential for repeat or expanded business, and the permanent loss of that customer, not only to the service department, but as a buyer for any future new cars. The service station is always an alternative once the warranty expires, and if the car dealership is to maximise its bottom line, that alternative should not be made too tempting by a service administrator whose job is simply to write up the order.

Parts

The parts situation is not nearly as complex but still should involve some sales ability, which it most often does not. Certainly there is an order taking and inventory aspect to the parts counter job. But, when a customer is at the counter, a sales opportunity is presented. Failure to take advantage of that opportunity is not going to have the negative impact that service failure will have, because the customer is not likely to perceive that he or she has not been sold something even if that something would have been valuable to them. If the parts counter person is polite, competent and provides the product, the dealership is not hurt, although we should add that many parts counter people do not even possess these very simple attributes. The point, however, is that many opportunities do exist in the parts department that are not taken advantage of, but that could in a simple, most cost-effective way, add considerably to the dealership's bottom line. Many a part has been bought in a motorists centre or in a service station that could have and should have been purchased from the dealership if someone had bothered selling that part. In today's competitive world, it is simply too good an opportunity to be lost through mislabelling a potentially valuable function.

HAS THE INDUSTRY ADJUSTED?

We have talked about the enormous changes that have taken place in the industry, and how they have impacted on the issue of what it takes to succeed in sales within the retail car industry. While, though belatedly, and perhaps even today too slowly, the industry has reacted to the new product requirements, it has largely failed to react to the implications of these requirements to people.

With some dramatic exceptions, dealerships today are still examples *par excellence* of the warm body approach to hiring. They pay minimal starting wages and will hire most people who are 'willing to work hard', 'willing to put in the hours', and 'who like cars'. Many customers still hold a built-in fundamental contempt for the individual who is charged with the responsibility of selling that very high-priced, very complex, automotive product. In a perfect example of this, a large manufacturer asked us to do a study for them of a number of their dealerships to develop a salary-based compensation plan. This study was designed to determine whether dealers would be receptive to paying salespeople salaries if they could be provided with carefully selected, potentially productive people.

The proposed salary plan involved a base of £9,000 to £11,000 per year with incentives, and the reaction from most dealers, even with many built-in factory supports, was negative. Is it any wonder then that with literally little or no selection and offering salaries beneath any adult's ability to survive, even with all of today's requirements for sales success, the people entering the industry continue to be way below par, and the turnover rate continues to be at a staggering 60 per cent per year?

What is amazing to us is that virtually any dealer we speak to in a seminar or one on one articulates his or her belief that hiring top professional, productive salespeople and retaining those people is essential to their success and, yet, those same dealers continue to insist upon the minimal salary, open-door hiring process.

What is critical is that dealers take a hard look at the industry, their dealership and their products as they are constituted today, and adjust to the fact that they need consultative professional salespeople, and that these people are not likely to be found by offering £700 (or even £900) monthly starting salaries, even with the use of a car. People meeting today's needs in the car industry do exist and can be found through proper recruitment, selection and, of course, reward. But they need to be sought out and in doing so many old attitudes need to be changed as radically as the products themselves have been. The dealers who do this will not only survive but will thrive. The others will be gobbled up or go out of business, perhaps to the long-run benefit of the industry and the buying public.

CAN BETTER SELECTION REALLY WORK?

Earlier in this chapter, we mentioned our initial study of the car industry which was published in the *Journal of Psychology* in 1964. That study proved that even through simply measuring empathy, ego-drive, ego-strength and a few other qualities, car sales success could be predicted. Ten years later, we completed a far more ambitious study, the results of which were published in the October 1974 issue of *Automotive Executive*. This study, which has since been repeated several times, compared the performance of individuals whose particular personality dynamics matched the specific sales job against those individuals hired for other reasons, but whose dynamics did not match the job.

For the purposes of this study, we selected 100 dealer clients. These dealerships represented approximately 5 per cent of the more than 2,000 dealers with whom we have worked and are a cross-section of the industry in terms of franchise, size and geographical area.

Questionnaires were sent to each dealer which provided a complete list of all individuals evaluated over the past two years, and which requested performance information regarding each individual actually hired. We asked that the individual performance figures be expressed in terms of quarterly standing in the sales force so as to reduce the problem of individual dealer difference, ie reward plans, dealer volume and market potential. In addition to the performance data requested for each individual after 6 and 14 months on the job, the employer also was asked to provide information about those dismissed, including: (1) when dismissed; (2) productivity while on the job; and (3) reason for dismissal. The employer was finally asked to give us any information regarding any special situations pertaining to the individual that could affect his or her performance or our analysis.

Performance forms on 4,217 persons were received. Of these, 994 were recommended for hire by our evaluations, while 3,223 were not recommended. Of the recommended, 500 were actually hired, while 512 not recommended were hired. From these figures it can be seen that just over half the recommendables were hired, while less than one-sixth of those not recommended were employed.

After the performance data were gathered and tabulated, they were divided and redivided in order to establish comparative performance figures. The group was first compared in terms of their recommendability versus non-recommendability after 6 and 14 months on the job. The dropout figures were also compared both quantitatively — actual number and percentage of those dropping out by 6 and 14 months — and qualitatively — evaluating the reasons for dropping out. The groups were then divided by sex, age, race, experience and education to determine if any of these factors were related to on-the-job performance, and whether these factors affected the personality makeup of the group.

Predicting sales performance

Table 25.1 presents the comparative performance figures for recommended and not-recommended groups after 6 and 14 months on the job. It can be seen from this figure that there are substantial differences even at the 6-month level, and these differences become even greater after 14 months. Sixty-four per cent of those who were recommended are performing in the top half of their sales force after 6 months, while only 17 per cent of the non-recommended are performing similarly. On the negative side, 9 per cent of the recommendables dropped out within 6 months of their employment, while 30 per cent of the not recommended were either fired or left. In total, 83 per cent of those individuals hired in spite of their non-recommendation were either no longer on the job or in the bottom half of the sales force, while only 36 per cent of those who were recommended fall into these categories.

Table 25.1 Figure and performance of car salesmen (1973)

Caliper Recommendations		Quarter of Sales Force				
Sales Personnel	*Total Number*	*1st*	*2nd*	*3rd*	*4th*	*Quit or Fired*
Performance after 6 months	Recommended N.500	21% 103	43% 217	16% 82	11% 54	9% 44
	Not recommended N.512	6% 30	11% 58	21% 109	32% 160	30% 155
Performance after 14 months	Recommended N.500	33% 166	40% 198	8% 41	3% 16	16% 79
	Not recommended N.512	4% 22	9% 43	20% 101	17% 88	50% 258

The differences became even more dramatic after 14 months. Seventy-three per cent of the recommended group was still performing in the top half of their sales force after 14 months, while only 13 per cent of the non-recommendables were performing on a successful level. Further, 50 per cent of those who were hired in spite of not being recommended were no longer on the job at 14 months, while 16 per cent of the recommendable group left or were fired prior to 14 months. Table 25.2, which will be discussed later, further shows that this dropout difference between the recommendable and non-recommendable groups is even greater when analysed qualitatively.

Table 25.2   Analysis of car sales turnover after 14 months

Total 337	Quit	Fired
no longer on job	116	221
Recommended	55	24
N.79	70%	30%
Not recommended	61	197
N.258	24%	76%

Another interesting group difference appears when only those remaining on the job after 14 months are examined. Of the 421 recommendables still on the job after 14 months, 86 per cent were in the top half of their sales force, while of the 254 non-recommendables remaining, only 26 per cent have managed to perform in the top half after this length of time (see Table 25.3). In other words, even of the 50 per cent (254 out of 512 hired) of the non-recommendable group who managed to survive on the job for 14 months, virtually three quarters (74 per cent) were performing in the bottom half of their sales force.

Table 25.3   Comparative performance of recommended versus non-recommended survivors after 14 months

After 14 months	Quarters			
T.675	1st	2nd	3rd	4th
Recommended	166	198	41	16
421	39.4%	47.0%	9.7%	3.9%
Not recommended	22	43	101	88
254	8.6%	16.9%	39.7%	34.6%

Since every hiring decision is a gamble, and some failure is inevitable, one has to examine the odds in making each hiring judgement. If we look at Tables 25.1 and 25.3, and we define success as performing in the top half of the sales force after 14 months, we see that the employer stands almost a three-to-one chance of success when hiring a recommended individual and about a one-in-eight chance for similar success if he decides to hire someone not recommended.

An examination of Table 25.2 reveals another important difference between the recommended and non-recommended groups. As has been indicated, approximately 50 per cent or 258 of the original 512 non-recommendables were no longer on the job after 14 months, while 16 per cent (79) recommendable individuals had similarly dropped out. Of these 258 non-recommendable dropouts, 197 (76 per cent) were fired due to poor production, while the remainder left for reasons not relating to productivity. On the other hand, of the 79 recommendables no longer on the job, only 24 (30 per cent) were fired due to poor production, while the remaining 55 (70 per cent) left for better jobs or other non-production related reasons. Thus, not only does the recommendable group turn over at a far lower rate than the non-recommendables, but they are far more productive while on the job than their non-recommended associates.

If, then, we were to compare the percentage of those fired due to poor production prior to 14 months, we see that 197 out of 512 (38 per cent) of the non-recommendables were similarly dismissed.

Clearly, when individuals are assessed and recommended for hire in car sales on the basis of their personality dynamics, their chance for success is greater.

From the results of this study, and from our ongoing work with thousands of dealerships, the answer is clear that better selection really does work, and that since approximately one in four people walking or driving past a dealership have good sales dynamics, regardless of what they are currently doing, the population from which to select is literally limitless. Dealers need only tap into the riches of that population and select from among those one in four people who have the personality attributes to sell their product in their dealership. Offer these people the necessary sales and product training, and the dealer is an excellent candidate for success in the 1990s and beyond.

CHAPTER 26

BANKING ON PEOPLE: THE KEY TO THE BOTTOM LINE

A few years ago, a bank asked us to do a study aimed at determining the reasons for a pattern of increasing job dissatisfaction among its employees. As they described the problem, it became apparent that not only was there increasing job dissatisfaction, but the bank was also experiencing the related problem of increasing turnover, particularly among long-term employees.

The first step we took was to conduct an attitude study, the results of which provided us with an early clue as to the nature of the problem. Many long-term employees, particularly loan officers, complained, to paraphrase, 'I was hired ten years ago to do one job, and today they are asking me to do something entirely different.' This led us to conduct extensive job analyses focusing particularly on the loan officer function and then to do a series of interviews, after which we concluded that the job analysis conducted at the time of the study would have been totally different if that same analysis had been conducted a decade earlier.

What had in fact occurred, and almost entirely without the awareness of the bank's management, was that the loan officer's job had evolved dramatically from a purely financial, decision-making capacity, to a heavily sales-oriented function. Thus, individuals who were doing an outstanding job, given the early definition, had evolved out of their competence as their job function changed.

Interestingly, when we presented these results, the bank's management resisted the implications. They really did not want to accept the fact, despite all the evidence, that a number of banking functions had become, in effect, sales and marketing activities.

Although this particular institution continued to resist the concept that sales and successful banking were rapidly becoming inextricably connected, many other commercial banks have become increasingly aware of marketing as a major differential between the outstandingly successful and the mediocre. Millions of pounds are spent on advertising designed to focus on the aspects of institutions' services which might differentiate them from their competitors.

- No minimum balance required for free banking.
- Lower car loan rates if you have more than a certain amount in your current account.
- Overdraft protection line of credit.
- Your own private business banker.
- Automatic transfer of funds from current to savings account.
- Ready credit if you set up a 'special' account.
- Automatic teller machines capable of dispensing cash, making deposits and transferring funds at any hour.
- An open door to the bank manager.
- Special focus on small and medium-sized businesses.
- Discounts on car loans for depositors.

The list goes on and on.

The implicit assumption underlying these campaigns is that all banking institutions are basically safe and insured, provide current and savings accounts, and can make loans. Given these rather obvious assumptions, it is generally felt that the only way to gain a competitive edge is to offer something slightly better than the others. Like most absolutes, this thinking is only half true, as it neglects a variable that can be the competitive edge.

ADVERTISING ATTRACTS PROSPECTS

Advertising, no matter how persuasive, rarely sells a product such as a bank. The most a successful advertising campaign can be asked to do is to bring potential customers into a commercial bank. Whether or not prospects developed through expensive advertising are converted to customers is directly dependent upon the quality of the people within the institution to whom these prospects are exposed. It is important to understand that few customers have any real idea as to the structure, policies or financial strength of their bank. The bank, to the average man or woman and even to more sophisticated business customers, is the cashier, the loan officer or the bank manager with whom that customer happens to deal.

Too often, the enormous amount of time, money and effort devoted to bringing a prospect in is undone in the first 30 seconds if that prospect deals with the 'wrong person'.

Unfortunately, as Robert Frost wrote, to many people, 'A banker is someone who will give you an umbrella when the sun shines and takes it back when it rains'. Advertising works to set aside this negative image, but that one bad contact with a rude, discourteous cashier or a loan officer who acts more like a computer than a human being will quickly reinforce, and perhaps set permanently in the prospect's mind, a negative view that could have been turned around by a smile or just a bit of empathy.

PEOPLE GIVE THE EDGE

What we are suggesting here is that if an institution wishes to develop and maintain a competitive edge, the key to that edge is the people working in that institution.

Part of the problem that a commercial bank faces by definition in its people selection is the obvious necessity for banking personnel to be financially/business oriented. A cashier must be able to handle money. A good loan officer must be able to judge credit and be comfortable with figures. Often, these fiscal abilities run counter to the skills required to perform their people-oriented job responsibilities.

ANALYSE PEOPLES' SKILLS

In order to understand this point, let us backtrack and look for a moment at the psychology of occupational choice. A young man or woman becomes an accountant or financial analyst often because he or she is not comfortable with the pressures and ambiguities of human relationships. That accountant or finance person derives enormous ego-gratification from balancing the books, developing financial plans that work, effecting cost savings and the like. If that person is properly matched to a job requiring these financial skills, he or she will be happy and successful in that job.

On the other end of the continuum is the individual who is far too restless to cope with numbers and detail. This individual has ego-drive and so derives his or her gratification from the successful persuasion of another human being. The ego-driven individual wants and needs the victory of a successful persuasion as a powerful enhancement of his or her ego. Financial planning usually offers no challenge to the ego-driven individual. In fact, it is generally viewed as boring.

Can these two ends of the continuum be found in the same person? The answer is: to some degree in some cases, but certainly not in most. The first type, the financially oriented individual, has traditionally predominated bank staffs. The need for the cashier to have good people skills, for the loan officer to have excellent persuasive skills, and the bank's staff to include people with financial, persuasive and people skills has only recently begun to be realised, and the problem is that all too many employees are simply incapable of doing all of what today's banking job requires. They view their position as solely a financial one. In many cases, this view is reinforced by tradition and by management, as employees receive promotions for their success strictly on the basis of the financial aspect of their work. Yet, no deposit will be made unless an individual agrees to make that deposit. No loan will be made unless someone chooses to borrow, and no mortgage will be provided unless the borrower chooses that institution to provide it. The bank's need, then, is clearly for people who have not only financial skills but people and persuasive skills as well.

COMBINED SKILLS ARE RARE

This is not an easy task we are describing. Based on our research across industry, we have determined that about one in four individuals possesses really good detail ability, ie very good potential as a finance person. About the same number, one in four, possess good persuasive skills. But in less than one-third of the cases do the combinations overlap. Thus, as a bank recruits cashiers and loan officers etc, it has to begin by selecting people with certain competency in terms of their financial abilities; it also has to be willing to eliminate at least three out of four of these financially competent people who do not possess the needed people and persuasive skills.

This means that a financial institution would probably be able to successfully hire one really good cashier or loan officer out of ten superficially qualified applicants. Is this expensive? Of course it is, but how much less expensive is this rigorous hiring than the loss of that one customer with the multiplied effect of that loss? How much better is it to concentrate just a little more effort on bringing in the right people for the right jobs to begin with, and spending the necessary time and money to train and supervise these appropriate people, than to spend the enormous money and efforts required in continually recruiting and firing, and continually losing customers not only for your own institution but for the entire industry?

COSTS OF THE WRONG PEOPLE IN THE WRONG JOB

A simple method by which the costs can be measured is to compare the productivity of the top loan officer and that of a person near the bottom. The difference between those numbers represents pure cost in terms of reduced revenue. Clearly, what a banking institution's top people produce can be produced by others, and if other individuals are not doing so, they are literally throwing revenue away.

Another major cost stemming from the lack of effective salespeople in banking institutions relates to cross-selling. A recent study discloses that 75 per cent of the people who opened an account or took out a loan at a financial institution within the past year were not told about any additional services that might benefit them. Beyond this, 25 per cent of those who said their financial institutions did attempt to cross-sell a product indicated that the product was a pension plan; and only 10 per cent of those approached actually took up the offer of this service.

With the enormous and rapidly increasing array of products and services offered by banking institutions, this failure to cross-sell has an enormous negative impact on a bank's bottom line and, so, on its ability to compete.

A SALES CULTURE

For a banking institution to maximise sales opportunities, even on one product, and certainly for it to take full advantage of cross-selling opportunities, a sales culture must exist within that bank, which, as we have discussed earlier, is often lacking in tradition-bound organisations. What will it take to create this new sales culture in an institution?

First, for there to be a sales culture, there must be sales-oriented individuals within the institution. Also, a culture has to be developed which fosters, promotes and rewards successful cross-selling.

Management can set the tone for whether the employees of a commercial bank will possess:

- an understanding and problem-solving approach toward each customer's needs;
- an attitude that selling is mutually beneficial to the bank and the customer;
- a team, rather than an individual, effort toward completing a sales transaction; and
- a feeling that the institution is special and worthy of a superior effort.

Sales can only flourish if goals are clearly spelled out. The simpler and clearer these goals are, the greater the likelihood that a culture can develop around those goals.

Setting these goals is probably more difficult in the banking industry than in many others because of the duality of the banking relationship. When an individual discusses a possible loan with a loan officer, a sales goal would obviously be for that loan officer to make the loan — to sell the loan. On the other hand, the loan officer's fiscal responsibility includes making a judgement as to the efficacy of the loan. Simply put, not every loan should be made. Clearly then, the goal is not simply to put as many loans as possible on the books, but rather to sell loans that are good for the bank.

Thus, as the banking industry increasingly recognises the sales and marketing aspects of its overall function, it must also develop a valid performance appraisal system that can include balancing sales with the very necessary fiscal responsibility to make top sales realistic and profitable.

To be truly effective and to enhance the development of a sales culture, sales goals need to be followed up with periodic performance appraisals. If performance criteria are clearly defined and transmitted to employees, the potentially productive individuals will respond positively to periodic objective measurement of their performance. Personally motivated, driven salespeople want to be judged and so, knowing that a system is in place to do just that will serve as a real, positive motivation for them.

IMPLICATIONS FOR THE FUTURE

When discussing commercial banks it is safe to say that the banking industry has undergone tremendous change in the last couple of decades, which is likely to continue at a rapid pace well into the 1990s. An industry that was marked by regulation, simply defined products and services, and clear separation of services among the various institutional categories is now rapidly becoming deregulated, with multiple product offerings and enormous overlap in services, not only among banks, but between banks and other financial services institutions. How, even a few years ago, could one read in the newspaper or see on television a building society proclaiming itself as a one-stop financial shopping centre?

The intense competition resulting from these factors has led to the demise of many institutions, including some very large and well-respected ones, the acquisition of others, and the bankruptcy and restructuring of still others. And the competition among banks and between banks and competing industries is only going to get more intense.

So, we return to the beginning. With the evolution of the industry has come the evolution of the job, though, as we said, the latter evolution has not always been well recognised. Where the job of the loan officer might some time ago have been described as simply approving loans, today few would deny that a loan officer needs some sales ability. Although there are elements within the industry still looking down their nose at sales, viewing banking as just a little above the need to sell, most, perhaps reluctantly, now recognise that to succeed, they had better sell, and many have even set up sales forces to do just that. There are even positions in some banks called sales, and some branch managers' job descriptions prominently include sales. The casualties are the individuals who were suited to their jobs 10, 15 or 20 years ago, as they were then described, but who are, through no fault of their own, made redundant by their new job description. They are the same people, but what they are now expected to do is radically different. What can be done for these people?

Perhaps there are other jobs within the institution that still fit their personalities, and hopefully, if they have provided loyal service to their bank, they would be offered the opportunity to fill those positions. Others, of course, may retire, but what is critical to a bank's survival is that these jobs that do require sales be filled by individuals who possess the dynamics of a salesperson, while, again, still possessing the necessary financial orientation to perform the banking aspects of their jobs. Thus, while an individual must have detail ability, organisational skills and good financial orientation, he or she must combine these skills with the ability to sense the reactions of others, the motivation to persuade them and the sense of self (ego-strength) to sell, and even be rejected where necessary.

The banking salesperson must also have the motivation to service since that is what banking, after all, is still all about. Yes, as we said, though it is not easy, the people with this combination of abilities do exist, if the industry will actively seek them.

The challenge then, is to turn traditionally unaggressive financial institutions, which may have prospered in yesterday's highly structured, rate-protected marketplace, into lean, hungry and highly professional sales organisations that provide outstanding service, and have the capability of selling that service.

CHAPTER 27

HIGH-TECHNOLOGY/CONSULTATIVE SALES: THE NEW BREED

As our economy shifts from producing products to delivering services, the nature of selling is changing dramatically. To meet the challenges brought on by selling intangible services, a new breed of salesperson is emerging. These individuals come across as consultants. Rather than being perceived by their clients as product suppliers, consultative salespeople are viewed as problem solvers and profit improvers. These new, emerging salespeople are particularly evident in high-technology sales, but are now being seen in many new and old industries.

What is occurring in high technology is condensed into a shorter period of time than any other development in history. High technology has already permeated every aspect of our lives and changed the way we do things, from paying our bills to preparing a marketing strategy.

All of this is occurring at head-spinning rates. Today's high technology will be tomorrow's state-of-the-art, and the day after will be merely commonplace. Along the way, our future is reshaped. Certainly, the nature of sales is changing. And there is much the sales profession at large can learn from those who are on the frontier of new developments.

That is why, some time back, we undertook a study of sales forces in client companies selling new technologies, ie micro, mini and mainframe computers, telecommunications and office automation, computer time-sharing networks, application software, and biotechnical and medical equipment. Among successful salespeople of such high-tech products, and they are a rare breed, we found some striking differences from salespeople who thrive in almost every other field. These distinctions have important ramifications for everyone trying to sell in today's marketplace.

As John Hoffman, vice president of sales for Computer Sciences Corporation, put it: 'When it comes to high-tech products the old rules of selling no longer apply. This is because successful high-tech salespeople are not really selling products or services. What is actually sold are solutions . . . solutions which have to be customised to meet the unique needs of each client.'

In most sales situations, as we have described elsewhere in this book, the need for persuasive drive cannot be overemphasised. Enough is never too much. However, for someone selling high-tech, information or professional services, we found that if the need to persuade is too intense, it can be a hindrance rather than an asset. The reason involves the very nature of the consultative sale. In consultative selling the salesperson must be willing to build the sale in a slow, step-by-step process.

The intensely ego-driven salesperson wants to close right now. He or she wants the instant gratification that the close brings and will have difficulty delaying that gratification. It certainly is impossible to convey the image of the concerned consultant when the need to close immediately is too intense.

We want to be clear here. Successful high-tech salespeople must have some ego-drive, or else they will never close a sale, but their drive must be tempered. Ultimately, a high-tech sale takes time—which means it takes patience, follow-through, persistence, empathy and the ability not to take rejection too personally.

What evolves is an individual who is extremely attentive to a client's needs and totally intent upon seeking an ideal solution to each client's unique problems.

The consultative sale is the classic example of 'the sale beginning after the sale is made.' Once the system, service or programme is installed, the salesperson's job has just begun.

Since each client has unique needs, each high-tech product or service must be tailored to meet those needs completely, or else the sale will be lost to a competitor.

A high-tech salesperson, then, should be perceived by clients as a technically knowledgeable, sincere and competent professional with a strong sense of personal integrity.

Clients are looking for a salesperson who has a consultant's demeanour because once the system is installed, the salesperson's responsibility does not end. The sale forms the basis for a continuing, long-lasting relationship in which the salesperson troubleshoots any problems that might arise and implements new facets of the system as needs expand.

Clients are keenly aware that they are not simply buying another piece of equipment. In fact, in many ways they are acquiring an ancillary employee. The ability to develop a trusting, long-lasting relationship is essential to success in high-tech sales since additional products and services will be expected by a client for a long time to come.

To provide solutions to problems, an individual must convey the solid, stable, reliable image of someone who has credibility, keen intelligence and who conveys the feeling that she or he can be trusted to alleviate problems and concerns, and really help to come up with the best possible solutions. The qualities that we uncovered which most differentiate the successful high-tech salesperson from the rest all add up to this solution-oriented consultant's image.

'There is an enormous amount of consulting involved with every high-tech sale' says Donald Walker, vice president of sales for Comshare Inc, which provides a computer time-sharing network. 'Each client has unique needs — there is no one widget for all problems — and our service must be tailored to meet those needs completely, or we will lose a sale to one of our competitors.'

Clients ask informed questions, and the salesperson who does not know his or her product and understand the client's needs inside out is going to be perceived as being poorly prepared, and will reflect negatively on the product and the company.

We have found that most productive high-tech salespeople are also extremely well organised. They have to be able to handle details well and organise their work effectively. This personal organisation gives them the capacity to keep many things in mind simultaneously, including the technical aspects and capabilities of a wide spectrum of products and services.

High-tech salespeople also need to be bright, articulate and confident enough to deal with key executives in major corporations. Since the purchases are substantial and the products will have tremendous impact on the overall effectiveness of an entire company, the sale is generally made at the highest level of an organisation.

To excel, high-tech salespeople must have the ability to get their point across strongly and confidently without appearing pushy or overly aggressive. Such an individual should also be unpretentious, because of the diversity of people encountered. There is a precarious balance between presenting a professional consultant's image, while simultaneously being open to meeting with people in all types of corporate situations.

High-tech salespeople have to have the flexibility to adjust their communication to the particular individual with whom they are dealing. As a manager from Prime Computer, one of the first manufacturers of minicomputers, put it, 'High-tech salespeople do not have to convince just one individual, such as a purchasing agent, within a firm.' They have convincingly to speak the language of programmers, systems analysts and controllers, as well as chief executives and boards of directors.

Our research findings underscore that people who excel in high-tech sales are excellent communicators, both verbally and in writing. They must have the ability to compose letters, proposals and reports clearly, concisely and convincingly. This is distinct from salespeople in almost every other field, who, for the most part, view paperwork as drudgery and an obstacle to closing additional sales.

Over time in this kind of selling, one has to be technically oriented to succeed. The problem is that not all people who are technically oriented can sell. In fact, from the point of basic personality characteristics, the successful salesperson and the successful technician are almost polar opposites. So, simply moving people from the technical side to the sales side would be corporate suicide.

Still, a technical background is a necessary starting point, as is pointed out by Marty Sanfelter, an IBM marketing manager. He describes a scenario where one's technical credibility is being challenged all along the way. Innocently enough, a high-tech salesperson starts out by asking, 'What kind of collection basis are you using?' But as the prospect responds with a curt 'Ten bit BCDs', the sale could come to a grinding halt — unless the salesperson could say something like, 'Our binary code decimal base ranges from point one to point zero, zero one, which could significantly increase your capabilities.' But what does the salesperson say when the technician responds, 'The floating exponent range of my calibration is more than your system can handle'?

At this point, most salespeople would have to excuse themselves, saying something like, 'Well, that is a very good point ... let me get back to my technical people and I'll have an answer for you first thing in the morning.' But, of course, the next morning the prospect may be hard to find. You can see why the successful high-tech salesperson is a rare breed.

The individual must be a long-timer, because the firm's investment will not be recovered in six months or even a year. He or she must have enormous perseverance. Attention must be paid to the slightest detail or solutions will not be complete. And such an individual must be thoroughly knowledgeable about their products as well as the business world. Meanwhile, the high-tech salesperson needs persuasive ability, but, as we said, it must be tempered.

Where do you find this new breed of salesperson? Short of hiring twins, one adept in technology and the other in sales, and working them as a team, it is difficult to uncover someone who can stand out in the technical as well as the sales end of the business world.

Most good people who have both attributes are not looking for new jobs, and even if they were, there are not enough of them to go around.

So, where do you look for those who are not looking? One of the most overlooked places for finding high-tech salespeople is in a company's own backyard. A potentially record-breaking salesperson might be working in the company, doing something completely different, wasting his or her natural ability.

One recent study found that nearly 90 per cent of scientific programmers and analysts are interested in exploring new computer jobs. Certainly some of these technical wizards will also have the innate ability to sell. Many of them may be at a dead end, with no clear path for advancement from their present positions. Selling might give them a fresh start. Once you have identified those who have the requisite technical background, and the desire and ability to sell, sales training can be effective.

Now, we have just described a unique individual — the successful high-tech salesperson — and from the start we said that by getting a clearer understanding of what it takes to succeed on the leading edge of new developments, there would be lessons for all of us in sales. What are those lessons, and how can they be translated into other sales situations?

The common thread winding through the field of high-tech sales is that clients are becoming increasingly sophisticated and knowledgeable before making purchases.

Studies in numerous other industries show that this trend in consumer awareness is having far-reaching consequences throughout the entire sales profession. Well-thought-out and researched questions are being asked before even the most minor acquisitions are made, and there is little patience with the salesperson who tries to gloss over any concerns or objections.

Just as high technology has affected all aspects of our lives and made consumers demand quality, value and high performance in everything they buy, so the high-tech, consultative salesperson appears to be the first of a new breed.

Ultimately, we can all learn from those who are succeeding on the frontier of new developments.

PART 6

CHANGING SALES IN A CHANGING WORLD

CHAPTER 28

CHANGING SALES IN A
CHANGING WORLD

In order to understand and define the role of the salesperson in the future, it is worthwhile to examine the changes that have occurred in the past few decades. Where we were once dominated by mass production and smokestack industries, we are now dominated more and more by service, information and high-tech industries. In addition, our marketplace is no longer an isolated one, but has become global.

The baby boomers (those born between 1949 and 1963) today are 73 million strong, and they dominate the adult population. They are computer literate and are more adaptable to the speed of change than the generation before them. Many have highly sophisticated educational backgrounds, and as a group they control nearly half of all aggregate income. More than 50 per cent belong to dual-income households. They represent a greater diversity of life-style than has ever existed before. These are the clients, customers and sales and management work force in today's and tomorrow's economy.

This group of new achievers has high expectations and high demands. As clients and consumers they want to deal with professionals who know their products, have innovative solutions to complex problems, and provide service and support.

As employees they want more than a nine-to-five job with security and classic upward mobility. They will bring their analytical, creative and persuasive skills to companies that are willing to challenge them sufficiently, reward them adequately and provide them with an environment where they can grow and further develop their skills. If treated insensitively, challenged insufficiently or rewarded inadequately, they will move to a more rewarding environment. They seek recognition both financially and psychologically. They want to know what their contribution can mean to the total picture of an organisation. In other words, they want to feel their corporate worth, and have the opportunity to develop and expand their skills.

Companies that hope to compete successfully for these top people will make a commitment to undertake innovative approaches. We have already begun to see the signs of a shrinking workforce. This trend will continue as baby boomers continue to mature, and the lower numbers of potential employees available in the next generation slowly enter the workforce. Increased competition for qualified applicants will only intensify.

If these highly productive people are to be retained, companies will make certain that communication will be open not only from the top down, but from the bottom up. Managers will include their people in brainstorming sessions, strategic planning and policymaking decisions because management can benefit significantly from the input of this group, and because it knows that such active participation is the way to tie these valuable human resources psychologically to their company. To achieve this, there is likely to be an acceleration of the trend that has already begun: a flattening of corporate structure and a decentralisation of the decision-making process.

Additionally, employees will be encouraged to attend seminars and courses at the company's expense as a way to improve performance, demonstrate the company's interest in the employee's personal and professional development, and bring new resources and skills to the company. Companies will understand that it is good business, and essential to attracting and keeping top-notch people, to provide opportunities for growth and development, and to create an environment where employees feel that their individual growth is vitally linked to the success of the company. A genuine partnership will exist between the people and the organisation, in which each has an important influence on the other. These companies will have arrived at the realisation that with labour costs in most organisations running 50 per cent (and even higher in some service industries), the importance of strategically managing and developing this asset, their people, is critical.

PREPARATION FOR THE FUTURE

All of this points to the fact that human resource development, especially in the sales and sales management area, will continue to be the key component of corporate success. For in this rapidly changing economy, the goals of the company will only be fully achieved when management thoroughly understands its people-resource potential, and employees understand that their growth is vitally linked to the success of the company.

Both the salesperson and the consumer of the future will be better educated, more skilled, technologically sophisticated and highly selective in the products and services they represent or purchase. Meeting their high demands and high expectations will be the challenge.

Our work with start-up entrepreneurial firms tells us there is no single formula for building a successful enterprise. The most successful organisations, however, do share one thing: an emphasis on people — on their development and proper selection. Ultimately, that emphasis is the key reason for their brilliant success.

INDEX